EAST
WINDS

EAST WINDS

Recipes, history and tales from the hidden Caribbean

Riaz Phillips

Breakfast

Vegetables
Fry Bake
Roast Bake
Sada Bake

FILLINGS

Bodi

Salt Fish

Ochro/Okra

Pumpkin

Roasted Melongene

Tomato Choka

Bhaji
Soup

Bush Tea
Coffee
Chocolate Tea

LITTLE PARADISE ♥

PUJA STORE

PH: 292-9735

OPENING HRS
MON-SAT-10am-5pm.
SUN-8am-10am

Introduction

"We are all Jamaican here", an émigré to Britain from Barbados declares in the fictional tale *Small islan' complex*. Thanks to a number of street carnivals around the world, TV personalities and restaurants, Caribbean cuisine has slowly entered the mainstream in its large diaspora regions. Ultimately, the country sending the most people to Britain – Jamaica – has dominated British Caribbean culture. Georgetown, the capital city of Guyana, is 1,500 miles from Kingston, the capital city of Jamaica. That's roughly the same as a flight from London to Istanbul in Turkey. So, given this continental magnitude of distance, how did the food and cultures of both countries become so conjoined?

In the early–mid-20th century, promising job and life prospects were touted by numerous recruitment drives set up in cities and towns across all corners of the British West Indies (though I will mainly be referring to the Caribbean in this book). British services like the NHS (National Health Service), London Transport and British Rail, targeted young Caribbean men and women to fill labour shortages and help rebuild a Britain decimated after the world wars. Wars that numerous Caribbeans themselves had been enlisted to fight in. On arrival, the jobs and the lifestyle in Britain were far from those promised in the advertisements and many of those who arrived sought solace and support from within their local communities.

The recruitment drives, and the mass migration they effected, tore apart families back in the Caribbean. Facing the dreary weather and, at times, bigoted reception in Britain, the people of the different Caribbean islands came together on an unprecedented scale. As a result of prejudiced landlords, many people, regardless of which country they came from, and including those from other British colonies such as Nigeria, Ghana and Kenya, often lived together, worked for the same employers and frequented the same social hangouts where they were welcomed.

While such countries may seldom intermingle back in the homeland, here in the diaspora they lived shoulder to shoulder.

When families like mine came to the United Kingdom from the 1950s onwards, for the British media of the day and the white community of the country they were all just "Black", even if some of them were ethnically Indian. People saw no nuance or really engaged with the cultural difference of migrants, be they Ghanaian or Guyanese, Jamaicans or Trinbagonians (Trinidad and Tobago herein often referred to as Trinidad and the people of the dual-island nation as "Trini"). That said, they did have numerous cultural similarities born out of the shared legacy of enduring an age of colonialism, from which the indelible result was the English language and often a devoutness to Christianity, which no doubt made forming a community easier.

The communities that centred around church, the informal residential parties called "shebeens" and the restaurants and bars begat the vibrant Caribbean community we see in the UK today. From the 1950s onwards, establishments in London such as Dougie's Hideaway club in North London's Archway and The Mangrove in West London's now famed Notting Hill, opened by staunch civil rights activist Frank Crichlow, were crucial social hubs that provided an inviting safe space for Black people from all walks of life, as well as homely sustenance.

A vintage issue of *New Musical Express* (*NME*) magazine touted Dougie's as "having the best Dhal pouri in town" and Crichlow himself was a native of Trinidad and Tobago. However, rather than being called "Trinidadian/Trinbagonian" restaurants, both Dougie's and The Mangrove (like many others then and now) were simply called West Indian or Caribbean. Following the post-war migration, most Guyanese and Trinbagonians ended up in the same neighbourhoods as other British–Caribbeans and found a growing

The aim was to give the wider public a clue about what's on offer inside. Despite this, these shops will take any chance to let you know exactly where they are from and the fact that they are definitely NOT Jamaican, be it via the flags or vibrant soca or chutney music in the background.

As a kid growing up in the UK with no formal education about where my family had come from, these people were all just one people. They were just my family. It never occurred to me that many of them came from different places. Different aunties and uncles would have different maps and flags at home or seat-head coverings and flag-adorned mini boxing gloves on their car mirrors and so on. At the dinner table and hall parties, family would discuss events "back home" or get into fierce but funny debates over island stereotypes: "*You Jamaicans are always doing that...*" responded to with, "*Yeah well, Trinis always do this...*" Though I could see Jamaica, St. Lucia, St. Vincent and the Grenadines, Trinidad and Tobago, and Guyana (where my family hails from) were seas apart on my little spinning globe, because of the closeness of my family and their friends I always thought they were next-door neighbours, who could just hop on a boat and be at the others' place in no time.

This togetherness was encapsulated at special occasions like birthdays, christenings and even funerals, where a spread of Caribbean food was always guaranteed. As my family skews heavily to Jamaican descent, I was accustomed to the usual spread of jerk chicken, rice and peas, fried fish, stew chicken and so forth. However, any time at least one family member from Trinidad or Guyana (or sometimes even not) was involved, there would be roti. This amazing soft but crumbly bread was able to save even the worst-tasting fillings and ferry them through the mouth directly to the soul. In addition, "goat curry" or "curry goat" (depending on where you're from) was a unifying force that all could agree on.

From the first time I had roti and curry goat, I sung its praises constantly – in the school playground or playing out in my area, although it usually fell on deaf ears. For those who know roti, it is quite time-consuming to make (think Aunty in the kitchen for eight

amount of their commerce coming from people of other islands, and so this trend stuck. Rather than segregating or dividing, many of these initial spaces aimed to form a bridge for the whole community and usually catered to all. Trinidad-style curries and roti were added to Jamaican-flavoured menus, and calypso and soca sounds incorporated into the DJ rotation of rocksteady and reggae.

In Britain, the Caribbean food that dominates the everyday life of the Eastern reaches of the region, such as *chokas*, dhal and *talkaris*, has always been its own subsection, alien even to other Caribbean people. For businesses hailing from the Eastern (or hidden) Caribbean – Trinidad and Tobago, Guyana and less represented islands like Grenada – appealing to other Caribbean people has sometimes proven tricky. Reaching a wider audience has been even harder. As well as dominating the populace of the diaspora in the West, Jamaica is by far the number one long-stay tourist destination, which adds to its supremacy.

Across the Atlantic Ocean, in the other main diaspora of the Caribbean, the USA, the diaspora of the Southeasterly Caribbean is larger and thus this shapeshift has been less necessary in places like South Florida and New York. As in the UK, the majority of Guyanese and Trini shops suffered the fate of non-Jamaican-island-derived shops in having to call themselves "West Indian" or "Caribbean" rather than Guyanese or Trini.

hours) and my working single mum who descends from Jamaica was never going to make it. I definitely was never going to share it on the few occasions I had it either. Whether it was slightly soggy, having been procured in a doggy bag at a family event, or on the joyous occasions a family member would pick up a fresh pack from Horizon Foods, a family owned Trini bakery based in Hackney, East London at that time.

These deaf ears baffled me. Not only had so many of these kids not tried roti, but they'd also never even heard of it! Something piqued my interest at the time though. The kids from parts of Asia – particularly places like India and Pakistan – hadn't just heard of roti, they knew different kinds and recalled how they had it on the weekends; it was very much a staple part of their cuisine. The fact that we Caribbeans and other people of Asia shared this food escaped me at the time. I also discounted the fact that they have sandwiches in France just like they have sandwiches in Japan, a notion I probably gathered from textbook images.

When twelve-year-old me thought about it some more, people like my Uncle Salahudin, his mother Salima and other family members and friends, did have Indian-sounding names (not discounting the fact that my own name Riaz comes from the Indian subcontinent also) and they did *look* Indian. Similarly, other family members had surnames such as Sankar, Gafoor, Ishmael and Maharaj. However, they mostly referred to themselves as Black, be it with paler skin or less coarse, straighter (unfortunately at times labelled "good") hair, so I left it at that. There was no Google at the time and I was never the type to ask older family members many questions, which is why I am playing catch up now.

My uncle would annually wish the family "Happy Diwali" and numerous Trini people in the UK mentioned the Hindu festival (anyone Caribbean can instantly tell the difference between a Jamaican and Trini or Guyanese accent!). In school, this holiday was reserved for people from India but here I knew that this was more than coincidence. Why were "Black" people in the Caribbean celebrating Diwali? I didn't ask my uncle, but I did ask shortly afterwards at my local kids' community

centre. He paraphrased a kid-friendly answer that suggested a turbulent tale of Indian cross-ocean migration to the Caribbean. A story reminiscent of the West Africans that preceded it but very different in many ways. I wasn't completely ignorant of African slave history at this time as I had seen the infamous *Roots* TV show with Kunta Kente, and the transatlantic slave trade era was something that was mentioned in the house and occasionally at the dinner table.

The dots had been loosely connected, though in my adolescent years my heritage took a back seat to other more interesting and time-consuming activities like playing video games and going to music festivals. Growing up and moving out of my mum's house, I still continued to regularly eat Caribbean food. More diverse Caribbean food spots were springing up around London, and whichever part of town I was in I could use my mental Caribbean food map to reach whatever spot was closest, be it a jerk or roti shop.

After my grandmother Mavis passed away, I realized I didn't know too much about her background and why she was always so devoted to cooking the Jamaican food of her homeland. That being said, looking back I sensed a reticence from her and other elders to share parts of their background they perhaps wanted to forget. I realized the same was true, perhaps even more so, of other family members, like my Uncle Sal and his home in East Bank Demerara, Guyana, and other family members from Trinidad and Tobago, Grenada and beyond. Through the research for my first book, *Belly Full: Caribbean Food in the UK*, I was able to find answers to these questions I had never asked, and I began to understand the nuances of Caribbean culture and food. Questions like why Jamaicans hardly ate doubles, why jerk chicken wasn't a big deal for the Guyanese and so on. What I found consistently was that in the diaspora where I grew up, the cultures from the other, less discussed, reaches of the Caribbean were often subsumed into that of (chiefly) Jamaican, even though they were markedly different. Again, "We are all Jamaicans here."

Save for a few known snacks like roti and doubles, the gamut of Trinbagonian and Guyanese culture has seldom been explored and celebrated in the UK in the same way as that of other Caribbean nations. With the UK having an enormous Asian community, this was a poser to me. But as the population of Trinidad and Guyana combined is less than Jamaica, this does make sense. Statistics on the demographics of the famous 1948 Windrush ships' passengers illustrate the pattern of migration seen in the UK: Jamaica at the top, Trinidad below that and Guyana lower still. Jamaican, specifically Black Jamaican, culture and voices rose above all others. Subsequently, it was arguably this subsumption of culture that has prevented the food and culture of the rest of the Caribbean becoming more well known.

Often lost in a culinary quagmire between the Caribbean and South America, and frequently labelled as "Indian" on search websites, seemingly little is known about Guyana, which borders Spanish-speaking Venezuela, Portuguese-speaking Brazil and the former Dutch colony of Suriname. Guyana holds an interesting position in South America as the region's only officially English-speaking nation (and English plug socket user!), having once been a British colony called British Guiana from the early 18th century.

Guyana is known for having six broad cultures, which themselves encompass a wide range of rich tradition and history, including that of the Amerindian Indigenous peoples, West Africa, North India, South China and elements of Portuguese, amongst the evident influence of the colonial European nations. This is, of course, a simplification and the diversity of the region contains many more stories. That being said, while Jamaica and Guyana are often both thrown under the same Caribbean umbrella in Britain, Jamaica is over 90 per cent Black (composed of African descendants), while Guyana's Black population comprises a third of the total populace, with those of Indian heritage representing nearly half. Likewise, in Trinidad, a former Spanish colony and French-dominated region, the population of African and East Indian people each take up about one third of the entire population. Suriname's ethnic make-up is similar, with around 40 per cent of Indian heritage and 30 per cent African or Creole.

This is largely a result of British colonial forces' dependence on indentured Asian labour after the abolition of transatlantic slavery. The British sought cheap labour to keep their plantation system afloat. For this, they brought over additional West Africans, as well as Chinese and European but mostly Indian labourers to work across Southeast Africa, in places like Kenya and Uganda, as well as over 9,000 miles across the oceans to the Caribbean. The British Raj encouraged recruitment drives in Indian cities such as Calcutta (now Kolkata) and Madras (now Chennai). Wanting to escape extreme poverty, Indians who lived in destitution and famine-stricken regions signed these contracts in the hope of returning home with the fruits of their labour, rather than intending to migrate permanently. Labour conditions were bleak, riots often occurred and various problems ensued when workers tried to return, including planters lobbying for them to stay to avoid paying their settlement costs, as well as lack of ships due to the world wars.

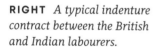

RIGHT *A typical indenture contract between the British and Indian labourers.*

As a result, many ended up in the Caribbean permanently, adding to the already kaleidoscopic Creole melting pot of Caribbean ethnicities and identities. As the existing populations of Trinidad and Guyana were small compared to Jamaica, the culture, customs and norms that Asian workers brought with them had a greater impact on the development of the country compared to other European-controlled islands. For instance, in Jamaica, most foods are commonly referred to by their English or American names, however in the Southeast many words emanating from the Indian subcontinent have become mainstream. Aubergine (eggplant) is *baigan*, chickpeas are *channa*, cumin is *jeera* and so on. The shared, complex demographics of the Eastern Caribbean lead to the similar cultures seen in Guyana and Trinidad today spilling over into neighbouring countries like Suriname, hence why their cultures and cuisines are often grouped together. Whether you're in a roti spot in South London or South Florida, this is overwhelmingly evident. With

While this great diversity has not always been effectively unified in terms of politics and society, or in private and public, food is one of the few parts of the culture (in addition to music and carnival) that unites all peoples in the Caribbean.

Like all Caribbean food, there are regional differences and endless family debates about "correct" ingredients, recipes and meal names. It's highly likely that, even if I don't mention a certain country, many foods in this book are consumed there under a different name. Not just in the "British West Indies" but countries such as Belize, Panama, Honduras and the Dominican Republic, as well as in the original hinterland. In Asian culture, like African culture, which informs the majority of today's Caribbean food culture, formal written recipes are just not a thing. Recipes are passed down through oral traditions, learned via being summoned to cook for the rest of your family as a child.

I did not take advantage of these free lessons as a youngster, so again I was playing catch-up. Fortunately, meticulously recording the movements of my mother cooking in the kitchen before she passed away was a great help. This was then supplemented by lurking at numerous aunties' houses, who found humour in my new-found interest in their cooking methods but were, also more than happy to oblige. Recipes also arose from the many "internships" (for lack of a better term) that I have had over the past few years, including working at my favourite Trini-London outpost – Roti Stop in Stoke Newington, North London – and on a lovely family farm in Moruga to the south of Trinidad, as well as shadowing my "Uncle" Dom, a benne-ball maker and vendor based in Penal, whose wife Janet could effortlessly make every recipe in this book like a great actor can recite entire acts. Also not forgetting hundreds of kitchens where I was a fly on the wall while writing *Belly Full* and the many chefs and owners who shared numerous insights and tips (though rightfully withheld their family recipes!).

While the number of novel ingredients may cause a few issues for newcomers, this will be less of a problem than it was some

all this being said, with the indelible fingerprint left by the European countries in this region, this isn't some far and away distant culture and history that should only be glanced at in Black History month. This is European (British, Spanish, Dutch and French) history as much as it is Caribbean history.

RECIPES

So, what and where is the hidden Caribbean? (Or as some have called it, "The Other Windrush".) I don't propose it is a specific place, but rather putting a magnifying glass to the myriad cultures that have been obscured in both the Caribbean and the diaspora. Despite this, I would purport that much of it isn't Black, Asian or Caribbean history but, in fact, British history. A history which is inextricably linked and can't be separated. These cultures, be they a result of varying Indian backgrounds, Chinese, European, Amerindian and numerous African tribes and multiple religions, such as Hinduism and Islam amongst others, can be found in every nation of the Caribbean, including Jamaica. It just so happens that the former on the list are more heavily concentrated in the southeastern reaches of the Caribbean, in the likes of Trinidad and Tobago, Guyana and Suriname. So that is where I travelled to learn more about my own family and heritage, and therefore these are the countries that contribute the majority of the incredible food I have attempted to recreate in this book.

years ago, with new high-street restaurants and recipes from the Indian and Chinese subcontinents being championed by even those with no familial lineage, making it easier to source regional foods.

Even for those wishing to learn the mythical ways of roti-making, for which I have dedicated an entire chapter, there are no advanced cooking techniques here. What readers will find, similarly to *West Winds* (my previous book on Jamaica), are slow, sometimes time-heavy, but relaxing and engaging recipes, many of which I feel are almost meditative. Really, more time here is spent cleaning, gathering, peeling and chopping fresh fruit, vegetables and herbs. These are then mixed with seasoning and combined with starches, meat and fish, then left to rest for some hours. Here you'll find incredibly simple food but you will be astounded by the aromas of these recipes, which will transform your home in mere moments. I often wonder if the people who hailed from such scorching hot climates could ever have suspected that their descendants would end up in such drastically colder locales, and that the same foods they enjoyed in said heat would produce so much solace in the depths of winter.

Coming from Caribbean kitchens where community is at the heart of all culinary endeavours, these meals that utilize a pantry of a few packs of powder, plus leftovers and spare produce will feed friends and family alike for days. Tupperware to save leftovers for days to come is highly recommended.

THE BOOK

This book looks to celebrate a culture that has been hidden but not lost, in fact, the opposite. For those who are from it, preach it and live it, the culture is as strong as anywhere else in the Caribbean. While you are more likely to see the red, gold and green of the Rastafari in Jamaica, in the hidden part of the Caribbean

you are more likely to see the trinkets and Jhandi flags of Hinduism and Islam, and this is reflected in the food. For those of the hidden Caribbean, pitting their food against the likes of Jamaica is no contest. This book aims to pull that food and culture out from the shadow of Jamaican cuisine and give it the limelight it deserves, rather than just sharing the one or two recipes which show up again and again.

This book mirrors *West Winds* by focusing on food norms that people in the UK and Europe very much understand now. Ideas that have been touted as fresh and innovative but, in fact, as the stories, tales and even song lyrics show, have occurred in the Caribbean for centuries. Chapters such as *plant-based, seeds & pulses, preserves & juices, nose-to-tail* and notably the one dedicated to *curry* will hopefully provide an easy passage of understanding for newcomers. The sections on *seafood* and baking or frying in *flour & water* do not feature any recipes that are wildly different to baking or cooking found in Europe and, in many cases, dishes are remnants of the continent's legacy in the Caribbean. The trickiest techniques are to be found in the *roti* chapter (see pp198–219), which features half a dozen delicious roti recipes alongside step-by-step photos to help guide you through the making process. In all these chapters and recipes, I will tell of the hidden Caribbean and its heritage in a way that will hopefully resonate long after you've pored through this book.

RIGHT *Great Aunty Salima Ishmael and Great Uncle Oscar Ishmael (front); Uncle Salahudin Ishmael (back).*

Pantry

This list is a collection of items I found no homely kitchen or small cookshop from Port of Spain down to Paramaribo was without in some form. These ingredients crop up again and again in the recipes and are often used liberally without measurement, meaning that they are frequently purchased in the largest available quantity. Unless you live in New York City or South Florida, it will be quite rare that you'll find a Guyanese, Trini or Surinamese owned shop. However, the roots of these ingredients likely mean that your nearest Southeast Asian store will carry the majority of the items and more. Online specialists are also a great way to acquire otherwise hard-to-find ingredients.

ALL-PURPOSE SEASONING

This classic Caribbean spice blend is easy to source at any diaspora grocery shop or larger supermarket. Do not confuse all-purpose seasoning with allspice.

AMCHAR MASALA

A unique spice mix used commonly with mango dishes and preserves.

CARDAMOM

Also known as *elaichi* and used in both whole and ground form.

CHICKPEAS

Also known as *channa*. For expediency and convenience, this book refers to chickpeas in their pre-cooked can form. In every instance, you can use dried chickpeas which you soak for a minimum of 6 hours, or overnight, before boiling for 45 minutes and then cooking as the recipe instructs. If you have a pressure cooker you can boil them without soaking for 2 hours.

COCONUT MILK

Fresh coconut milk is always preferred but for many in the diaspora is a luxury. Canned versions are good as they keep in storage for a long time, as do the powder packet and solid block versions. If you buy these, simply follow the instructions on the packet to approximate an equal weight.

CUMIN

Anytime you see cumin mentioned in this book it is interchangeable with what you or the products in your area may call *jeera* (*geera*). Both ground and seed versions are used in this book, the former mainly for seasoning and the latter for cooking in oil.

CURRY LEAVES

These are the dried leaves and so can travel, and as such are easy to find online.

CURRY POWDER

Discussed on p77. You can also use masala curry powder, which is a pre-made mixture of curry powder and masala spice mix.

FENUGREEK

Any time you see fenugreek mentioned in this book it is interchangeable with what you or the products in your area call *methi*. Both ground and seed versions are used, the former mainly for seasoning and the latter for cooking in oil.

FRESH CORIANDER (CILANTRO)

When you see fresh coriander mentioned in this book, I'm actually intending to use *shado beni* (see p26). *Shado beni* is extremely hard to come by outside of the Caribbean or India, so fresh coriander is the de facto replacement. Used to season everything and anything.

GARAM MASALA

Spice mix including black pepper, cardamom, bay leaves and nutmeg amongst others, which is used to add to the flavour of curries. Packets of this ground spice mix can be easily found at most supermarkets.

GARLIC

If you can, I'd highly recommend buying bags of frozen pre-peeled garlic or set aside some time with a bag and garlic to peel and freeze it in an airtight bag. It's a time investment but will save a lot of hassle down the line.

GHEE

If you want to be true to traditional Indian-influenced recipes you can use ghee as your base oil or where recipes (such as baking) call for the use of butter. Regular oil, such as vegetable or sunflower oil is fine, as is coconut oil or rapeseed.

GREEN MANGO

Green mangoes are a specific type of sour, tough mango that aren't easily edible like regular mangoes. These can be found often at Indian grocery stores and, if not, you can use unripe regular mangoes.

GREEN SEASONING

See p26.

HOT SAUCE

A few recipes call for a drop of hot sauce in them or as a serving addition. The Lime &

Pepper Sauce on p235 is suggested for this. If you haven't made any, then any Scotch Bonnet-based hot sauce is a good option.

MUSTARD SEEDS

Otherwise known as *sarsa*, these are commonly used to flavour oil before sautéing onions and garlic when cooking a curry.

PEPPERS

Any references to pimento aren't for the small seeds but rather the small fresh peppers visually akin to jalapeños but which taste more similar to bell peppers. These are usually added for bulk, seasoning and colour, however, for availability, this book leans on using bell peppers instead.

SCOTCH BONNET PEPPERS

Since the famed Guyanese *Wiri Wiri* and Trini *Scorpion peppers* aren't that readily available outside of their host nations, all recipes rely on Scotch bonnet peppers. If you can find the aforementioned peppers, feel free to use them.

SPRING ONIONS (SCALLIONS/GREEN ONIONS)

Often referred to as *cives* or chives (not to be confused with the small thin chives), these are a common seasoning across all heritage food in the Caribbean as well as a garnish.

SUGAR

Both white and brown sugar are used throughout the book. The former is used in more modern versions of bakery snacks and the latter in all manner of sweet and savoury dishes. Brown sugar is largely used as a substitute for *jaggery*, an Indian sugar.

TURMERIC

In some parts of the Caribbean, turmeric is called *saffron powder* even though turmeric and saffron are two different spices. In your local Southeast Asian store it may be called *haldi* or *hardi*, however, the majority of supermarkets carry ground turmeric.

YELLOW SPLIT PEAS

Known as *dhal*. Often sold in packets of 1kg (2¼lb) and appear in many recipes (see p210).

PLANT -BASED

"Here vegetables are not the forgotten side elements of the meal. Rather plants are literally the root of all meals."

According to the folklore of Carib peoples – one of the Indigenous tribes of the Caribbean – when man arrived on earth the central tree of the first garden bore cassava and plantains, in addition to other fruits. Folk tales suggest that this tree was discovered by a tapir who fattened himself on its fruits. The Caribs were eager to find out the tapir's secrets, so one by one they sent a variety of other animals, but each failed to come back with the secret until they finally managed to coerce it from the last animal. They then felled the tree with axes and each Carib took a piece and planted it. It grew and matured, and thus harvest was born. Another Carib account of the first cultivation of a *"cloudlike mass of brilliant green"* and *"fruits that had never before been seen"*, recorded in *Legends and Myths of the Aboriginal Indians of British Guiana* reads:

"Lower down – its trunk surrounding,
Plantains grew, bananas sweet:
All choice plants were there abounding
Which we now (in gardens) meet.
Golden maize, so fresh and fair,
Waved its plumy tresses there

Sweet cassava one might find there,
With the bitter, 'neath the fruits;
Yams, potatoes, every kind, where
Widely spread its mighty roots.
There was found, in pristine state,
All that men now cultivate."

While the various Amerindian collectives of the Caribbean were markedly different in their make-up, culture and traditions, other tribes have a similar philosophical relationship with cultivation of the land and consumption from it. Legends of the Arawaks, another tribe whose existence in the Caribbean dates back many millennia, also speak on the reverence, and even preference, for fruit and vegetables over meat. Like the Caribs, the Arawaks' way of life was a process of accommodation with nature. Anthropological studies of their descendants note: *"They may scrounge, pilfer and kill too, if need be, but none against the laws of nature and they never hoard. Their concern for ecology and the environment and the balance of nature is part of their belief system."* The ecology of their surroundings was, and is for their descendants, woven seamlessly into the fabric of their culture. Everything in the forest, from the roots of the trees to the bark and leaves, as well as the surrounding area, has a role to play and nothing is wasted. They live in harmony with nature and do not adulterate the landscape or endanger plants or wildlife.

Gradually, over the centuries, the many Amerindian tribes' status as the dominant populace of the Caribbean was eroded. The arrival of European looters meant disease, war and genocide. Today, a comparatively diminished fraction of these tribes remain in the likes of Trinidad and Tobago and Jamaica, with the dense inland regions of Guyana sustaining them somewhat. However, many aspects of their ideological outlook provided a fertile ground for those who would take on stewardship of the islands afterwards.

Today the majority of people who reside in the Caribbean are the direct descendants of various generations of the enslaved transplanted by force from a myriad of European colonies, initially West Africa. Regardless of whether the colonizers were Spanish, Dutch, French or English, agriculture always played a pivotal role in the economic development of the region. The enslaved worked tirelessly under the relentless sun producing sugar, rum and cotton, and some but not all were limited to the diets centred on foods cultivated from areas of varying quality of soil called "provision grounds". While there wasn't a uniform size for these grounds nor were they guaranteed, in the likes of Tobago they were legislated at one quarter acre for adults. Here, the enslaved grew starchy root vegetables like yam and cassava, which provided the base of their diets and were bulked out with infrequent extras they were given or able to buy. The recorded heights of the enslaved (a commonly used metric of health) and high mortality rates suggest, however, that eating throughout this period was purely for sustenance, and took precedence over awareness of health, as it may have in their original hinterland.

"Vegetable and fruit-based dishes are often the stars of the show, with meat sometimes being the sideshow and filler."

After the transatlantic slave trade was disbanded in the early 1800s, production of sugar essentially continued with indentured workers, primarily from northern India and southern China. At the turn of the 20th century, with consecutive waves of migrants, a new way of looking at health and food was arguably informed by religion. Notably Hinduism and Islam in Trinidad and Tobago and Guyana, and Seventh-Day Adventism and Rastafari, both Christian-centred religions overwhelmingly practised by West African descendants, in Jamaica.

The presence of these religious customs is reflected in the food shops on high streets and markets. In Islam, certain behaviours might be considered *haram* (forbidden), such as pork consumption. In Hinduism, a legacy of Ayurvedic consumption and the idea of *ahimsa* – an ideal of non-violence influenced by Buddhism and Jainism – informs the popularity of vegetarian diets, beef avoidance due to the sanctity of the cow, as well as the concept of pollution of self as applied to consuming impure foodstuffs like chicken, eggs and pork, which bears similarity to the ideals of *haram* in Islam. In Hinduism, fruits such as coconuts, limes and bananas play an extensive role in the elaborate offerings that make up the *puja* ceremony, which takes place at home with the aim of blessing and protecting the host family. In Jamaica a great deal of the awareness of veganism and conversations around healthy eating are rooted in Rastafari culture and Seventh-Day Adventist vegetarianism, which exists in a smaller way in other parts of the Caribbean.

"In many of these recipes, plants are given the same or more attention than meat dishes and are to be savoured."

Freed from the bounds of chattel slavery, small village shops – often in the front of houses – and market stalls became high-street shops. Many of these shops and the composition of the foods they sold were a reflection of the foods the owners ate at home. Here, vegetables are not the forgotten side element of the meal. Rather plants are literally the root of all meals. The British notion of "meat and two veg" is subverted to almost "two veg and meat". Vegetable and fruit-based dishes are often the stars of the show, with meat sometimes being the sideshow and filler.

In many of these recipes, rather than being an unadorned side boiled in salted water and gulped down with haste, plants are given the same or more attention than meat dishes and are to be savoured. The hard line sometimes seen between fruits and vegetables is blurred in the Caribbean. Callaloo (see p38), a grander, richer cousin of spinach, is cooked down in coconut milk; tomatoes and aubergines (eggplants) are seasoned and grilled, and squash are cooked with herbs and hot peppers. Mangoes can be enjoyed straight off the tree but the greener ones are fused with masala (see p41) and made into a tart, tantalizing quasi-condiment, almost mandatory with lunch or dinner in Trinidad.

The idea of naming any meal or diet "plant-based" would cause bemusement in many corners of the Caribbean. In shops dotted across the region, be they Indian family shops, Rastafari vegan eateries or Seventh-Day Adventist vegetarian outposts, such a way of life is commonplace, and all have in some way influenced the diet of each other. The dishes in this chapter are classics enjoyed for generations and the ease with which they can be made with rudimentary cooking equipment is testament to this. The majority are great standalone dishes, perhaps with pulses or dense starchy vegetables, though most traditionally tend to feature as one of a minimum of two dishes (but sometimes four or five) to comprise a meal with rice and curry.

Green seasoning

Stop! As in Monopoly, do not pass go, do not collect £200 and do not continue to pass through this book without making this green seasoning and keeping some handy at all times. Green seasoning is, in essence, a concoction of herbs, bulbs and citrus fused together to create the ultimate one-stop seasoning shop. From exploring the lush green of Paramin to the north-west of Trinidad, known as the green seasoning capital of the island, to helping fetch greens in gardens down south in St. Mary's, I've found no two green seasoning recipes are the same. While some people prefer the consistency and ease of store-bought versions, many find the time to make their own – and the deep green bottles aren't easily found in the diaspora.

Brian, owner and head chef of Fish, Wings & Tings in Brixton, South London, once shared with me a rudimentary version of green seasoning but gleefully let me know he was withholding a few secret ingredients. I would never dare reveal a magician's secrets, but I do know for sure that absolutely no green seasoning in Trinidad, Guyana and beyond is complete without the leafy base of the ubiquitous, subtly prickly plant known as *shado (chadon) beni*, also known as *culantro* or *bandhania* (*dhania* is the Hindu word for coriander seed) as well as countless other names. The first name comes from the French *chardon beni*, loosely translated as "blessed thistle", and so *shado beni* is likely a Creole-leaning name from when the French presided over the island in the 1700s. *Shado beni* can be extremely hard to find in the West and so in this recipe, as well as often in the rest of the book, the fresh coriander (cilantro) is acting as a quasi-replacement for *shado beni*.

Green seasoning should be considered a staple in your fridge; however, you can adapt it to your taste and create your own recipe that you'll pass down to your next of kin, be it adding twice as much or half the listed garlic or increasing the heat with more peppers. The only suggestion I would make is not to make it too watery or you will struggle to properly season anything with it. After seeing how easily you can fuse such depth of flavours into any dish, you'll want to drop a few tablespoons of green seasoning into any and everything you make.

Please note that at some point you will be adding ingredients to dishes that already exist in your green seasoning but that works to overload flavour. Lastly, if you come to a dish with green seasoning as an ingredient and you haven't pre-made it, use a combination of 2 tablespoons fresh coriander (cilantro), 2 garlic cloves, a dash of salt, a dash of chilli powder, a bit of citric juice and a dash of water and mash together to make 2–3 tablespoons.

MAKES 800ML (3¹/₂ CUPS)

5 spring onions (scallions/green
  onions), roughly chopped
1 large onion, roughly chopped
1 green bell pepper, deseeded and
  chopped (optional)
3 ribs of celery (leaves included),
  chopped
1 Scotch bonnet pepper, deseeded
  and chopped
2.5cm (1in) piece of fresh root
  ginger, peeled and finely
  chopped
8–10 garlic cloves, peeled
1 bunch of parsley (100g/3½oz)
1 bunch of fresh coriander
  (cilantro) (80g/3oz)
1 bunch of thyme (15g/½oz),
  leaves picked
½ tsp sea salt or all-purpose
  seasoning
juice of ½ lime or lemon
  (optional)
1 tbsp apple cider vinegar
  (optional)
1 tbsp light soy sauce (optional)

Wash all the vegetables and herbs, then add to a food
processor with 3 tablespoons water and seasoning and
blend until smooth. Stir in the citrus juice, vinegar and/or
soy sauce, if using. If you don't have a blender, then finely
chop or grate all the ingredients and mash together with a
pestle and mortar. Pulse until the sauce reaches your
desired consistency and then decant into an airtight jar
and store in the fridge. Use within 2 weeks. If you add
citric juice and/or vinegar, the mixture should last for up
to a month.

NOTE *If you're not planning to use the seasoning for a while,
you can store it in the freezer and then defrost half a day
before use.*

Choka

Possibly the worst thing that has ever happened in the food world is Western-driven sugary wheat snacks doused in dairy milk becoming synonymous with the first meal of the day: breakfast. So much so that we're almost at the point where consuming anything savoury is now seen as a bit odd. But when you delve into the history of most cultures, this is, in fact, very common. Indians who came to the Caribbean brought savoury breakfasts with them and for the indentured servants the first meal of the day from rations included roti and curried vegetables or *choka*. Like anyone who enjoys an English breakfast or a Sunday roast, I've always enjoyed roasted vegetables, and *chokas* take this roasting another step. Produce, commonly *baigan* (aubergine/eggplant) or tomatoes, or even both together in the case of *Murtani*, are roasted and then mashed with garlic and pepper before being doused in hot oil and served up with some Sada Roti (see p218).

A fellow guest of Eastern European descent at a guesthouse I stayed in in Trinidad, tells me that the aubergine *choka* reminds her of her grandmother's baba ganoush and I hope these recipes provide a warm, family-cooked feeling to your early morning routine. If you aren't averse to spice, you can increase the amount of chilli peppers or refrain from deseeding them, which will certainly perk up your morning.

Preheat the oven to 180°C (160°C fan/350°F/Gas 4).

Place the vegetables, Scotch bonnet peppers and garlic on a tray lined with foil and roast for 10–15 minutes until the skin begins to blacken and char. Remove from the oven and peel off some of the charred skin from the vegetables and Scotch bonnet peppers but leave some on for taste. Place everything in a bowl or a large pestle and mortar and mash until smooth or your desired consistency.

Next, in a small frying pan, heat the oil on medium-high heat and add the cumin seeds, if using. When the oil starts to sizzle (and the seeds start to turn dark brown), carefully pour the oil into the bowl of vegetable mash and gently stir. Season to taste.

Serve hot or warm with Sada Roti (see p218).

NOTE *If you want the choka to be less peppery and hot, deseed the Scotch bonnet peppers or feel free to omit them completely.*

SERVES 2–4

FOR THE TOMATO CHOKA

6 tomatoes
½ onion, chopped
1–3 Scotch bonnet peppers, tops removed
3 garlic cloves, peeled
4 tbsp cooking oil of choice
½ tsp cumin seeds (optional)
sea salt, to taste

FOR THE AUBERGINE CHOKA

2 large aubergines (eggplants), tops removed
1–3 Scotch bonnet peppers, tops removed
½ onion, chopped
3 garlic cloves, peeled
4 tbsp cooking oil of choice
½ tsp cumin seeds (optional)
sea salt, to taste

FOR THE MURTANI

2 large aubergines (eggplants), tops removed
3 tomatoes
6–8 okra, topped and tailed
½ bell pepper of choice, deseeded and finely diced
½ onion, chopped
1–3 Scotch bonnet peppers, tops removed
3 garlic cloves, peeled
4 tbsp cooking oil of choice
½ tsp cumin seeds (optional)
salt, to taste

RIGHT *Tomato Choka* (right), *Murtani* (bottom)

Okra & tomato

On my various food journeys, I've been surprised by how divisive okra is. For many people, the thought of the slimy, slithering okra fingers sliding down their throats brings immediate repulsion. For okra fans, however, the same sensual experience and taste brings joy. I'd also suggest the prior crew have possibly never had any variation of okra apart from its basic form – boiled in lightly salted water. Be it in West African chop bars, Southern American soul food diners or Indian restaurants, the combination of fried okra and tomatoes rears itself. The geographical disparity of these regions tells a story of food movement but also gives credence to my thesis that only those who can bring out the magic of okra fully appreciate it.

This dish (shown on p33) is like a cousin of the gumbo of Louisiana and the *bhindi masala* of Northern India, frying okra in herbs and spices to give a certain crunch, with the flavour balanced by comparatively sweet onions and tomatoes. While it makes a great lunch or dinner side, I highly recommend it with roti (a common theme you'll see throughout this book), particularly Sada Roti (see p218) for a warming, belly-arousing breakfast.

In a large frying pan, heat 3 tablespoons of the oil over a medium heat. When hot, add the okra and stir-fry for 10 minutes until slightly browned and crisp. Sprinkle with ½ teaspoon of salt, then remove with a slotted spoon and place onto a plate lined with kitchen paper.

Add the remaining 2 tablespoons of oil to the same pan and heat again. When hot, add the cumin and mustard seeds and fry until they darken slightly. Next, add the onion and sauté for 3 minutes before adding the garlic, ginger and green seasoning. Sauté for another 2 minutes. Then add the tomatoes and stir to combine before adding the turmeric, chilli powder and garam masala. Then add 60ml (4 tablespoons) water and cook for 5–7 minutes. After this, the paste should start to bubble slightly. Finally, add the okra back in and stir gently to combine.

Sprinkle over pepper and salt to taste.

NOTE *For a simple okra dish, reduce the amount of tomato and water by half.*

SERVES 2–4

5 tbsp cooking oil of choice
500g (1lb 2oz) okra, topped and tailed and cut into 2cm (¾in) slices
½ tsp cumin seeds
½ tsp mustard seeds
½ onion, chopped
4 garlic cloves, finely chopped
2.5cm (1in) piece of fresh root ginger, peeled and grated
1 tbsp Green Seasoning (see pp26–27)
200g (7oz) tomatoes, chopped into 2cm (¾in) chunks
½ tsp ground turmeric
½–1 tsp chilli powder of choice
½ tsp garam masala
sea salt and freshly ground black pepper

Caraili (bitter melon)

When expanding on the great foods of Trinidad, a taxi driver waxes lyrical about growing up eating *balongie*, the name for stuffed caraili (or karela), otherwise known as bitter melon. Perhaps one of nature's cruellest culinary tricks is that the bitterest foods are often so good for us. Furthermore, it seems that being accustomed to eating an entire side of caraili can perhaps only be achieved by a childhood of eating it. From the Indian subcontinent to China, the fruit grows embedded in a network of weedy vines. In the sequel to Rudyard Kipling's renowned novel *The Jungle Book*, Mowgli seeks vengeance on the villagers who wish to harm his adoptive parents and in *Mowgli's* "song against people" he repeats numerous times their *"house beams shall fall and the Karela, the bitter Karela, shall cover you all"*.

As with lots of produce, caraili comes with a great deal of variety. In the Caribbean, you are more apt to find larger, lighter green caraili with softer bumps, whereas in the diaspora you'll find smaller, darker green ones with more defined bumps, which can tend to be slightly more bitter. For those without the generational taste buds for caraili, adding tomatoes, especially sweet tomatoes, to this easy sauté dish (shown on p33) gives it a fine balance. This is commonly eaten as a side or with Sada Roti (see p218) for breakfast.

To prepare the caraili, cut off the tops and tails and then halve them lengthways. Then, using the back of a spoon, scrape out the insides as well as the white skin left behind. Slice into half-moons ½–1cm (¼–½in) thick.

In a large frying pan, heat the oil over a medium heat. When hot, add the onion and sauté for 3 minutes, then add the spring onion, garlic, Scotch bonnet pepper and green seasoning, if using. Continue to sauté for 2 minutes, then add the caraili and fry, stirring occasionally for 5 minutes. Add the tomato and fry for another 3 minutes. Finally, add salt and pepper to taste and serve.

SERVES 4

500g (1lb 2oz/3 medium) caraili (bitter melon)
4 tbsp cooking oil of choice
½ onion, finely chopped
2 spring onions (scallions/green onions), chopped
3 garlic cloves, minced
½ Scotch bonnet pepper, deseeded and finely chopped
1 tbsp Green Seasoning (see pp26–27 – optional)
1 tomato, cored and finely chopped, or 10 cherry tomatoes, halved
sea salt and freshly ground black pepper

Fry aloo

At a soul food diner in America's Mississippi, the breakfast I'm served comes with the option of grits and "breakfast potatoes". The latter immediately gives me a flashback of being in Trinidad where Fry Aloo (fried potatoes) also serves as a breakfast dish, which I have enjoyed numerous times. The soul food version, while incredibly moreish, has most of its added taste derived from salt and pepper. As you'll discover in this book (and pretty much any Caribbean recipe), absolutely nothing is consumed without at least a small army of seasoning. In Northern parts of India, breakfast potato dishes, like dry Aloo Ki Sabzi (essentially this recipe), have been enjoyed for centuries and another form of fried potato, Aloo Tikki – a patty of grated and boiled potatoes – looks to me to have directly influenced hash browns.

This dish can take some attempts to get the desired level of crispiness on the potatoes, however, with the support of that army of herbs and spices, it always makes for a great, filling early day option.

In a large frying pan or Dutch pot, heat the oil, mustard seeds and asafoetida, if using, over a medium heat. When hot, or when the seeds and powder start to brown, add the onion and sauté for 3 minutes. Then add the garlic, Scotch bonnet pepper and green seasoning, if using. Sauté for 2 minutes, then add the potatoes. Stir to combine, cover with a lid and cook for 10 minutes.

Remove the lid and note that the bottom of the potatoes will have started to stick to the bottom of the pan, which is fine as you want to ensure they are cooked and crispy. Now, add the salt, pepper, turmeric and flour, if using. Gently stir to combine and cook for another 10 minutes, stirring halfway through until the potatoes are golden yellow with a brown crisp.

Garnish with the fresh coriander.

SERVES 4–6 AS A SIDE

5 tbsp cooking oil of choice
⅓ tsp mustard seeds (optional)
⅓ tsp asafoetida (optional)
1 onion, chopped
3 garlic cloves, finely chopped
1 Scotch bonnet pepper, deseeded and finely chopped
1 tsp Green Seasoning (see pp26–27 – optional)
800g (1¾lb) white potatoes, peeled and cut into 1cm (½in) dice
1 tsp sea salt
1 tsp freshly ground black pepper
½ tsp ground turmeric (optional)
1 tsp chickpea flour or cornflour (corn starch) (optional)
2 tsp finely chopped fresh coriander (cilantro)

RIGHT *Fry Aloo* (top), *Okra & Tomato* (middle) *and Caraili* (right).

Bhaji

In *bhaji* (*bhagi* or *bagee*), blended green leaves are sautéed in seasoned oil before being wilted with (ideally fresh) coconut milk. The *bhaji* I ate in the UK relied on spinach (or partly kale), however, in its original form it may be made up of a number of different plants, including the young leaves of sweet potato, cassava, pumpkin, saijan or moringa, as well as those of cocoyam (taro), which we know as dasheen bush or callaloo leaves (shown overleaf.)

A study of the edible plants used by the East Indians of Trinidad and Tobago notes that *"they take the saijan leaf to make bhaji and the fruit to make talkari"*. This tradition lives on and is the reason you see the combination often plated together. It's rare, for me at least, to have one without the other, either as part of a lunch/dinner plate or caressed in a soft roti.

SERVES 2–4

5 tbsp cooking oil of choice
3 garlic cloves, finely chopped
1 Scotch bonnet pepper, deseeded and finely chopped
1 tsp Green Seasoning (see pp26–27)
500g (1lb 2oz) dasheen bush leaves (callaloo) or flat-leaf spinach, finely chopped
½ tsp sea salt
1 tsp freshly ground black pepper
200ml (¾ cup) coconut milk
1 tsp all-purpose seasoning (optional)

———

In a large frying pan, heat the oil over a medium heat. When hot, add the garlic, Scotch bonnet pepper and green seasoning and sauté for 2 minutes. Add the dasheen bush leaves or spinach and stir, then add the salt and pepper and stir to combine. Pour in the coconut milk and stir again.

Cook for 10 minutes, stirring every few minutes until the mixture thickens. Adjust for taste using all-purpose seasoning or salt and pepper. Serve with rice and dhal or alongside Bodhi (opposite), Pumpkin Talkari (right) and roti (see pp204–219).

Pumpkin talkari

Working on a farm in South Trinidad, I'm called to help the crew harvest their pumpkins for the following weekend's market stall in Princes Town. This day is the best day for it, a local tells me, as it's three days after a full moon, which provides the best yield. Though the majority of the pumpkins are headed for sale, some are kept behind, primarily to make pumpkin talkari. Talkari is a word you'll see throughout this book and is essentially any kind of vegetable or meat stew, where the main ingredient is combined with other ingredients such as mango, and cooked down for some time, producing a marvellously smooth dish (shown overleaf.)

SERVES 2–4

4 tbsp cooking oil of choice
3 garlic cloves, chopped
1 spring onion (scallion/green onion), chopped
½ Scotch bonnet pepper, deseeded and chopped
750g (1½lb) pumpkin, peeled, deseeded and chopped
½ red bell pepper, deseeded and finely chopped (optional)
2 tbsp light soft brown sugar (optional)
sea salt

———

In a large saucepan, heavy-based pan or Dutch pot, heat the oil over a medium heat. When hot, add the garlic, spring onion and Scotch bonnet pepper and sauté for 2 minutes. Add the pumpkin and bell pepper and stir to combine. Cover and steam for 20 minutes. If the pot is dry, add 60ml (4 tablespoons) water and then the sugar, if using. Stir again, cover and continue to cook for another 15 minutes. After this time, the pumpkin should be completely smooth. Use a potato masher to mash to your preference. Add salt to taste.

Serve as a side with curry or alongside Bhaji (see left), Bodhi (opposite) and roti (see pp204–219).

Bodhi

China and India lead the world in the production of green beans, where they have been cultivated for generations. With certain varieties growing several feet without much assistance, it's no surprise that their crunchy wholesome taste became part of the diet of those regions and then travelled with people wherever they moved. In the Caribbean, yard-long stringy pods hang off market tables and are scooped by vendors into scandal bags, poking out of the top for all to see. The most common form of green beans across the Caribbean is chopped, seasoned and sautéed, with a different role depending on where you are. In Guyana *bora* is often served entangled with chicken or shrimp and potatoes; in Suriname *kousenband* finds itself with minimal additions as a side to Bami (see p154) or Nasi (see p56) and in Trinidad and Tobago, to which I owe this recipe, *bodhi* is often paired with tomatoes to accompany a meal platter or give body (apologies for the pun) to vegan roti filling options (shown overleaf.)

In a large frying pan, heat the oil over a medium–high heat. When hot, add the onion and sauté for 3 minutes before adding the garlic, Scotch bonnet pepper and green seasoning, if using. Continue to sauté for 2 minutes and then add the green beans. Sprinkle in the salt, black pepper and curry powder, if using, and stir to combine. Turn the heat down to medium, cover with a lid and cook for 15 minutes.

Remove the lid and stir. Turn the heat down to low, add the tomatoes and cook for another 15 minutes. At this point the tomatoes will have cooked down and the green beans should have turned a dark green colour with some charring.

Serve as a side with curry or alongside Bhaji (see left), Pumpkin Talkari (see left) and roti (see pp204–219).

SERVES 2–4

4 tbsp cooking oil of choice
½ onion, chopped
3 garlic cloves, minced
½ Scotch bonnet pepper, deseeded and chopped (optional)
1 tsp Green Seasoning (see pp26–27 – optional)
700g (1½lb) green beans, chopped
½ tsp sea salt
½ tsp freshly ground black pepper
1 tsp curry powder of choice (optional)
2 tomatoes, chopped

OVERLEAF *Bhaji* (left), *Pumpkin Talkari* (centre) *and Bodhi* (right).

Callaloo

Of all the dishes I've come across where the final product does not visually convey the array of ingredients within, the dish known as callaloo found on the Caribbean's Eastern shores, may be amongst the best examples. This deep green stew is different from the sautéed callaloo found in the likes of Jamaica. Here, the callaloo leaves (also known as dasheen bush leaves) are cooked down alongside copious amounts of okra and diced squash amidst a swirl of coconut milk, before being blended, traditionally with a *dhal gutni* or swizzle stick. Those familiar with West African food may find interesting similarities between this and *ogbono* soup or okra soup, in the way the dish oozes and draws when clinging to the surface of a dipped piece of starch or bread.

I'm not sure exactly which dish was cooking when the term "melting pot" was coined, maybe it was Pepperpot (see p140) but perhaps it was callaloo, as all the ingredients "melt" and combine into one. The dish has become something of a symbol of social representation in the Caribbean, illustrating the multiplicity and democracy of all parts (or ingredients) within. As Trinidad is described in an archive of the region's world famous carnival: *"strange design of time and space, history and geography, the races, the religion, the cultures of the world are here on this island. We are a marvelous twentieth-century hybrid. We are a callaloo..."*

This dish has many different forms. Sometimes it's a hearty stew, enjoyed by itself or on top of a hill of rice or if there's some leftovers, then it has no problem playing the role of a side.

SERVES 4–6

4–5 tbsp cooking oil of choice
1 onion, chopped
3–4 garlic cloves, minced
3 spring onions (scallions/green
  onions), chopped
1 tbsp Green Seasoning (see
  pp26–27)
500g (1lb 2oz) dasheen bush
  leaves (callaloo) or flat-leaf
  spinach
8–10 okra, topped and tailed
½ bell pepper of choice, deseeded
  and chopped
250g (9oz) pumpkin, peeled
  (optional), deseeded and
  chopped
1 tbsp dark brown sugar
  (optional)
400ml (13.5fl oz) can coconut
  milk
1 Scotch bonnet pepper, whole
sea salt and freshly ground black
  pepper

In a large saucepan, heavy-based pan or Dutch pot,
heat the oil over a medium–high heat. When hot, add
the onion and sauté for 3 minutes. Next, add the garlic,
spring onions and green seasoning and continue to sauté
for a further 2 minutes. Then add the dasheen bush
leaves (callaloo), okra, bell pepper, some black pepper, the
pumpkin and the sugar, if using. Stir quickly to combine
and then pour in the coconut milk. Stir again and then
drop in the whole Scotch bonnet pepper. Turn the heat
down to low/medium–low, cover with a lid and simmer
for 30 minutes.

Remove the lid and test the pumpkin by piercing it
with a knife or fork and turn the heat off. Now for the fun
part, if you have a traditional *dhal gutni* or swizzle stick,
submerge it into the pot and twist the handle quickly
with the palm of your hands to blend. If, like me, you are
looking for a shortcut, use a stick blender, submerge it to
the base of the pot and pulse until completely smooth or
your desired consistency. Add salt to taste.

Serve by itself in a bowl or on top of rice.

NOTE *If you have neither of these tools, you can either
attempt to use a potato masher or wait for it to completely
cool and blend it. If you want the dish less "gooey", then use
less okra.*

Masala mango

Two things seem to happen every time I go back to the Americas. One, I find out I have a new cousin and two, I find a new mango I've never heard of. Both immediately become like family to me, and I act like I've known them forever. In Jamaica, mangoes, usually soft and bursting to the touch, are seldom used for anything apart from eating and juice; however, towards the southeastern shores of the Caribbean, the use of mangoes is taken to another level. The green mango found here is a consistently dense fruit that can't really be eaten any other way apart from cooked or preserved, as seen with numerous hot condiments like Kuchela (see p229), Mango Sour (see p232) and this masala mango.

This dish, sometimes known as mango talkari or mango amchar, sits somewhere between a main, a side and a condiment. The former comes with the addition of much more water, making it a mango curry of sorts, while the latter (represented here) uses minimal water combined with sugar and amchar masala to create a subtly spicy syrup. Sometimes it dominates the plate beside a pile of rice and sometimes just a tablespoon or two is dished out amid a number of other bites.

Wash the mangoes. Then halve them, place them flat and slice into 3–4cm (1¼–1½in) strips. Serrated knives are good for slicing through mango stones. Place the mangoes into a large saucepan and cover with water. Add the salt and boil for 20 minutes. Drain and discard the water.

In a heavy-based saucepan or Dutch pot, heat the oil and fenugreek seeds, if using, over a medium–high heat. When hot, add the garlic and Scotch bonnet pepper and sauté for 2 minutes. Next, add the curry powder, green seasoning and 60ml (4 tablespoons) cold water. Stir to combine, then add the mango. Thoroughly stir to combine, ensuring you coat all the mango. Add another 60ml (4 tablespoons) of cold water and stir. After a few minutes, add the sugar, stir and add the amchar masala and ground cumin. Stir again to combine, then turn the heat down to medium, cover with a lid and cook for 8–10 minutes.

Remove the lid and turn the heat down to low. Simmer, uncovered, until it is your desired consistency. It should be smooth and thick but not overly stiff and sticky. Stir in the fresh coriander and serve a few tablespoons on the side of a curry or any plant-based meal.

SERVES 6 AS A SIDE

4 green mangoes (700–800g/ 1lb 9oz–1¾ lb)
2 tsp sea salt
5 tbsp cooking oil of choice
½ tsp fenugreek seeds (optional)
3 garlic cloves, chopped
1 Scotch bonnet pepper, finely chopped
1 tbsp curry powder
1 tbsp Green Seasoning (see pp26–27)
100g (½ cup) brown sugar of choice
2½ tsp amchar masala
½ tsp ground cumin
1 tbsp chopped fresh coriander (cilantro)

Limin'

For centuries, leisure was a restricted concept for the people of the Caribbean. The Indigenous tribes, under waves of European invasions, were constantly on the move. For the enslaved, their time was owned by someone else, as was that of their unborn children, and the early indentured worked tirelessly under the premise they may return home one day. Even today, the harsh economic climate in the region means that for many, work seldom stops. According to anthropologist Keith E. McNeal, accounts of the limited "free time" of the enslaved describe *"each Saturday night (or frankly any day away from cane field or mill), as play-play"*, which involved dance, music, costume, food and drink. This came to dominate the culture and heart of enslaved societies and became *"a carnival in miniature"*, according to Professor Richard D. E. Burton. This space offered a communal focus and embodied an idea of freedom. As Keith E. McNeal argues *"all play is oppositional and all oppositionality is 'playful' or contains a 'play element'."* The ability to just do nothing was a dream and an act of resistance, and it's now a reality savoured by many in limin'.

Limin' is one of those words that bends from verb to noun, though when used in a certain way people understand its meaning. To give a technical definition, limin' is *"an informal gathering of two or more people characterized by semi-ritualized talking and socializing, drinking and eating."* There are many guesses about the origin of the phrase. One account tells that American sailors carried citrus fruit to prevent scurvy and with their loitering habits around Port of Spain came to be known as "limeys". Another, in the 1940s, tells of a strict code for fetes (parties) – you couldn't go if you were not invited. If someone not invited was outside the house feeling sour, you'd say *"suck a lime"*. Later on, you invited friends to *"bus [have or join] a lime"*, and that became "lime", as defined in the *Dictionary of the English/Creole of Trinidad & Tobago*. These old school limes went on deep into the night with *"ole talk and Caribbean music and a little baddening of the head"*, as described by Learie Alleyne-Forte in the short story collection *Jokers on the Abyss' Edge*.

None of this fully describes the essence of the lime. It's hanging out, any time of day, though as the description in the *Dictionary of the English/Creole of Trinidad & Tobago* rightly states, *"It have all kinda lime: sweet lime, sour lime, short lime, long lime, impromptu lime, formal lime and regular lime. You name it we have it."* You might cook all day, then walk to the shop because you forgot something, then end up on someone's veranda limin' for the whole night, eating their food and forgetting all you had made the hours before. This can seem strange to those visiting the Caribbean for the first time, but sharing, especially the sharing of food with "the village", is a staple act of all the creeds that make up the region.

Sometimes the lime may be flyered around the village, weeks in advance of someone's birthday or a fundraising BBQ. Here there will be a table for drinks, a manned row of bain-maries or insulation boxes serving food, and pulsating music vibrating the entire locale for the night. If the music is too loud, you can lime across the side of the road on a deckchair or the bonnet of the car and still feel the vibe.

Sometimes you're walking down the lane and someone says, *"Yo, we avin' a lime tomorrow boy!"*. This can sometimes feature raucous debate but in other instances a word might not be uttered for an hour as everyone simply enjoys the pleasure of being in the company of other people as the night breeze wanders through the front yard. That being said, it only takes Winston or Everett from down the road, Mrs Palmer and her friends, and a bottle of puncheon to turn a quiet lime into what Farmer Nappy would call a *"Big people party."* As soon as the music cuts on, neighbours driving by park up and see *"wah happnin"* and the next few hours become a blur. People once separated by plantations, by

scheming overseers and by divisive racial colonial politics, all come together.

For us in the diaspora, the act of getting together for no real reason is something I find waning and is becoming limited to birthdays, public holidays, weddings and now, more frequently, funerals. For people in cities like London or New York, I'd ask when was the last time you said hello to your neighbours, let alone strolled over to hang out for no reason. In towns like Moruga, this is a weekly event. I'm often asked why Caribbean food in the UK is so important and, to me, it seems that for the diaspora the spaces in which Caribbean food is served offer the last vestige to recreate this community spirit in their new home.

Boil 'n' fry yam

For the great majority of the enslaved in the Caribbean, the cultivation of starchy vegetables like yams represented their first small sphere of autonomy and a modicum of freedom. In what were known as the provision grounds, a small allotment was allocated to individuals where they could tend the land unsupervised. The produce grown – primarily cassava and yam – provided the basis of their diets, rather than rations, which were usually a weekly occurence. It also became possible for the enslaved to sell any excess produce in the town and city markets, which provided an income. A number of generations later, yam is arguably still as important to the descendants of those people. But unless it finds its way into a hearty soup or stew, like my grandmother made, many have mainly consumed it via boiling it in salted water, a method which made it relatively hard for the 10-year-old me to chow down.

Attending cookouts in Trinidad was the first time I really saw this incredible alternative use of yam. Considering how many times I've eaten mashed potatoes, I can't see why it never came to mind before. This is no simple mash though, a second stage of sautéing it with seasoning and peppers turns what is meant to be a side into a dish that can be enjoyed by itself. If you can't find yam, feel free to try this recipe with potatoes.

Place the yam in a large saucepan with a dash of salt and cover with water. (The size to which you chop the yam will dictate the ease of boiling and the consistency when frying.) Boil over a high heat for 25–30 minutes. To test the consistency of the yam, simply prod with a knife or fork and the ease with which you penetrate through the yam will let you know. When it slides through easily, the yam is ready. Discard the water, drain the yam and set aside.

In a large frying pan, Dutch pot or wok, heat the oil over a medium–high heat. When hot, add the onion and sauté for 3 minutes before adding the spring onions, garlic, Scotch bonnet pepper, carrot, red bell pepper, salt or all-purpose seasoning and green seasoning, if using. Now, add your boiled yam and stir, using your utensil to mash while you stir for 5 minutes. Keep stirring and mashing until it is your desired consistency. You can add a splash of water if it isn't mashing easily. When it is starting to mash easily, then add the fresh coriander and mash it into the mix. Add salt and black pepper to taste and serve.

SERVES 4–6

1kg (2¼lb) white or yellow yam, peeled and roughly chopped
5 tbsp cooking oil of choice
1 onion, sliced
2 spring onions (scallions/green onions), chopped
3 garlic cloves, finely chopped
1 Scotch bonnet pepper, finely chopped
⅓ carrot, peeled and grated
½ red bell pepper, deseeded and finely chopped
1 tsp sea salt or all-purpose seasoning
1 tsp Green Seasoning (see pp26–27 – optional)
2 tsp finely chopped fresh coriander (cilantro)
sea salt and freshly ground black pepper

Corn soup

On main roads between St. Mary's, Barrackpore and Penal in Trinidad, cars and pickup trucks parked along the highways hang signs promising the sweetest Canadian corn. My "uncle" Dom is conflicted, while he believes the country should make an effort to support home-grown sweetcorn, the hint of sweetness that emanates from Canadian corn can't be beaten, he tells me. For him and many of his generation, working trips to Canada in harvest season were a way of life and the abundance of the country's sweetcorn left an unforgettable taste.

Whatever the origin, corn is a way of life, so much so that an entire soup was created as a way of devouring as much corn as quickly as possible. Corn on the cob is an amazing vessel for flavour, with elements of spice, herbs and coconut nestled up in the grooves of the corn. While the soup can be found throughout the week, most shops and homes reserve soups for the weekends. In the diaspora, in places like Toronto and New York City, where I think no amount of time can ever pass for Caribbean descendants to be able to truly embrace the winter cold, you can also find it throughout the week.

———

In a large saucepan or Dutch pot, heat the oil over a medium–high heat. When hot, add the onion and sauté for 3 minutes before adding the garlic and spring onion.

Next, add the cornmeal or split peas along with the bell pepper and fresh coriander. Pour in the hot water and stir before adding all the seasoning ingredients. Turn the heat down to low and simmer for 30 minutes until the split peas are soft to the touch. If you like, you can use a hand-held blender and pulse until completely smooth at this stage. If you use cornmeal, skip this pulverizing step.

Add the corn, coconut milk, carrot, pumpkin, plantain (if using), whole Scotch bonnet pepper and stir. Cover with a lid and cook for 20 minutes.

Meanwhile, cook the dumplings following the instructions on p195. When the dumplings are cooked, drain the water and place them into the soup pot. Remove the thyme stems, whole scotch bonnet pepper and serve.

NOTE *You can either boil the dumplings in a separate pot as per the instructions or you can place them gently into the soup pot. Doing the latter may mean they take slightly longer to cook – 25–30 minutes – since the soup pot is on a low heat. If so, the latter part of the cooking method will take 30–35 minutes rather than 20 minutes.*

SERVES 6

5 tbsp cooking oil of choice
1 onion, chopped
6 garlic cloves, chopped
2 spring onions (scallions/green onions), chopped
70g (½ cup) cornmeal or yellow split peas, rinsed
1 red bell pepper, deseeded and chopped
1 tbsp chopped fresh coriander (cilantro)
800ml (3½ cups) boiling water
5 corn on the cobs (ears of corn) (about 900g/2lb), silk and husks removed
400ml (13.5fl oz) can coconut milk or water
1 carrot, peeled and sliced or diced to preference
500g (1lb) pumpkin or sweet potato peeled and chopped
1 plantain, peeled and chopped (optional)
1 Scotch bonnet pepper, whole
Coconut Boil Dumplings (see p195)

FOR THE SEASONING

5 sprigs of thyme
2 tsp vegetable bouillon or 1 vegetable stock (bouillon) cube
1 tsp sea salt
1 tsp freshly ground black pepper
½ tsp all-purpose seasoning (optional)

SEEDS
& PULSES

"Legends passed down over generations recount how African women on their journey to the Americas hid rice grains, which could serve as seeds if they were still husked."

Be it the gungo beans of West Africa, the split peas of India or the green beans of China, every people that came to the Caribbean either brought with them a foodstuff or knowledge of particular foods – ingredients like the rices, grains and seeds that bolster dishes, and which today we often see as relatively unremarkable. These foods are on record as being consumed for centuries, and for new residents of the Caribbean they represented not just a meal but a way of reconnecting with their former homes.

Scholars suggest that many African ethnic groups possessed the techniques for rice cultivation generations before the transatlantic slave trade. For this reason, it's suggested ethnic groups from rice-growing regions of Africa, such as modern-day Sierra Leone and Senegambia, were specifically favoured by planters who sought to capitalize on their agricultural skills in the New World, from South Carolina down to Suriname. Legends passed down over generations recount how African women on their journey to the Americas hid rice grains, which could serve as seeds if they were still husked, and so dishes like *waakye*, seen today all over Ghana, were reworked into comparable versions such as Rice & Peas (see p59). Moreso, the porridges that people from all over the Caribbean enjoy, such as peanut, hominy and Cornmeal Porridge (see p70), seem to be reimagined versions of the pap enjoyed in the mother continent of the enslaved.

Access to these types of foods was still very limited at this time. Grains were usually only provided to the enslaved when tropical climate-induced floods or droughts caused the depletion of soil and led to the failure of the provision grounds where their root vegetables were grown. Where planters were usually expected (and often compelled by law) to supply weekly food rations to their workers, they imported foodstuffs such as grains and cornmeal. These types of food were favoured, especially amongst the enslaved and poverty stricken, due to their ability to feed people en masse. One study in the Caribbean recorded in B. W. Higman's *Jamaican Food* remarked, *"Rice and cornmeal are apparently our cheapest foods and most used, because they swell in cooking and provide large quantities of food at a cheap rate."*

Both rice and beans feature in many West African legends in the Caribbean. A chapter in *Tall Tales of Trinidad & Tobago* tells the story of Ti Piggi. Here rice grains scattered on the floor prevent the completion of the blood-sucking, shapeshifting soucouyant Ti Piggi's mission. This hampers the spirit as picking up and eating each grain of rice distracts it from its mission by which time the sun rises and evaporates the evil spirit. Both West Africans and Caribbeans of a certain generation know stories of Anansi. In one particular tale, *Anansi and the pot of beans*, Anansi's impatience regarding his grandmother's stewing pot of beans leads to him being scalded. I think it's no coincidence that the moral of these tales is that there are negative consequences to eating food that has been cooked to feed many others!

"They too saw power in foods like rice and its role in sustaining people."

For the most part, the majority of the enslaved Caribbean diet consisted of starchy vegetables and stews. Stews were innovative and utilized what was available, and this habitually included the likes of kidney beans, whether it was red pea soup in Jamaica or Bruine Bonen (see p75) in Suriname.

This shifted markedly with the arrival of indentured labourers from India and China. Rice provided the bulk of the diet for these workers on their voyages to the Caribbean, which lasted for around 4 months at sea. A revised dietary scheme for Indian workers included 14 *chataks* of rice and 2 *chataks* of dhal (1 *chatak* = 60g/2oz) as well as ghee, turmeric, onions, salt and tobacco. Beyond sustenance, the people of Indian heritage also had a legacy of reverence towards grains like rice. In ceremonies like the Matikor/Dig Dutty ritual originating in North India, it is used as part of the array presented to deities in order to receive earthly blessings. They too saw power in foods like rice and its role in sustaining people. Kitchri (see p58), a dish that combines rice and split peas and a famed part of the holistic ayurvedic way of life, has been consumed for centuries for this very reason. Rice was also a staple ingredient in the sweet Kheer (see p65) served at religious functions like *pujas*.

While the experience of Indians, especially in Guyana and Trinidad and Tobago ran quite parallel, a key difference came in Trinidad with the government offering to trade their right to a return journey to India for five or ten acres of land. This provided an agrarian source of income and set the impetus for rice cultivation and consumption on a larger scale. This turned many of the indentured into landowners, which led to land development and increased agro-production that benefitted the government as it led to higher overall productivity. This was bolstered by the increase in migrants sent for by their families and also growing rice imports at the turn of the 20th century. By the end of the 19th century, when sugar profits had plummeted on the estates, a few Indian workers were allowed to use some of the less productive land for plantation-style rice farming. This also led to the wider availability of pulses like split peas and chickpeas, both of which have become essentials in Caribbean food, specifically in the countries with a high Indo-Caribbean populace.

Split peas or *dhal*, used throughout this book, also act as a way of reconnecting with history. Dhal (see p72), also the name for the split pea soup, was a meal enjoyed for centuries in the Indian motherland of indentured workers, and today in the Caribbean it is commonly recreated using the same age old techniques like chounkay-ing (see p73).

Though they came in smaller numbers, many of the Chinese and Indonesian people who arrived in the Caribbean also had exceptional rice-cultivating skills, as well as a cooking prowess that immediately wowed their new compatriots. The popularity of fried rice in various forms, such as Nasi (see p56), whether in an Asian-Caribbean or Afro-Caribbean restaurant, is testament to this. All these cultures came together layer on layer to form cook-up rice dishes like Pelau (see p62), which are served at "Creole" restaurants and loved the region over.

Long before the "innovation" of zero waste stores took hold in the West, the likes of Stabroek Market, Central Market and Centrale Market

"Hopefully this chapter can help reframe what breakfast means and tastes like."

(and the markets of Asia and West Africa before them) had open baskets and tubs of lentils, kidney beans, chickpeas and rice. Here you could come with your own containers and be served by weight. This system lives on today, however, I know many people don't have the time to soak seeds and pulses overnight. Bearing that in mind, most recipes in this chapter refer to the pre-cooked canned versions of their relevant ingredient. If you would like to go the more traditional route, simply use roughly the same weight as a "drained can", soak and continue according to the recipe.

Another thing mentioned over and over again in this chapter is that many of these simple dishes, the majority savoury, were eaten for breakfast or early lunch, similarly to the plant-based recipes and some of the curries (see pp82–101). Breakfast is my favourite meal of the day when I'm in the Caribbean and hopefully this chapter can help reframe what breakfast means and tastes like. Hopefully, so that we can be open to options beyond sugary-oat crisps and dairy milk, which in many cases is not even cheaper than these traditional dishes (definitely not in the Caribbean, West Africa and Asia where prices for imported Western cereal brands are astronomical).

URINAAMS ETEN

BOILED RICE
PRODUCT OF GUYANA

Fry channa

The history of chickpeas dates back multiple thousands of years, traversing many world routes starting from the Caucasus and modern day Turkey before reaching the Mediterranean and then India. In all those places the chickpea or *channa* (chana) as it's known in Hindi, was prepared and consumed in myriad different ways. Now, some millennia later, I find there are still novel ways of consuming chickpeas when I go back to Trinidad and see new flavours of chickpea snacks on the shelves.

While the predominant use of *channa* in the Caribbean is in its curried form, which ends up in rotis and *doubles* (see p166), the pulse makes a great snack and side on its own. Roasting gives all the goodness of chickpeas without the extra-curricular tasks needed to make a curry. The fried version, like those seen jam-packed into bottles, are a fantastic bite for chain-snackers.

Drain the chickpeas and lay them in a bowl or on a plate. Place them in the sun for an hour or so or use kitchen paper and try to dry them as much as possible.

In a frying pan, heat the oil over a medium heat and, when hot, add the onion. Sauté for 3 minutes and then add the spring onion, garlic, green seasoning, Scotch bonnet pepper or chilli flakes and the cumin. Stir to combine and sauté for an additional 2 minutes. Next, turn the heat up a notch and add the chickpeas, salt and pepper. Fry while stirring for 3 minutes and then remove the pan from the heat.

Garnish with the fresh coriander.

SERVES 2 AS A SIDE

2 x 400g (15oz) cans chickpeas
5 tbsp cooking oil of choice
1 onion, finely chopped
1 spring onion (scallion/green onion), finely chopped (optional)
4 garlic cloves, chopped
1 tsp Green Seasoning (see pp26–27 – optional)
½ Scotch bonnet pepper, deseeded and finely chopped or 1 tsp dried chilli flakes
½ tsp ground cumin
½ tsp sea salt
½ tsp freshly ground black pepper
1 tsp finely chopped fresh coriander (cilantro)

Roast channa

SERVES 2

2 x 400g (15oz) cans chickpeas
1 tbsp cooking oil of choice
1 tsp dark brown sugar
1 tsp chilli powder of choice
1 tsp mixed herbs
½ tsp ground cumin
½ tsp sea salt
½ tsp freshly ground black pepper
½ tsp all-purpose seasoning
   (optional)

Preheat the oven to 190°C (170°C fan/375°F/ Gas 5).

Drain the cans of chickpeas and, if time permits, remove as many skins as you can. Then dry them with a dish towel and place in a bowl. Add the tablespoon of oil and use your hands to combine the oil with the chickpeas. Then add in all the remaining ingredients and mix again.

Place the chickpeas onto a lined baking tray and roast in the oven for 10 minutes. Turn the chickpeas and cook for a further 10 minutes. After this, turn up the heat to 220°C (200°C fan/425°F/Gas 7) and place your oven on grill (broil) and cook for a final 5 minutes.

Remove the tray from the oven. The chickpeas should be orange and browned in some spots and they also should have shrunk.

Leave to cool for 5 minutes, then taste. If you want a deeper taste, you can sprinkle over oil and add further dashes of brown sugar, chilli powder, pepper and all-purpose seasoning and toss to combine.

Store in a sterilized bottle (see p223) or container and eat within a week.

Nasi (Fried rice)

The Dutch colonists who once controlled what we know today as Guyana, lost much of their sway in the Caribbean through physical and economic wars, leaving Suriname as one of their last cultural holds in the region. (Others include Aruba, Curaçao and Sint Maarten.) Here, patterns of human movement to power the transatlantic slave trade followed the textbook set by other European nations. This included seeking replacement labour for the freed West Africans. The Dutch, too, turned to India but to supplement this they further ravaged Indonesia, a place they had colonized for four centuries. The predominantly Muslim Javanese people, descending from the island of Java (the largest island of Indonesia today), worked the plantations until the labour initiatives ceased. The legacy of their descendants is impossible to miss in Suriname. With 5 per cent of the population identifying as Javanese descendants, it makes sense that on every street you'll find food spots serving Nasi – deftly sweet fried rice that, like its Chinese culinary sibling, has a current of soy sauce running through it (shown on p60). Easy to whip up for lunch or dinner when paired with some stewed meat.

In a medium saucepan, add the rice and 400ml (1¾ cups) water and boil over a high heat. Add 1 teaspoon of salt and stir. When hot and bubbling, turn the heat to medium, add the butter and stir, then cook for 5–8 minutes until the liquid evaporates. Stir intermittently to ensure the rice isn't sticking. Then turn the heat down to low and simmer with the lid on for 25 minutes. Remove the lid, fluff the rice with a fork and set aside.

In a large frying pan or wok, add the oil and heat over a medium heat. When hot, add the onion and sauté for 3 minutes. Then add the spring onions, garlic, lemongrass, if using, ginger (or galangal) and pimento, if using, and sauté for another 2 minutes. Next, add the pre-cooked rice and mix for a few minutes to thoroughly combine. When combined, turn up the heat a notch and add the oyster sauce, soy sauce, brown sugar and 1 teaspoon of salt and continue to stir thoroughly. After this, the rice should have turned brown. Continue to stir-fry the rice for a further 7 minutes. The rice will continue to get a darker shade of brown as you continue to cook. Add a pinch of black pepper and garnish with chopped fresh coriander.

This is commonly served with Guyanese chicken or Brown Stew Chicken (see p138).

SERVES 6 AS A SIDE

350g (2 cups) basmati rice, thoroughly washed and drained
2 tsp sea salt
1 tsp butter, margarine or coconut oil
5 tbsp cooking oil of choice
1 medium brown onion, finely chopped
2 spring onions (scallions/green onions), chopped
3 garlic cloves, minced
1 piece of lemongrass (optional)
2.5cm (1in) piece of fresh root ginger, peeled and minced, or 2.5cm (1in) piece of galangal root
½ tsp crushed pimento seeds (allspice berries) or allspice powder (optional)
1 tbsp oyster sauce
1 tbsp dark soy sauce
1 tbsp brown sugar or 2 tbsp black soy sauce (see p146 – instead of brown sugar and dark soy sauce)
pinch of freshly ground black pepper
2 tbsp chopped fresh coriander (cilantro)

Bhaji rice

Bhaji rice or spinach rice (see photo on p60), a cook-up rice of sorts, is often traditionally made with salted pork cuts such as pigtail, or saltfish. However, as partners to main meals they are great without. At most Caribbean takeout spots, you are offered a side of rice with your order and at places like Sybil's, my go-to when in the Queens borough of NYC, it sits gleaming under the lights of the cabinet with options aplenty. Throughout the book I've suggested serving most main dishes with white rice, though if you have the capacity, this dish also makes a great companion to most mains.

Wash the spinach and set aside.

In a medium saucepan or Dutch pot, heat the oil over a medium heat. When hot, add the onion and sauté for 3 minutes until it starts to brown slightly. Then add the garlic and green seasoning, if using, and sauté for a further 2 minutes. Next, add the spinach and stir for 3–5 minutes until the leaves wilt and darken. Then add the rice and stir for 2 minutes. By this time the onions will have started to brown.

Next, add the coconut milk, 100ml (⅓ cup) water and salt and stir to combine. Turn the heat up a notch until the liquid starts to boil and when it does, turn it down to medium and cook for 5–8 minutes to let the liquid evaporate. Stir frequently to ensure it doesn't stick to the bottom of the pan. Finally, add the whole Scotch bonnet pepper.

Turn the heat down low to a simmer, cover with a lid and cook for 25 minutes. Serve as a side with any curry (see pp82–101) or 2–3 plant-based recipes (see pp26–47).

NOTE *When covering the pan, place a layer of foil under the lid to ensure the heat is trapped in the pan.*

SERVES 6 AS A SIDE

150g (5 cups) baby spinach or dasheen bush leaves (callaloo), stems removed
4 tbsp cooking oil of choice
½ onion, finely chopped
4 garlic cloves, minced
1 tbsp Green Seasoning (see pp26–27 – optional)
350g (2 cups) basmati rice, thoroughly washed and drained
400ml (13.5fl oz) can coconut milk (or 400ml/1¾ cups water)
1 tbsp sea salt
1 Scotch bonnet pepper, whole

Kitchri

There are as many regions across Southeast Asia who enjoy this meal as there are different spellings – *kitchri, kichdi, kitchri, khichiri, kitchari* – each with its own unique variation and method of preparation (shown on p61). Those of you familiar with the "English" dish of kedgeree will immediately draw a parallel, which then makes sense when you say any of the aforementioned names in a slow blighty accent. The baseline of the dish that appears non-negotiable is rice and dhal – often mung but sometimes (as in this recipe) the easier-to-find yellow split peas. *Kitchri* has been at the forefront of the recent wave of popularity that has accompanied the traditional Indian ayurvedic way of healthy living. Perhaps rightly so, the dish is equally as satiating in its rudimentary form for breakfast as it is loaded with greens and veggies for dinner.

In a pressure cooker, heat the oil over a medium heat. When hot, add the cumin seeds, cinnamon and cardamom. When they begin to turn brown, add the onion and sauté for 3 minutes before adding the spring onions, garlic and ginger. Next, add the split peas and sauté for a minute before adding the rice and carrot, continuing to sauté for another two minutes.

Then add the water, turmeric, vegetable bouillon and salt. Stir to combine and boil for 2 minutes. Secure the lid and cook for 15 minutes. Release pressure and unsecure according to the manufacturer's instructions. Remove the lid and, using a potato masher or *dhal gutni*, mash to your preferred texture. Leave to cool for 5 minutes, remove the cinnamon stick if used and serve.

NOTE *You can soak the split peas in water and leave for a minimum of 6 hours to overnight, which will make the peas softer. You can also use a regular saucepan, though you'll need to boil the peas first for 10 minutes and cook for 30–45 minutes for the final cook.*

SERVES 6 AS A SIDE

- 5 tbsp cooking oil of choice
- ½ tsp cumin seeds
- 1 cinnamon stick or ½ tsp ground cinnamon
- ⅛ tsp ground cardamom (optional)
- ½ onion, chopped
- 2 spring onions (scallions/green onions), chopped
- 3 garlic cloves, minced
- 2.5cm (1in) piece of fresh root ginger, grated
- 250g (1¼ cups) yellow split peas, soaked and washed
- 250g (1 cup) basmati rice, thoroughly washed and drained
- 1 carrot, peeled and finely diced or sliced
- 900ml (scant 4 cups) boiling water
- ½ tsp ground turmeric
- 1 tsp vegetable bouillon or 1 vegetable stock (bouillon) cube (optional)
- 1 tsp sea salt
- 3 tbsp chopped fresh coriander (cilantro)

Rice & peas

At this point I should mention something I've concealed like secret government intel. There are many people who don't consider rice and peas with kidney beans to be the "true" rice and peas (shown on p61). While the scale of affinity toward a particular legume shifts from island to island, it seems wrong to definitively say, for example, kidney beans is Jamaican style and gungo peas is Trini style, as you'll likely aggrieve someone. In my family the division is clear (but that's just mine). The kinship toward gungo peas makes sense when delving into the archives. Gungo, a Creolization of "Congo", became the umbrella term for the many peoples emanating from West and Central Africa who brought either foods or the knowledge of the cultivation of certain foods to the Caribbean, which included these peas. This dish makes a great foundation for a vegan platter, with many of the recipes in the plant-based chapter, as well as underpinning any curry, especially goat.

SERVES 6 AS A SIDE

400g (15oz) can gungo peas (or pigeon peas) in salted water
400ml (13.5fl oz) can coconut milk or 200ml (scant 1 cup) water and 200ml (scant 1 cup) coconut milk
300g (1½ cups) basmati rice, thoroughly washed and drained
1 tbsp butter
2.5cm (1in) piece of fresh root ginger (optional)
1 Scotch bonnet pepper, whole (optional)

FOR THE SEASONING

2 tbsp Green Seasoning (see pp26–27)
5 sprigs of thyme
½ onion, peeled
1 tsp dark brown sugar
1 tsp sea salt or all-purpose seasoning
¼ tsp freshly ground black pepper
6 pimento seeds (allspice berries)
1 tbsp browning (optional) or dark soy sauce

Empty the peas and any liquid in the can into a saucepan or pot. Add 3 tablespoons of water to the can to loosen any stuck peas and pour into the pan. Next, add the seasoning ingredients and then bring the pot to the boil over a medium–high heat. Turn down to low–medium heat and cook for 10–15 minutes with the lid on, until the peas are heated through.

Remove the lid, add the coconut milk (or coconut milk and water) and rice and stir (the liquid should be about 5mm/¼in above the rice). Cook over a medium heat for 7–10 minutes until the liquid evaporates. Stir intermittently to ensure no rice is burning and sticking to the bottom of the pan. When the liquid has evaporated, turn the heat down to the lowest setting, stir in the butter, add the ginger and whole Scotch bonnet pepper, if using, put on the lid and simmer for 25–30 minutes.

Remove the onion, Scotch bonnet pepper, ginger and thyme and then you are ready to serve.

NOTE *When covering the pan, place a layer of foil under the lid to ensure the heat is trapped in the pan.*

OVERLEAF *Nasi (Fried Rice)* (top left), *Bhaji Rice* (bottom left), *Kitchri* (top right), *Rice & Peas* (bottom right).

Cook-up rice

Cook-up rice is an umbrella term for any one-pot rice dish that includes any number of additions – be it vegetables, meat or pulses. In some sense, any of the prior rice dishes in this chapter could be considered cook-up rice, however, cook-up rice is most commonly associated with the one-pot dish known as pelau. Like a great deal of dishes that we, the descendants of the poverty stricken Caribbean peoples, enjoy today, it has its origins in providing sustenance and a means of survival. In his culinary memoir *Pig Tails 'n' Breadfruit*, Bajan novelist Austin Clarke describes pelau as "slave food", noting it being a "make-do kind 'o food". This is a philosophy that runs all through this book.

Pelau is another dish that embodies the fusion of cultures in the Caribbean. The name is considered to be a Creolization of the Middle Eastern pilaf that had made its way to various parts of Asia, and the Persian *polow* which preceded that. From these people came mass cultivation of rice in the Caribbean. The process of browning meat in sugar for pelau arguably came from the West Africans who were in turn mimicking the Amerindian tribes' *cassareep*, and the use of ketchup, which could only arise after interaction with the West.

This recipe for pelau is attempting to replicate one I had in a neighbour's house in Trinidad that was similar in many ways to a risotto. Ideally the rice is on the moister side, so you don't need to scrutinize the cooking of it too much. This is a real larder, bottom-of-the-fridge, leftover type dish, so do use what you have even if that's a different meat from chicken, just ensure you cook it amply.

SERVES 6

1kg (2¼lb) chicken breasts or
thighs, cut into bite-sized
pieces

4–5 tbsp cooking oil of choice

50g (¼ cup) light soft brown
sugar

500g (2¾ cups) basmati rice,
thoroughly washed and
drained

400g (15oz) can pigeon peas
(gungo peas) or kidney beans

1 carrot, peeled and chopped to
preference

1 white onion, finely chopped

3 spring onions (scallions/green
onions), chopped, white and
green parts separated

2.5cm (1in) piece of fresh root
ginger (optional)

3 garlic cloves, grated (optional)

1 tbsp tomato ketchup (optional)

1 tbsp light soy sauce (optional)

400ml (13.5fl oz) can coconut
milk

1 tsp sea salt

1 tsp freshly ground black pepper

1 tsp vegetable bouillon or 1 stock
(bouillon) cube of choice
(chicken, beef or vegetable)

1 tsp all-purpose seasoning

500ml (generous 2 cups) boiling
water

1 Scotch bonnet pepper, whole

1 red bell pepper, deseeded and
finely diced

2–3 tbsp chopped fresh coriander
(cilantro)

1 avocado, peeled, pitted and
sliced (optional)

FOR THE SEASONING

2 tbsp Green Seasoning (see
pp26–27)

1 tsp all-purpose seasoning

1 tsp sea salt

½ tsp freshly ground black
pepper

Place the chicken in a bowl with all the seasoning ingredients and mix in. Cover and refrigerate for a minimum of an hour but ideally 6 hours to overnight.

In a heavy-based pan or Dutch pot, add the oil and heat over a medium–high heat. When hot, add the sugar and gently make sure it's all submerged in oil but don't stir. After 5 minutes the sugar will start to bubble. When it does, use tongs to take the chicken and shake off any excess marinade before you place it in the pot piece by piece.

Stir the chicken and coat in the sugar mixture for 5 minutes. The chicken will take on a brown coated appearance. Turn the heat down to low, cover the pot and simmer for 10 minutes.

The chicken will have released its juices into the pot – stir for 30 seconds and then add the rice. Start to combine the rice for 3–5 minutes and then add peas. Stir for 2 minutes and then add the carrot, onion, white part of the spring onions, ginger, garlic and ketchup and soy sauce, if using.

If the pot starts to get dry, add a splash of water to the base and stir. Next, add the coconut milk, salt, black pepper, stock powder or cube and all-purpose seasoning and stir to combine. Pour in the hot water.

Turn the heat up to medium–high and cook until the liquid starts to bubble. When it does, turn the heat to medium and cook until the liquid evaporates – this should take about 5–7 minutes. When the liquid has evaporated, turn the heat to low, then add the whole Scotch bonnet pepper. Next, place a layer of foil over the top of the pot, put on the lid and cook for 25 minutes. Slowly open the lid and add the bell pepper, green part of the spring onions and chopped fresh coriander. Replace the lid and cook for a final 5 minutes.

If you like your rice a drier consistency, feel free to cook for an extra 5 minutes. Remove the whole Scotch bonnet pepper and serve with sliced avocado.

Kheer

Elaborate desserts aren't a huge thing across the Caribbean. Either the dinner has a sweet element to it, or it's being washed down by a sweet drink. With that said, I find *kheer* – a sweet rice pudding – bookending the proceedings of numerous Hindu events. Amongst the most captivating was my Guyanese neighbour's *puja* in his home in Central Florida. This hours-long intricate ceremony is a ritualistic offer to Hindu deities, though can only be really explained by observing or being part of one.

The Hindi word *kheer* is said to derive from the Sanskrit *ksheer* for milk and *khsirika* for any dish prepared with milk. It has its earliest mentions in Indian scriptures of the 14th century and since then has been associated with festive occasions. To describe this dish as a rice pudding does seem like underselling it. The drop of ghee or coconut oil adds a completely new dimension, as does the cardamom and cinnamon used to season it. The toppings are where individual tastes or familial traditions make their mark and no two *kheer* ever seem the same, so feel free to play about. This is mainly eaten solo in a cup, though I've seen numerous people eat it with *dhal puri* roti and even though I'll eat *puri* with anything, I've yet to try that particular combo.

SERVES 4–6

1.3 litres (5½ cups) milk of choice (usually dairy milk)
1 tbsp ghee or coconut oil (optional)
¼ tsp ground green cardamom
1 cinnamon stick or ¼ tsp ground cinnamon (optional)
¼ tsp grated nutmeg
¼ tsp vanilla extract
70g (⅓ cup) basmati rice, throughly washed and drained
100g (½ cup) granulated brown sugar
¼ tsp sea salt (optional)

FOR THE GARNISH (OPTIONAL)

10g (2 tbsp) desiccated coconut
10g (2 tbsp) pistachios, chopped
20g (3 tbsp) raisins or currants
dried rose petals
a few strands of saffron

Heat the milk and ghee, if using, in a saucepan over a medium–high heat, stir in the cardamom, cinnamon, nutmeg and vanilla extract and boil for 8–10 minutes until the milk has reduced by half. Stir intermittently to prevent it boiling over. Add the rice and stir. Now stir in the sugar and let the mixture boil up for a minute before turning the heat down to medium and cooking for another 15 minutes, continuing to stir every minute or so. The milk should continue to evaporate, and the mixture become thicker. Take off the heat and let cool before serving. If you would like the dish to be thicker, turn the heat down to low and continue to simmer for a further 15 minutes.

Stir in the salt, if you like, and garnish with your choice of ingredients. Serve hot, warm or cold.

Sawine

The proportion of Hindus to Muslims in Trinidad in the last decade of the 19th century essentially mirrored that in the regions of Uttar Pradesh and Bihar in India, which accounted for the majority of indentured labourers. This proportion was around 85 per cent Hindu and 14 per cent "Muhammadans". Since that time, the latter has been supplemented by Muslim West African descendants of the Hausa, as well as relatively recent phenomena like the Nation of Islam. While overall the percentage of Muslims in Trinidad and Tobago and Guyana remains comparatively small at 5 per cent and 6 per cent respectively, the overall numbers still dwarf most other Caribbean nations. This is seen in the number of beautiful mosques that colour the region as well as the fanfare that accompanies the national holiday of Eid – the finale of Ramadan. Deals for *iftar* boxes adorn advertisement boards and word of feasts abounds.

As a result of the melting pot that is the Caribbean, while many may not be of the Islamic faith, they'll still observe some part of the tradition (in much the same way as non-Christians enjoy Christmas trees and presents). On the most recent Eid, I was in Trinidad in the morning and was greeted by a silver cup of hot sawine, essentially an alternative version of *kheer* (and even called *Seviyan kheer* in Pakistan), which utilizes vermicelli noodles instead of rice. The idea of noodles cooked down in a sweet milk may take some bites to get used to but surely only a few.

If you like, you can dry-fry the vermicelli in a large frying pan or wok for around 5 minutes until the majority of it turns a brownish hue. Turn off the heat and set aside.

Heat the milk and ghee, if using, in a saucepan over medium–high heat, stir in the green cardamom powder, cinnamon stick, nutmeg and vanilla extract and boil for 8–10 minutes. Stir intermittently to prevent it boiling over. The milk should have reduced by around half. Turn the heat down to medium–low, add the vermicelli, then stir in the sugar. Next, cover the pot with a lid and cook for 10 minutes. Remove from heat and you are ready to serve. If you would like the dish thicker, you can continue to simmer over a low heat for 10 minutes.

Stir in the salt if you wish and garnish with your choice of ingredients. Serve immediately.

NOTE *If dry, add 100ml (scant ½ cup) of milk and reheat over a low heat with the lid on.*

SERVES 6

100g (1 cup) dry vermicelli pieces of broken thin spaghetti
1.3 litres (5½ cups) milk of choice (ideally dairy milk)
1 tsp ghee (optional)
¼ tsp green cardamom powder
1 cinnamon stick or ¼ tsp ground cinnamon (optional)
¼ tsp grated nutmeg
¼ tsp vanilla extract
80g (⅓ cup) granulated white sugar
¼ tsp sea salt (optional)

FOR THE GARNISH (OPTIONAL)

30g (¼ cup) maraschino cherries
10g (2 tbsp) almonds, chopped
20g (3 tbsp) raisins or currants

Pardna

Seeds, grains and pulses are the lynchpin, the foundation, the unsung heroes of this book. Diminutive alone but together they grow and expand into something a magnitude greater than the sum of their parts. A single grain of rice is insignificant, however, when filling a bag the grains become immovable, able to suppress surging waters and traffic. This same philosophy, strength in numbers, is what gives a community power and helps it flourish. One indelible childhood memory is my mother on the phone to her sisters and cousins constantly talking about the "pardner" money. It was something I always knew about but I had no idea what it was or what it meant.

Pardner money is where an informal group of individuals all periodically (weekly or monthly) pay a set amount of money to an informal "banker" and then periodically each individual collects the total pot. A first-hand account from Caribbean people setting up a new life in 20th-century Britain describes:

"There may be six or seven of you and every week or every month you 'throw' a pound or whatever the group decide they can afford and when. One person called the 'banker' collects money from everyone in the group and every week or month they give each person in the group that 'hand' collected from everyone. You would get your 'draw' and it would rotate like that for maybe six or seven weeks or months until everybody in the group got a hand or draw and then it would start all over again."

This informal savings system that my mum and aunties used was far from new. Known to those of Indian heritage as a *chit fund*, or to Chinese as a *hui*, throughout the Caribbean in the 1800s it was noted that as well as being a place to make income, African-Caribbean women used the marketplace for organizing the West African Yoruba-derived *asue*, a monetary system used to save for, and meet financial obligations.

Asue turned into *sou sou* (or *susu*) which then had other names such as "partner hand", from which *pardner/pardna* derives. The

trust needed for this informal finance is something that can only be fostered by a solid community. Whether it was Africans or Jahaji (Indian indentured groups transported to the Caribbean), or Caribbeans transplanted to Britain, there exists a constant chain of fostering community and family in a new land, which aided the foundation of the *pardna*. Parents' friends became your "aunties and uncles" and their kids were now your "cousins", irrespective of zero biological link.

As the earlier account continues, *"We called it 'pardner hand' or 'Susu' or 'Club'. That's how West Indians were able to buy houses, because you lend a friend or relative your draw and then they use that to put down a deposit, which was only a couple hundred pounds in those days. And when they got the house you would then rent a room from them."*

Many lower-middle class and well-educated middle class people from the Caribbean became working class or underemployed when they arrived in the UK and found limited opportunity, and some believed there was a kind of class shift as they moved. Couple this with extremely limited access to finance and loans, which even persists to this day, and the importance of these informal community support structures can be seen.

As the above passage shows, one of the main goals of the scheme was for everyone to be able to afford a home and as my mum and her companions all secured houses through hard work boosted by the pardna, I heard it discussed less and less over the years. What it birthed was what Michael McMillan beautifully depicts in his book *The Front Room*, describing how *"the front room was recreated as the spiritual, moral and social centre of the public presentation of the family towards the outside world."*

The community support led to the cultivation of a space – the home – where living was free from public persecution, where patois and Creole could freely roll off the

tongue and "proper" English could be folded away in the drawer with the work uniform. Here, people could continue to foster Caribbean culture with joy. In my family, Sundays especially were, and continue to be, the day when you can go to a certain "auntie's" house to just lime (see p42). No questions asked, no invite needed, you know around a certain time there will be a bottle of something on the table and some debate or discussion to jump into. Of course, it goes without saying that there will be food, not just any food, but the food found throughout this book, and so I hope these recipes can in some way help continue this for another generation.

Cornmeal porridge

As far back as the 17th century there are records of West Africans eating rudimentary forms of porridge that appear to be related to pap, a dish consumed the continent over. These early versions usually centred around farina – a flour derived from the cassava tuber. The process of turning the cassava into flour was a lengthy one but prepared this way, it lasted, and could be stored for a long time. The coarse flour provides the base of the cassava bread Jamaicans know well as bammy; however, it could later be made into a porridge by mixing it with water and milk, then stirring for a few minutes, adding salt and nutmeg and sweetening to taste. Over time, this recipe evolved to utilize pretty much anything people could get hold of, be it American imported oats, ground nuts or cornmeal – all milled fine into powders. The latter is much acclaimed due to its expansion when cooked and so its ability to feed more mouths.

Growing up I came to realize there was a great disconnect between the porridge I was raving about and the porridge that my non-Caribbean friends at school were berating. My version would appear on Saturday mornings and any time I had to stay with aunties after school. In the method I've noted that you keep stirring to avoid clumping but looking back I always loved those small clumps hidden like golden nuggets in the bowl, so don't take that as gospel.

Add all the ingredients, except the salt and sugar, together with 700ml (2¾ cups) water to a saucepan and heat over a medium–high heat. When the mixture starts to boil, turn down the heat to medium and simmer for 20 minutes, stirring intermittently with a whisk or fork to prevent lumps of corn forming.

Turn the heat down to low, add the salt and sugar and stir until they dissolve. You can continue to simmer over a low heat until the porridge is your desired consistency if it is not already. Remove the cinnamon stick (if used) and bay leaf and serve hot.

SERVES 6

250g (2 cups) fine cornmeal
400ml (13.5fl oz) can coconut
　　milk or milk of choice
1 cinnamon stick or ¼ tsp ground
　　cinnamon
¼ tsp grated nutmeg
¼ tsp vanilla extract (optional)
1 bay leaf (optional)
¼ tsp sea salt
2 tbsp brown sugar of choice

Dhal

Not to sound like a broken record, but like the overwhelming majority of recipes in this book, there is no definitive way of making dhal. A dish that is cooked with a number of different whole or split pulses, it has a rich history and is highly regarded in the communities who savour it. While the likes of curry and roti can be relatively time consuming in terms of prep and cooking, dhal's comparative ease of making has helped it keep its status as a staple for centuries.

In *A House for Mr Biswas* famed Trinidadian-British writer V. S. Naipaul wrote: *"Trinidad Indians are now part of a Caribbean culture, and they find the effort to work backwards and 'rediscover' India difficult"*. I think there's much to say about recipes that help us tap into the lives of our ancestors and dhal provides an opportunity to do just that. Be it the use of a *dhal gutni* (wooden hand-blender) or – as you'll see throughout this book – the call for a final chounkay-ing. To chounkay, from the Hindi *chaunknā* or *chaumk*, is described as deep-frying a select few seasonings in oil or ghee in a *kalchul*, which is then thrown over food, particular curries, *choka* and dhal. This can be a light fry or cooked to the point where the seasonings are completely blackened – just be careful how you pour!

One thing to note, you may like dhal as a more solid stew-type dish that sits on top of the rice, while some prefer it as a translucent soup that seeps, permeates and disappears into the caverns of a rice pile. To adjust this, simply cook with more or less water as suits.

PRESSURE COOKER

Add all the ingredients to the pressure cooker and heat on high. When bubbling, turn the heat down to medium, attach the lid and pressure cap, then cook for 15–20 minutes. After this, depressurize the lid and test the split peas. You should be able to crush them between your thumb and index finger. If you can't, simply cook for another 5 minutes.

When done, submerge a *dhal gutni* or hand-held blender into the pot and pulse until completely smooth. If the mixture isn't your desired consistency, you can cook on low heat until it is. Set aside.

SERVES 6

150g (¾ cup) yellow split peas
1.5–2 litres (6¼–8½ cups) water
2 tsp Green Seasoning (see
   pp26–27 – optional)
3 garlic cloves, finely chopped
½–1 Scotch bonnet pepper,
   deseeded and finely chopped
2 tsp ground turmeric
1 tsp sea salt

FOR THE CHOUNKAY

3 tbsp cooking oil of choice
1 tsp cumin seeds
1 tsp mustard seeds (optional)
3 garlic cloves, sliced

POT

Add all the ingredients into a large saucepan or Dutch pot and heat over a high heat. When bubbling, turn the heat down to medium, cover with a lid and cook for 1 hour. After this, remove the lid and test the peas. You should be able to crush them between your thumb and index finger. If you can't, simply cook for another 20–30 minutes.

When done, submerge a *dhal gutni* or hand-held blender into the pot and pulse until completely smooth. If the mixture isn't your desired consistency you can cook over a low heat until it is. Take off the heat and set aside.

CHOUNKAY

When the dhal is nearly ready, make the chounkay. In a small frying pan, heat the oil over a medium–high, and add in the seeds. Fry the seeds for 2 minutes until they start to brown. Add the garlic and cook for 5 minutes until the garlic browns. Some people prefer to keep cooking the garlic until completely black but it's up to you how long you cook it for.

Now carefully pour the oil into the pot of split peas being careful that no garlic goes in (the seeds are fine). Mix to combine.

Serve the dhal with plain rice, any Choka (see p28) or Bhaji (see p34). In the image above it's served with Sada Roti (see p218), plain rice and chopped tomatoes.

NOTE *Please do not attempt to blend the split peas and hot water after cooking – even when warm – as the blender may explode from the hot air pressure.*

You may have to cover the pot with one hand while pouring in the chounkay oil with the other as it can splash back.

Stew lentils

In Trinidad, my neighbour Monty, an affable man who tells me his kids are probably my age, doesn't have a lot but when he does, he adamantly shares it, including his various dinner cooking sessions throughout the week. Growing up in London where neighbours can hardly talk to each other, this concept can still feel extraordinary from time to time, but when food is involved I'm not going to be shy. One particular breezy day, Monty has a huge Dutch pot of lentils stewing. Though the dish is basically another form of dhal, for some reason it reminds me more of an East African stew – the likes of Ethiopian *misir wot*. For vegans or those hoping to reduce their reliance on meat, this is a stout everyday dish – whether it's a grey day in European winter or the burgeoning sun of the Caribbean spring.

Soak the lentils for anywhere from 1 hour to overnight – for most lentils the longer you soak them, the less time you need to boil them. Drain the lentils, add to a saucepan with 500ml (generous 2 cups) water and cook for 20–25 minutes. Turn off the heat and leave the lentils in the pan – the water will have reduced somewhat but there will still be liquid in the pan.

In a large frying pan, add the oil and heat over a medium–high heat. When hot, add the onion and sauté for 2 minutes before adding the garlic, spring onion and Scotch bonnet pepper. Sauté for a minute, then carefully pour the lentils and their cooking liquid into the frying pan. Stir to combine and then add the green seasoning and carrot before adding the coconut milk or hot water. Turn down the heat to medium and stir again. Now cook for 10 minutes, stirring intermittently until the mixture starts to become mushy. If the pan is getting too dry or the lentils are sticking, add a splash of water.

Add the salt or all-purpose seasoning and pepper to taste and continue to cook for a further 10 minutes, stirring every 5 minutes.

If you prefer, you can mash a quarter of the lentils and stir in to finish. Serve with white rice for a good vegan meal or with white rice and Brown Stew Chicken (see p138).

SERVES 4 OR 6 AS A SIDE

200g (1 cup) green or brown
  lentils
4 tbsp cooking oil of choice
1 onion, chopped
2–3 garlic cloves, chopped
1 spring onion (scallion/green
  onion), chopped
½ Scotch bonnet pepper,
  deseeded and chopped
1 tsp Green Seasoning (see
  pp26–27 - optional)
½ carrot, peeled and chopped
  (optional)
200ml (scant 1 cup) coconut milk
  or boiling water
sea salt or all-purpose seasoning,
  to taste
freshly ground black pepper

Bruine bonen

I sit by the kitchen in Cyriel's Snack, a small eatery to the rear of Centrale Market in Paramaribo, Suriname's capital, between the heat of the day and the steam from the dozen or so pots simultaneously on the go. I try to brush off my profuse sweating as the two cooks are, of course, unaffected. As someone who has worked in hospitality for years, I commit my own cardinal sin by asking "What's the best dish?" It's laughed off, and in a flash, I'm served a plate with rice, a side of cassava and some fried fish, topped off by a simple but luscious bean stew.

Speaking above the loud music which sounds exactly like Congolese rumba, in Creole the cook explains this kidney bean dish can be served with beef, pork or pork tail. At this moment it becomes clear to me that this dish is directly related to what is known in Jamaica as red pea stew – a dish based on kidney beans. With the chef looking just like me, the moment seems as if I'm peering at myself in a parallel universe, a butterfly effect moment of ships departing one port in Africa with different destinations. In these destinations, the differing nuances of the region and peoples make for different takes on the same base ingredients. Here, rather than the deep-stewed, soupy form found in Jamaica, this lighter version, not swimming in liquid, makes for an incredible morning meal that fills you up without immediately sending you to sleep.

SERVES 2–4 AS A SIDE

4 tbsp cooking oil of choice
4 garlic cloves, minced
2.5cm (1in) piece of fresh root ginger, peeled and minced
1 tsp onion powder or ½ onion, finely diced
1 tomato, cored and finely diced
2 tbsp tomato purée (tomato paste)
2 x 400g (15.5oz) cans kidney beans
1 tsp dark brown sugar
1 tbsp Black Soy Sauce (see p146)
1 tsp sea salt
1 vegetable stock cube or 1 tsp vegetable bouillon (optional)
100ml (⅓ cup) water or coconut milk
1 Scotch bonnet pepper, whole
freshly ground black pepper

In a large saucepan or Dutch pot, heat the oil over a medium–high heat. When hot, turn the heat down to medium and add the garlic, ginger and onion powder and sauté for 2 minutes. Next, add the tomato and tomato purée and continue to sauté for 2 minutes. Add the kidney beans and use a few tablespoons of water to loosen any stuck beans and pour into the pan.

Then add the brown sugar, black soy sauce, salt, pepper, stock, if using, and water or coconut milk. Mix to combine and then turn the heat down to low–medium. Add the whole Scotch bonnet pepper and cook for 30 minutes, uncovered.

Serve with white rice.

CURRY?

"In the Caribbean, curries developed over time, with a distinctive British undertone."

Curry? The question mark is there for a reason – what exactly is curry? The question is so loaded with social, economic and political history that it deserves an entire academic syllabus dedicated to it. Unfortunately, there's not enough space to investigate it thoroughly here, so instead the focus will be on curry in the Caribbean, primarily made the Indo-Caribbean inspired way. The curry that came to dominate the Caribbean is very much the anglicized version, in both name and composition.

Curry is said to originate from the Tamil word *kari*. This was, in its simplest form, a mixture of dry spices but one that wasn't fixed. It contained a rotating roster, including roasted and ground black pepper, cumin (*jeera*) and mustard seeds (*sarsa*), fenugreek (*methi*) and *kari patta*, which we recognize as curry leaves. *Kari* then came to denote any spiced dish that accompanied southern Indian food, and was first referred to by the term *caril* (or *carel/carriel*) by Portuguese colonists as early as the 1500s. Subsequently, British imperial forces came to the Indian region looking to disrupt the trade and profits which the Iberian peninsula were reaping. Their naval forces destroyed rival ships, allowing them to get a foothold in the Indian subcontinent. The impact of the British in the region was extensive (the British East India Company was formed shortly afterwards) and fills libraries and museums. How it affected this particular topic is that the word *caril* soon, for many different reasons, became stylized as "curry". This word was greatly widened in usage to include a liquid broth, a thicker stewed preparation, or even a spiced dry dish. Whether the dishes were from the south or north, regardless of ethnic differences or dissimilar spice mixes, they all became curry.

The British, having become accustomed to this array of flavours, which may well have been a revelation compared to what they were eating prior, wanted to import this taste back to Europe. So they began to standardize spice mixes and thus uniform curry powder was born. There was also an impact in India as British-owned hotels, restaurants and communities in India usually ran with the word "curry". As proximity to Britishness and British ideals were popularized, it's suggested that many people in India internalized the catch-all term curry. When those people migrated around the world, to help appeal to a wider audience who were potentially now aware of "curry" due to British influence, the term further stuck. In retrospect, when you think about the billions of people in India, the different terrains, ethnicities and so forth, it seems reductive, even ridiculous to reduce the foods of a vivid, varied continent to a single 400g (14oz) pack of spice powder, but this is what happened.

"Pretty much any ingredient can be curried, and the people of the Caribbean seem to have experimented with every creature and plant."

Dhal (see p72), bread and rice were the fundamental foods of Indian indentured labourers coming to the Caribbean, however, after the new arrivals became established it is documented that curry cooked in a *karahi* – a traditional cast-iron pan – was a constant part of their diets. However, similarly to the story in every chapter of this book, the vast and varied ingredients that were available back home or even just the specific herbs and spices of certain regions, were not readily accessible in the Caribbean. This, coupled with the influence of pre-existing Amerindian and West African cultures in the Caribbean, created something unique. Afro-Caribbean people too began to cook these curries in their traditional Dutch pots. What was noticeable in the Caribbean was that curries developed over time, with a distinctively British undertone that relied heavily on the use of "curry powders", a legacy that lives on today.

Irrespective of the British influence on curry, one element of its consumption that has survived the tens of thousands miles it has journeyed across oceans, is the omission and even disdain for using a knife and fork (or spoon) to eat it. At many houses I visited, from Trinidad south to Suriname, you won't be given cutlery unless requested. Knives and forks were seen as a supposed bastion of sophistication and using hands to eat became a synonym for the savagery and barbarism which the early Europeans ascribed to migrants to the Caribbean. The people of India, like those of West Africa, had a history of eating with their hands, and the peoples from other parts of Asia had their own cutlery, which Europeans superseded with their version. I'd like to reframe this and bring back the joy of eating with your hands. To get to know the meat before it's devoured, to fix the fingers to perfectly slide under and caress the skin of a roti, to clump a ball of rice and imbibe the streams of gravy. All are culinary skills honed over the years.

Pretty much any ingredient can be curried, and the people of the Caribbean seem to have experimented with every moving creature and stationary plant. The recipes in this chapter feature headline ingredients that can be found almost everywhere, like goat, chicken, shrimp and crab, plus vegan options such as chickpeas, aubergine (eggplant) and root vegetables. If they were more readily available I would have loved to highlight the likes of *katahar* (or *chataigne*, a breadnut), starfruit or banana stems, but they can be hard to come by outside of the Caribbean. When I said anything can get curried I meant it – deer, wild game, rodents, small mammals like armadillo and marsupials such as manicou, all feature in local curries. More commonly *pachownie*, a curry featuring offal like stomach lining, kidney and liver is still popular.

The combination of spices cooked here combusts into an eruption of aroma from the kitchen, which wanders throughout the house. In primary school, there was a shame attached to "smelling like curry" which the kids of Indian, Sri Lankan and Pakistani descent were largely the target of, though I too had such affronts lobbied at me with my "weird" food, which included curry goat and chicken. Now, looking back, I realize that, like mine, their parents were in a new land cooking food to recreate home comforts, and hopefully this collection of recipes, deep and rich with taste, with a well of spicy but flavourful gravies, can help create that link for many.

There are a million and one ways to prepare a curry, with many people swearing theirs is the true technique. I'm no arbiter of curry correctness, so what follows is an amalgamation of what I've seen in Caribbean kitchens from Amsterdam to the Americas. A process that is easy to follow and largely remains the same, whether you are making curry with chickpeas or crab. A curry paste is made in a small bowl and then added to hot oil and sautéed onions. This is cooked off to release a staggering aroma before your choice of curry undercards and headliners are added to the pot and cooked in whichever way and time frame are necessary. Water or coconut milk is then usually added and cooked before removing the lid and simmering away until your gravy needs are met. The thicker your pan, the longer it will take to cook down and for the liquid to reduce. If you want an additional depth of flavour in the curries, heat the oil and before adding the onions fry ½ teaspoon of mustard and cumin seeds, a dash of asafoetida, dried whole chillies, along with 2–3 curry leaves and 1–2 cinnamon sticks for 2 minutes. Conversely, if you want to keep things simple, you can just use curry powder (check to see if the ingredients include cumin) and forgo the additional cumin and garam masala. If you have an intolerance of heat, you can omit all use of chilli powder and Scotch bonnets and opt for mild curry powder instead.

LUNCH

Aloo & channa

Like many of the recipes in this book, these dishes are named after their base ingredients. In this case, the names come from Southeast Asian languages such as Urdu, where *channa* translates as "chickpea" and *aloo* (or *aluk*) means "potato". Though both ingredients feature in a host of other recipes, when you hear a reference to *aloo* or *channa* it is most likely their curried forms.

While *aloo* and *channa* curries are rarely the stars of the show, they act as a stabilizing, reliable force for any meal. *Aloo* and *channa* are often served together in a single curry, however, like any successful tag-team or duo, they can perform adequately when separated. *Aloo* is frequently used to bolster curries be they vegan, meat or fish and when those curries are ladled into a roti it can cause the roti to joyously burst at the brim. Given this, consider what you're making these dishes for. If you are preparing them for Doubles (see p166), omitting the potatoes is most common; for roti you want the potatoes diced smaller but not so small that they completely dissolve into mash. If making curry for dinner or lunch just for you, you can opt for larger potato chunks.

In a small bowl, add the curry powder, cumin, garam masala and green seasoning. In a pestle and mortar, mash the Scotch bonnet pepper and garlic and add to the bowl. Add 60ml (4 tablespoons) cold water and stir until the mixture resembles a paste.

In a Dutch pot or heavy-based saucepan, heat the oil over a medium–high heat. When hot, add the onion and spring onion and sauté for 3 minutes. Then add the spice paste and stir for 5 minutes. The paste may begin to stick to the base of your pan; if this happens, add 1 tablespoon of water and stir. Next, add the chickpeas and/or potatoes and stir to combine for 3–5 minutes. If the paste begins to stick to the base of the pan, either add another tablespoon of water or reduce the heat a notch.

Add the hot water and stir. Place the lid on the pan and cook for 25–30 minutes, stirring intermittently every 7 minutes or so to ensure nothing is sticking to the pan. Reduce the heat to low, then remove the lid. The dish is now ready to serve, however, you can leave it to simmer until the gravy is at your desired consistency.

SERVES 4-6

1 tbsp curry powder and 1 tbsp ground cumin (or 1½ tbsp madras curry powder)
1 tbsp garam masala
1 tbsp Green Seasoning (see pp26–27)
½ –1 Scotch bonnet pepper, deseeded and roughly chopped
6 garlic cloves, roughly chopped
6 tbsp cooking oil of choice
1 small onion, finely chopped
1 spring onion (scallion/green onion), finely chopped
500ml (2 cups) hot water

FOR THE CHICKPEAS AND POTATOES

400g (15oz) can chickpeas, drained
800g (1¾lb) white potatoes, peeled and chopped into bite-sized chunks

Baigan & eddoe

Sometimes the vegetables buried in stews and curries can lose their way in the pot, bogged down with water, forfeiting their own flavour and not providing much to the overall experience except extra fodder. *Baigan* (aubergine/ eggplant) and eddoe yam (cocoyam/taro) don't have this problem. Both have their own individual taste profiles. Aubergine (eggplant) needs little introduction and is able to soak up the essence of a curry while keeping its own flavour. Eddoe, meanwhile, comes in like a stauncher, firmer older brother of the potato, able to cook for longer and retain its shape and bite. This makes a pleasant but filling partner in this curry (shown overleaf). Eddoe yam is known as *suran* in parts of India, where taro root curries, while not wholly common, can be found. People of West African descent in the Caribbean had already been cultivating the root for generations before the arrival of people from India, so the continued popularity of this dish is apparent. For vegans looking for more modes of nourishment, I highly recommend that when your wallet allows, try incorporating yams into your diet. There's a reason they sustained those in the unrelenting working conditions of the Caribbean for centuries, not just in terms of taste but sustenance too.

In a small bowl, add the curry powder, cumin, garam masala and green seasoning. In a pestle and mortar, mash the Scotch bonnet pepper and garlic and add to the bowl. Add 60ml (4 tablespoons) cold water and stir until the mixture resembles a paste.

    In a Dutch pot or heavy-based saucepan, heat the oil over a medium–high heat. Add the onion and spring onion and sauté for 3 minutes. Then add the spice paste and stir for 5 minutes. The paste may begin to stick to the pan; if this happens, add 1 tablespoon of water and stir.

    Next, add the eddoes and aubergine and stir to combine with the paste. Add the salt and stir. Cover and cook over a medium heat for 15 minutes. Remove the lid and stir for 3 minutes, then add the boiling water. Stir again, cover with the lid and simmer over a medium–low heat for 20 minutes.

    Remove the lid and test the eddoes (yams) with a fork. The fork should pierce them with relative ease. The dish is now ready to serve, however, you can leave it to simmer until the gravy is at your desired consistency. Serve with white rice or Bhaji Rice (see p57).

SERVES 4–6

1 tbsp curry powder and 1 tbsp ground cumin (or 1½ tbsp madras curry powder)
1½ tbsp garam masala
1 tbsp Green Seasoning (see pp26–27)
½–1 Scotch bonnet pepper, deseeded and roughly chopped
6 garlic cloves, roughly chopped
6 tbsp cooking oil of choice
1 small onion, finely chopped
1 spring onion (scallion/green onion), finely chopped
900g (2lb) eddoe yams, cocoyams (taro), peeled and chopped into 5cm (2in) chunks
350g (¾lb) aubergine (purple eggplant), washed and chopped into 3cm (1¼in) cubes
1 tbsp sea salt
400ml (1¾ cups) boiling water

Curry corn

The sight of the words "curry" and "corn" together bemuse many, however, after spending any extended amount of time in Trinidad and Guyana the combination seems obvious given the love for both. While some ingredients can simply be passengers in a curry, not adding much to the show, the sponge-like traits of corn on the cob with its numerous crevices allow it to effortlessly hoover up the herbs and spices embedded in the coconut milk melange. Without the curry powder, this dish is very close to what some in Guyana know as "Gun Oil", which has many of the same characteristics. Straightforward and easy, this curry is best served as part of a platter amongst a few other dishes, perhaps a root vegetable curry or cook-up, some plant-based sides and, of course, rice (shown overleaf.)

SERVES 4

1½ tbsp curry powder of choice
1 tbsp garam masala
1 tbsp Green Seasoning (see pp26–27)
½–1 Scotch bonnet pepper, deseeded and roughly chopped
5 garlic cloves, roughly chopped
5 tbsp cooking oil of choice
1 small onion, finely chopped
1 spring onion (scallion/green onion), finely chopped
700g (1½lb) corn on the cob (about 6 ears), silks and husks removed and chopped
2 tsp sea salt
400ml (13.5fl oz) can coconut milk
1 tbsp finely chopped fresh coriander (cilantro)

In a small bowl, add the curry powder, garam masala and green seasoning. In a pestle and mortar, mash the Scotch bonnet pepper and garlic and add to the bowl. Add 60ml (4 tablespoons) cold water and stir until the mixture resembles a paste.

In a Dutch pot or heavy-based saucepan, heat the oil over a medium–high heat. Add the onion and spring onions and sauté for 3 minutes. Add the spice paste and stir for 5 minutes. The paste may begin to stick to the base of your pan; if this happens, add 1 tablespoon of water and stir.

Next, add the corn and stir to combine with the paste. Add the salt and stir. Pour in the coconut milk, cover with a lid and cook over a medium heat for 25 minutes, stirring every 5–7 minutes to ensure nothing is sticking to the base of your pot. You can cook for a few minutes less or longer than 25 minutes, depending on how soft or hard you like your corn.

The dish is now ready to serve, however, you can leave it to simmer until the gravy is at your desired consistency. Garnish with the fresh coriander. Serve by itself as a snack or with white rice or Bhaji Rice (see p57).

OVERLEAF *Baigan & Eddoe* (left) *and Curry Corn* (right).

Seven curry

At the end of their indentureship, over 80 per cent of the hundreds of thousands of Indians in the Caribbean stayed, whether by choice or not, and made the region their new home. There was originally a diversity of Indians, with the Bhojpuri/Hindi speakers the majority of the North Indian representatives and the Madrasis (Tamil-speaking people) from the south. There were a number of smaller ethnic and regional groups too, all with their own variations of homeland rites and traditions.

Indian immigrants brought with them memories of dozens of different religious festivals but tended to introduce just one or two to the community as a whole. In the context of the Caribbean, that included the Madrasi Fire Pass, the Muslim Hosey and the North Indian Hindu Phagwa festivities and carnival-esque street parades. These were given new meaning as unifying community celebrations in which everyone participated. Indians of all backgrounds joined in enthusiastically in each of these festivals. It is also suggested that because the events were very public celebrations they were also intended to function as a means by which the Indian communities could share their cultural heritage with the rest of the population, which could initially be hostile towards them for a variety of reasons.

The forms of religion that developed in the Caribbean were notably unique. As Gaiutra Bahadur details in her book *Coolie Woman: The Odyssey of Indenture*, Caribbean Hindus were able to craft a religious identity distinct from their ancestors in the Indian subcontinent, especially since Hinduism in rural India was often governed by cultural norms that significantly shaped interpretations of religion. Over the years, one tradition has superseded all, to in many ways become a showcase of heritage and that is Diwali (or Divali), the festival of lights that takes place annually towards the end of the year. At the end of the week running up to the weekend events, porches across the Caribbean are decorated with rows of candles and decorations. On my last trip, in Georgetown, Guyana's capital, the strip of Main Street was adorned with fairy lights and schoolkids gathered to draw *rangoli* (patterns drawn on the floor) on the pathway. Many smaller events take place to celebrate Diwali, but the main one is the motorcade. Here, various *mandirs* (temple or place of worship) from across the country design elaborate religious-themed trucks complete with performers and dazzling lights, which parade down the Rupert Craig highway parallel to the ocean. The end of the procession climaxes late in the night at a huge green with an abundance of festivities, and the notion of sharing cultural heritage is no more prevalently displayed than in the food. Hundreds of people of all backgrounds are seen with huge lily pad leaves in their hands eating Seven Curry, a mainstay of Indo-Caribbean special occasions, especially in Guyana. This dish (which Mauritians may recognize as Sept Cari) is almost a symbol of the Caribbean, a collection of every flavour, every taste and every colour.

1 lily pad leaf per person
1 large pot of plain white rice
Dhal (see p72)
Pumpkin Talkari (see p34)
Masala Mango (see p41)
Bhaji (see p34)
Aloo & Channa curry (see p82)
Baigan & Eddoe curry (see p84)
Kuchela (see p229)

Possibly with the aid of a few friends or family members, prepare all the dishes and cover with lids to keep warm. Dispense one lily pad per person (or plate) and scoop out a portion of rice. Cover the rice with dhal, then surround the rice with a large spoon of each and a smaller spoon of kuchela. Eat with your hands!

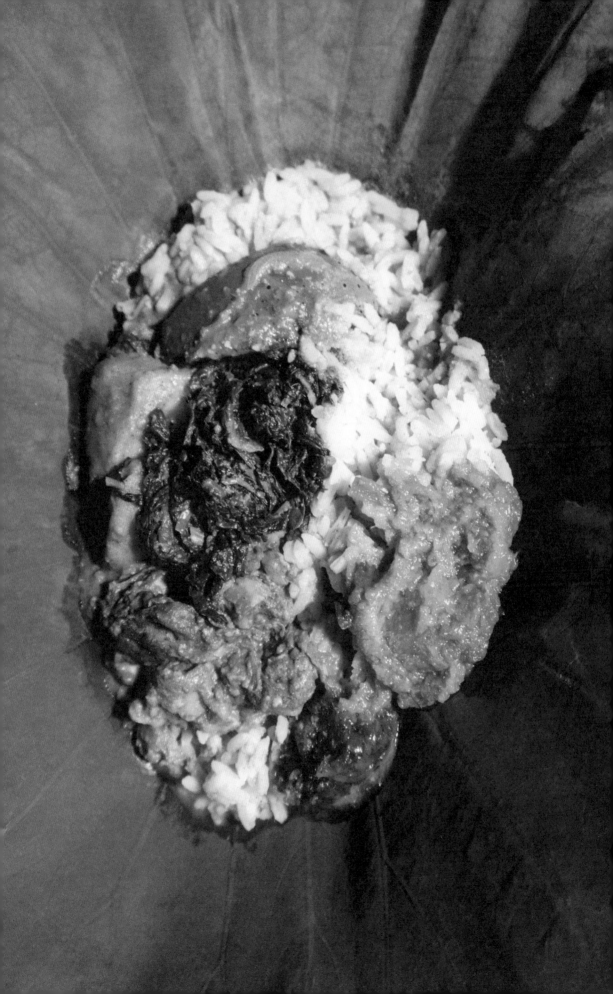

Curry chicken

At lunchtime in the covered yard of the farm owner's home I worked at in Trinidad, elders and kids alike artfully navigate chicken bones and roti skin – a plain piece of roti. I am usually a stickler for tradition and honouring those who came before me, however, in the case of curry chicken, I always prefer boneless chicken, much to the chagrin of friends and family. Like a cutthroat consultant or auditor, I have to eliminate anything that adds even milliseconds to my consumption of a curry chicken roti. I seem alone in this preference and give in to cooking it "properly", which means no parts of the chicken are favoured or frowned upon and you can use anything from thigh, breast, legs, neck and even foot. Curry chicken has always been the default carnivorous curry for most families, including mine. The meat was usually the cheapest to buy in bulk, it's much quicker to cook than darker red meats and it is the most forgiving meat to cook in large quantities, meaning it's a great choice for those new to cooking curries.

If you like, you can season the chicken in a large bowl with the marinade ingredients and marinate for a minimum of 4 hours, or overnight if possible by covering and refrigerating.

In a small bowl, add the curry powder, cumin, garam masala and green seasoning. In a pestle and mortar, mash the Scotch bonnet pepper and garlic and add to the bowl. Add 60ml (4 tablespoons) cold water and stir until the mixture resembles a paste.

In a Dutch pot or heavy-based saucepan, heat the oil over a medium–high heat. Add the onion and spring onion and sauté for 3 minutes. Then add the spice paste and stir for 5 minutes until it starts to get dry. The paste may begin to stick to the base of your pan; if this happens, add 1 tablespoon of water and stir. Next, add the chicken, turmeric and stir to combine before adding the hot water. Stir again, add 1–2 tablespoons of salt, place on the lid and cook for 10 minutes. Remove the lid, turn the heat down to medium–low and continue to simmer for another 10 minutes. If you want the liquid to be thicker, you can continue to simmer over a low heat for 10–15 minutes.

Add salt and pepper to taste and serve with roti (see pp204–219) and/or rice.

NOTE *You can add potatoes to this dish in the same way as the curry shrimp recipe on p99.*

SERVES 4–6

1kg (2¼lb) boneless chicken breast or thigh (or meat of choice), chopped into bite-sized pieces
1 tbsp curry powder and 1 tbsp ground cumin (or 1½ tbsp madras curry powder)
1 tbsp garam masala
1 tbsp Green Seasoning (see pp26–27)
½–1 Scotch bonnet pepper, deseeded and roughly chopped
6 garlic cloves, roughly chopped
1 small onion, finely chopped
1 spring onion (scallion/green onion), finely chopped
½ tsp ground turmeric (optional)
500ml (generous 2 cups) boiling water
sea salt and freshly ground black pepper

FOR THE MARINADE (OPTIONAL)

3 tbsp Green Seasoning (see pp26–27)
1 tbsp curry powder
1 tsp ground turmeric
1 tsp sea salt

Bunjal

Tracing the roots of dry curries in the Northern part of India, for which the Caribbean can largely thank for its curry prowess, turns up a dish entitled *bhuna*. *Bhuna*, described as a sauce in which spices are dry roasted, includes variations such as *bhuna* mutton and *bhuna* chicken. This *bhuna* seems almost identical to what's known in parts of the Caribbean as *bunjal* (*bounjal*) and perhaps the latter is a Creolization of the former word. *Bunjal* is still referred to as a curry, though its final cooked appearance may not resemble what a lot of people recognize as a curry. It's cooked with almost the same preparation as a curry but without the addition of ample water, relying instead on moisture from the juices of the meat itself and a bit of steam manufactured with a lid. The result of this process is more of a deeper, smokier burnt taste, which will certainly leave an indelible aromatic impression throughout your entire house. As for most curries, you can use any meat for *bunjal* – goat, duck or chicken liver and even innards like gizzards. Use the recipe below as a base and try it with whatever you fancy.

SERVES 4 OR 6 AS A SIDE

1 tbsp curry powder and 1 tbsp ground cumin (or 1½ tbsp madras curry powder)
1 tbsp garam masala
1 tbsp Green Seasoning (see pp26–27)
½–1 Scotch bonnet pepper, deseeded and roughly chopped
6 garlic cloves, roughly chopped
6 tbsp cooking oil of choice
1 small onion, finely chopped
1 spring onion (scallion/green onion), finely chopped
1kg (2¼lb) boneless chicken breast or thigh (or meat of choice), chopped into bite-sized pieces
1 tbsp sea salt

In a small bowl, add the curry powder, cumin, garam masala and green seasoning. In a pestle and mortar, mash the Scotch bonnet pepper and garlic and add to the bowl. Add 60ml (4 tablespoons) cold water and stir until the mixture resembles a paste.

In a Dutch pot or heavy-based saucepan, heat the oil over a medium–high heat. When hot, add the onion and spring onion and sauté for 3 minutes. Then add the spice paste and stir for 5 minutes. The paste may begin to stick to the base of your pan; if this happens, add 1 tablespoon of water and stir.

Next, add the chicken and fry for 8–10 minutes, stirring intermittently. Sprinkle over the salt, turn the heat down a notch to medium, cover with a lid and cook for a further 10 minutes. Remove the lid and stir the chicken. Now pour in 200ml (scant 1 cup) water, turn up the heat to medium–high and cook for 3 minutes until the water boils off and turns into a thick gravy. When the chicken is completely browned with light charring, it is ready. To double check, simply slice a piece and it should be white and cooked through.

Serve with white rice and roti.

Curry duck

In Jamaica and the surrounding Caribbean islands I think the battle for curry supremacy has just two main contenders – chicken and goat. But in Trinidad and Tobago and Guyana a third challenger enters the curry race: duck. Ironically, in St. Mary's, a town in Southern Trinidad, I find myself at a duck race – a literal duck race – that takes part as an annual community gathering. The event also features a duck curry competition, where teams work in duos in a timed contest to cook the best curry duck, adjudicated by a panel mostly composed of matriarchs who are evidently duck curry veterans.

Duck finds itself oddly placed in the hierarchy of British meat consumption. Frequently found on the menu of fine dining restaurants and the occasional gastropub, it has never crossed over to mainstream consumption like chicken. In this corner of the Caribbean, especially in rural areas, keeping a pen of ducks is relatively common and there are ample roadside services in every town and village to get your fowl and poultry plucked. Duck meat is tender and needs to be cooked for longer than chicken but not as long as goat meat, so duck finds itself perfectly placed in the middle of the two for your dining needs.

If you like, you can coat the duck with the marinade ingredients, cover and leave to marinate in the fridge for at least 4 hours, or overnight if possible.

In a small bowl, add the curry powder, cumin, garam masala and green seasoning. In a pestle and mortar, mash the Scotch bonnet pepper and garlic and add to the bowl. Stir in 60ml (4 tablespoons) water until the mixture resembles a paste.

In a Dutch pot or heavy-based saucepan, heat the oil over a medium–high heat. Add the onion and spring onion and sauté for 3 minutes. Then add the spice paste and stir for 5 minutes. The paste may begin to stick to the pan; if this happens, add 1 tablespoon water and stir.

Next, add the tomato and duck to the pan. Cook for 15 minutes, continually stirring and scraping the bottom of the pan. The duck should have released its own water into the pot. Add the thyme, salt, coconut milk and hot water. Now turn the heat down a notch to medium, stir, cover and cook for 10 minutes. Remove the lid and cook for a final 10 minutes. If you want the liquid to be thicker, you can continue to simmer over a low heat for 15 minutes. Serve with white rice and roti.

SERVES 4–6

1kg (2¼lb) duck, chopped into bite-sized pieces (bones included)
1 tbsp curry powder and 1 tbsp ground cumin (or 1 tbsp madras curry powder)
1½ tbsp garam masala
1 tbsp Green Seasoning (see pp26–27)
½–1 Scotch bonnet pepper, deseeded and roughly chopped
6 garlic cloves, roughly chopped
6 tbsp cooking oil of choice
1 small onion, finely chopped
1 spring onion (scallion/green onion), finely chopped
1 tomato, finely diced
a few sprigs of thyme (optional)
1 tbsp sea salt
400ml (13.5fl oz) can coconut milk
400ml (1¾ cups) boiling water

FOR THE MARINADE (OPTIONAL)

3 tbsp Green Seasoning (see pp26–27)
1 tbsp curry powder
1 tsp ground turmeric
1 tsp sea salt

Goat curry

For a time in the 19th century, many of the people residing in the Southeast Caribbean did not speak the same language, and I like to think food acted as a surrogate form of communication. Both West Africa and parts of Asia, from where these people descended, had climates and religions that prevented the mass farming and consumption of bovine and pork. As such, mutton (sheep) curries were enjoyed by the Bihari people of India, as were the peppery goat *asun* stews of Yorubaland. With this in mind, Caribbean goat curry (whether it uses goat, lamb or mutton) exists at the apex of all these amalgamated cultures.

By now, some of you may be unsettled by the fact I keep calling it goat curry and not "curry goat". Just like the "plantain" vs "plantin" debate, the correct answer at any given time is in the hands of whoever is wielding the large shiny spoon dishing out your portion. Code switch if you have to, to get your desired amount.

Goat meat and similar red meats take patience to cook, as do the multiple steps needed to fuse in the seasoning. Serve with Dhal Puri (see p210) or Buss-up Shot Roti (see p204) and white rice.

If you like, you can coat the goat with the marinade ingredients and leave to marinate for at least 4 hours, or overnight if possible. Cover the bowl with a lid and refrigerate.

In a small bowl, add the curry powder, cumin, garam masala and green seasoning. In a pestle and mortar, mash the Scotch bonnet pepper and garlic and add to the bowl. Add 60ml (4 tablespoons) cold water and stir until the mixture resembles a paste.

In a Dutch pot or heavy-based pan, heat the oil over a medium–high heat. Add the onion and spring onion and sauté for 3 minutes. Then add the spice paste and stir for 5 minutes. The paste may begin to stick to the base of your pan; if this happens, add 1 tablespoon of water and stir.

Next, add the goat to the pan and keep the marinade to one side. Fry the goat meat for 15–20 minutes, continually stirring and scraping the bottom of the pan to ensure nothing is sticking. Next, either continue using the Dutch pot or saucepan or, if you're short on time, then I highly recommend using a pressure cooker (see opposite).

SERVES 4–6

1kg (2¼lb) goat meat, bone-in
1 tbsp curry powder and 1 tbsp ground cumin (or 1½ tbsp madras curry powder)
1½ tbsp garam masala
1 tbsp Green Seasoning (see pp26–27)
½–1 Scotch bonnet pepper, deseeded and roughly chopped
6 garlic cloves, roughly chopped
6 tbsp cooking oil of choice
1 small onion, finely chopped
1 spring onion (scallion/green onion), finely chopped
1 litre (4⅓ cups) hot water
a few sprigs of thyme (optional)
sea salt and freshly ground black pepper

FOR THE MARINADE (OPTIONAL)

3 tbsp Green Seasoning (see pp26–27)
1 tbsp curry powder of choice
1 tsp ground turmeric
1 tsp sea salt

DUTCH POT OR SAUCEPAN

Add the hot water to the pot, scrape in the contents of the marinade bowl, add the salt and thyme, if using, and stir. Cover, turn down the heat and simmer for 2½–3 hours. Check the pot and stir every 20 minutes or so. The meat is ready when you can pierce it with ease and it is a deep maroon colour. When the meat is done, you can remove the lid and continue to cook for 5–10 minutes to get your desired gravy consistency.

PRESSURE COOKER

Add the hot water to the pot, scrape in the contents of the Dutch pot or saucepan and the marinade bowl, then add the salt and thyme, if using, and stir. Cover and simmer for 45 minutes–1 hour. Remove the pot safely as per the manufacturer's instructions. The meat is ready when you can pierce it with ease and it is a deep maroon colour. When the meat is done, you can unscrew the pot lid, transfer the contents back to your original pot or saucepan and continue to cook for 5–10 minutes to get your desired gravy consistency.

Fish, mango & okra curry

While most curries are happily tucked away inside a roti, concealed from the world, this fish, mango and okra curry is to be celebrated out in the open in all its glory. The combination of fish and mango may be confusing to a great deal of people except to those who descend from anywhere throughout India (*meen manga*, for example) to the southern reaches of Indonesia (*sambal mangga*) – cultures that today make up the fabric of many Caribbean locales.

For brevity this dish is often referred to as fish curry or oftentimes the popular fish for it, hassar (or *cascadoo*, a fascinating jet-black armoured fish, see p103) or gilbaka (curry), which is similar to catfish. If you hear of one of these curries being served and it doesn't have some kind of starchy veggie to bolster it, then it's usually coming with an abundance of okra fingers and sliced green mangoes. When seasoned and amalgamated with creamy coconut milk these three ingredients create a truly unique curry unlike any other in this book.

Unless you are in the Caribbean or on the US East coast it's rare to find gilbaka or hassar and so you can use the more readily available catfish or the likes of kingfish or snapper. Ideally, you'll use a tougher fish as soft fish can break down in the curry. Using sliced cutlets is a good way to avoid this. The tart mango really sets the tone for the curry, so if you aren't used to the taste, feel free to adjust it with salt and/or sugar.

———

If you like, in a large bowl you can coat the fish with the marinade ingredients, cover and leave to marinate in the fridge for at least 4 hours, or overnight if possible.

Heat 4 tablespoons of the oil in a frying pan and, when hot, fry the fish in batches for 3 minutes to slightly sear them.

In a small bowl, add the curry powder, ground cumin, garam masala and green seasoning. In a pestle and mortar, mash Scotch bonnet pepper and garlic and add to the bowl. Add 60ml (4 tablespoons) cold water and stir until the mixture resembles a paste.

In a Dutch pot or heavy-based saucepan, heat the remaining 2 tablespoons of oil over a medium–high heat. Add the onion and white part of the spring onion and sauté for 3 minutes. Then add the spice paste and stir for 5 minutes. The paste may begin to stick to your pan; if this happens, add 1 tablespoon of water and stir. Next, add

SERVES 6

1kg (2¼lb) fish, such as red snapper, kingfish or catfish, fillets sliced from whole fish
6 tbsp cooking oil of choice
1 tbsp curry powder and 1 tbsp ground cumin (or 1½ tbsp madras curry powder)
1 tbsp garam masala
1 tbsp Green Seasoning (see pp26–27)
6 garlic cloves, roughly chopped
½–1 Scotch bonnet pepper, deseeded and roughly chopped
1 small onion, finely chopped
1 spring onion (scallion/green onion), finely chopped (white and green part separated)
1 large tomato, chopped or 10 cherry tomatoes, halved
200g (½lb) hard green mango or red mango, quartered
30g (¼ cup) moringa, chopped into 5cm (2in) lengths (optional)
400ml (13.5fl oz) can coconut milk
1 tbsp fish seasoning (optional)
500ml (generous 2 cups) boiling water
8 okra, tops removed
sea salt, freshly ground black pepper and brown sugar (optional)

FOR THE MARINADE (OPTIONAL)

3 tbsp Green Seasoning (see pp26–27)
1 tbsp curry powder of choice
1 tsp sea salt

the tomato and continue to stir the dish before adding the fish and stirring intermittently for 7–10 minutes. Then add the mango and moringa, if using, and stir gently to combine. Now add the coconut milk, 1 tablespoon of salt, optional fish seasoning and hot water, stir to combine and cook for 15 minutes.

Turn the heat down to low and add the okra, stir gently, then cover and cook for 5 minutes. Remove the lid and continue to simmer for 10 minutes, at which point the liquid will have reduced and become thicker. If you want the liquid to be thicker, you can continue to simmer for 15–20 minutes. Add salt, pepper and brown sugar to taste. Garnish with the green part of the spring onion.

Serve with rice or roti or both.

NOTE *Serrated knives are good for slicing through the stone of mangoes. The brown sugar (or jaggery) is useful if the mangoes are overly sour for your liking.*

Curry shrimp

For pescatarians looking for a sumptuous curry, look no further than curry shrimp. Shrimp have long been a favourite of all the peoples of the Caribbean, particularly those from the coastal southern parts of China, Indonesia and waterway adjacent parts of India, which today account for the gamut of shrimp ranching. Shrimp, when multiplied in quantity and cooked in almost any way, provide a lingering taste on the tongue which begs for more. Since curry itself is a dish that flows effortlessly from pot to mouth too, the combination is a perfect union. Shrimp can be expensive, depending on where you are, but if so this is the perfect curry to shore up with a potato cut into chunks.

If you like, in a large bowl you can season the prawns (shrimp) with an extra 3 tablespoons of green seasoning, cover with a lid and leave to marinate in the fridge for a minimum of 4 hours, or overnight if possible.

In a small bowl, add the curry powder, cumin, garam masala and 1 tablespoon of green seasoning. In a pestle and mortar, mash the Scotch bonnet pepper and garlic and add to the bowl. Add 60ml (4 tablespoons) cold water and stir to form a paste.

In a Dutch pot or heavy-based saucepan, heat 2 tablespoons of oil over a medium–high heat. Add the onion and spring onion and sauté for 3 minutes. Then add the spice paste and stir for 5 minutes. The paste may begin to stick to the base of your pan; if this happens, add 1 tablespoon of water and stir.

Next, add the tomato and stir for 3–5 minutes. If the paste begins to stick, add 1 tablespoon of water and stir while scraping the bottom of the pan to loosen the paste.

Add the turmeric, salt and boiling water, coconut milk or stock and stir. Bring to the boil, then reduce to a simmer.

Heat the remaining 4 tablespoons of oil in a frying pan and, when hot, fry the prawns in batches for 3 minutes. Add the prawns to the sauce and cook for 10–15 minutes until the prawns change from grey to pink and firm.

The dish is now ready to serve, however, you can simmer until the gravy is at your desired consistency, although be careful not to overcook the prawns.

NOTE *You can use half to two-thirds the quantity of prawns and 400g (¾lb) potatoes peeled and cut into bite-sized chunks. Cook the potatoes in the water for 15–20 minutes, then add the prawns and follow the recipe as above.*

SERVES 4–6 AS A SIDE

1 or 4 tbsp Green Seasoning (see pp26–27)

1kg (2¼lb) raw king prawns (jumbo shrimp), peeled and deveined, heads removed and tails removed if liked

1 tbsp curry powder and 1 tbsp ground cumin (or 1½ tbsp madras curry powder)

1 tbsp garam masala

½–1 Scotch bonnet pepper, deseeded and roughly chopped

6 garlic cloves, roughly chopped

6 tbsp cooking oil of choice

1 small onion, finely chopped

1 spring onion (scallion/green onion), finely chopped

1 large tomato, diced

½ tsp ground turmeric (optional)

1 tbsp sea salt

500ml (generous 2 cups) boiling water, coconut milk or stock

Crab & dumplings

One of the ways I knew I was getting old was when my nephew started destroying me at video games without even trying. The memory was jogged as I sat prepping crabs in a family friend's yard in the southern reaches of Trinidad. I'm joined by a gang of kiddos all armed with knives no sharper than a butter spreader who scream that they want to join in. In a flash, they carve off the shells, scrape out the innards, discard them into a bucket and then are off on the way to their next adventure. My main mission is nothing but a side quest to these youths and that embarrassing feeling is doubled by the creak of my knees getting up from the stool.

On this day, the crab is going into a crab curry bolstered with boil dumplings. This curry, famed across the shores of Tobago, is a speciality usually enjoyed on the weekends or special occasions. You can source pre-shelled crab meat; however, the joy comes from navigating the curried coconut milk burrowed in the crannies of the crab shell that you bite through to access it.

To prepare whole crabs, slide a knife into the crevice between the eyes and wiggle or twist the knife to edge off the back. Chop the crab in half and, using a sponge or brush, clean off any ooze. Place the pieces into a large bowl with a tablespoon of vinegar and rinse/clean as thoroughly as possible. Repeat until all the crabs are done.

In a small bowl, add the curry powder, cumin, garam masala and green seasoning. In a pestle and mortar, mash the Scotch bonnet and garlic and add to the bowl. Add 60ml (4 tablespoons) cold water and stir to form a paste.

In a Dutch pot or heavy-based saucepan, heat the oil over a medium–high heat. Add the onion and spring onion and sauté for 3 minutes. Add the spice paste and stir for 5 minutes until it starts to dry out. It may stick to your pan; if this happens, add 1 tablespoon of water and stir. Add the crab and cook for 10 minutes, stirring continuously. Pour in the coconut milk and hot water. Stir, add 1 tablespoon of salt, cover and cook for 10 minutes.

Remove the lid, turn the heat down to medium–low, add the dumplings if you like, and simmer for 10 minutes. If you want the liquid to be thicker, continue to simmer over a low heat for another 10–15 minutes.

Add salt and pepper to taste and garnish with fresh coriander. Serve with rice and with the dumplings on the side, if you prefer.

SERVES 4–6

1kg (2¼lb) crabs of choice, preferably blue crab (about 8–10), whole, or 600g (1¼lb) shelled crab meat

1 tbsp vinegar for cleaning whole crabs

1 tbsp curry powder and 1 tbsp ground cumin (or 1½ tbsp madras curry powder)

1 tbsp garam masala

1 tbsp Green Seasoning (see pp26–27)

½–1 Scotch bonnet pepper, deseeded and roughly chopped

6 garlic cloves, roughly chopped

6 tbsp cooking oil of choice

1 small onion, finely chopped

1 spring onion (scallion/green onion), finely chopped

400ml (13.5fl oz) can coconut milk

500ml (generous 2 cups) boiling water

Coconut Boil Dumplings (see p195)

2 tsp finely chopped fresh coriander (cilantro)

sea salt and freshly ground black pepper

SEAFOOD

"Their limited access to meat meant those who lived in the Caribbean sooner ate fish."

A folklore in Southeast Caribbean passed down from generations reads:

"Those who eat the cascadura will, the native legend says,
Wheresoever they may wander, end in Trinidad their days,
And this lovely fragrant island, with its forest hills sublime,
Well might be the smiling Eden pictured in the Book divine."

This legend of the Cascadura, a black armoured fish which is a favourite of many across the Caribbean, is reimagined in Samuel Selvon's 1957 short story "Johnson and the Cascadura." This is the tale of an Englishman who ventures to Trinidad to get background material for a book he is penning. While there he meets an Indo-Caribbean woman named Urmilla, who works the land of the estate where he is residing. Love blossoms between the (Hollywood-esque) wealthy foreigner and the downtrodden rural girl, much to the chagrin of the locals. The night before he is due to depart, Urmilla prepares Johnson a fish curry in the hope that the legend of *those who eat the cascadura* is true. Johnson departs but some years later he develops an acute illness and so decides to return to Urmilla to live out the last of his days.

Although I guess I too was an Englishman venturing to the Caribbean to get background material for a book, I didn't meet an "Urmilla". However, I did meet many incredible cooks from shop owners to neighbours, who cooked fish curries so good you dream of returning. A glorious array of fresh fish, like the exceptional tar-black, armoured fish cascadura (or hassar), gilbaka, red snapper and kaleidoscopic rainbow trout, cooked with the freshest coconut milk were prepared just moments before serving, with spices milled that same week and green seasoning ingredients plucked from the yard an arm's length from the kitchen window. All this taking place amidst the beaming sun and wondrous breeze that passes through the covered garden shed like a brief visitor.

Though meat has arguably reached culinary supremacy throughout the world, if pressed I would give up meat before fish, and I think many in my family would do the same. Whether it's Green Fry Fish (see p123), Saltfish Buljol (see p112) nestled into fried bakes, or Jamaican ackee and saltfish, their limited access to meat over time meant that those who lived in the Caribbean sooner ate fish than meat. In Matthew Gregory Lewis's *Journal of a West India Proprietor*, the author notes:

"These vegetables [yams, dasheens, callalou, plantains, bananas] form the basis of Negro sustenance; but the slaves also received from their sources a weekly allowance of red herring and salt meat, which they seem to relish their

vegetable diet; and indeed they are so passionately fond of salted provisions that, instead of giving them fresh beef, I have been advised to provide some hogsheads of salt fish."

Planters began to observe the importance of saltfish in the diet of the enslaved, and throughout the 18th and 19th centuries it was particularly favoured by planters and enslavers as it could be shipped overseas for weeks and longer without spoiling. It also provided a relatively cost-effective way to feed and nourish their workers, in a way the constant provision of fresh fish would not (which would be the reserve of the elite).

When possible though, the island people did consume fresh fish. Surveys such as Mrs Carmichael's *Domestic manners and social condition of the white, coloured and negro population of the West Indies* describe how *"slaves exploited the fishing resources of the islands rivers,"* where local fish and crustaceans like crab and shrimp were sourced. It wasn't just Afro-Caribbeans who sought the waters. On the land indentured Indians traded for their right to return, it's noted that they would fish and catch crabs. And before all of them, the Amerindian tribes, like the Warrau, looked to the waterways as a key source of food. In a collection of *Legends and Myths of the Aboriginal Indians of British Guiana* a verse chants:

"On fish and crabs those Warraus chiefly live,
Which in abundance there the waters give."

While the story of the cascadura was based in Trinidad, I know first-hand that the delights of Caribbean seafood extend to every single corner of the region, and Guyana is no exception. The name Guyana is derived from the Indigenous word *Guiana* meaning *"land of many waters"* and the country has 276 waterfalls that pour into thousands of Amazonian tributaries, leading to its four main rivers: the Berbice, Courantyne, Demerara and Essequibo. Even though this chapter is entitled seafood, many peoples' relationship with water is seldom the oceans but rather the canals and rivers that meander through the islands and South American continent.

"All those who resided by the waterways incorporated seafood into their existing or ancestral modes of cooking."

All those who resided by the waterways incorporated seafood into their existing or ancestral modes of cooking. The Arawaks roasted their fish in clay, which is reminiscent of the sealed and roasted fish we eat today (see p128), those of Indian descent used fish and crab in their traditional curries (see p100), and the enslaved Africans used fish fresh or preserved it to fortify their starchy and root vegetable-laden stews like Metemgee and Oil Down when possible (see p120 and p124). In more modern times, after commercial amounts of fish became available, the devotion towards it grew with the prevalence of Christianity. The weekly tradition of eating fish on Friday and throughout the 40 days of Lent (as you are meant to abstain from meat-eating to focus on spiritual cleansing, prayer and sacrifice) led to Fish Friday being a mini weekly gathering that can now sometimes become a fully-fledged rave. While Christianity is still the most popular religion in the likes of Trinidad and Guyana, its many traditions like Fish Friday are less common due to comparatively higher numbers of other religions, whereas in the likes of Jamaica and Barbados, known for their dazzling fish platters, it can be a weekly event.

Today, of course, one does not have to venture to the waters to get fish. The cascadura man comes whizzing around the bend, down country lanes with ice pallets of fish and the markets are lined with hollering vendors with every cut, type and size of fish you can imagine on all but one or two weekdays. These are transported briskly to the shed – the second or sometimes main kitchen, which sits to the side or back of the house, protected from the elements with an angled sheet of galvanized metal. If not, then the kitchen may sit directly underneath the stilted raised house, most certainly with a hammock not too far away to rest in between. Here is where I witness most of the prep for fish dishes. In the heat of the day you don't want to be scaling, filleting or chopping fish indoors, attracting unwanted buzzing bugs and capturing the lingering odour inside. Outdoors, the fish waste is chucked to cats and dogs and rinsed away, with just the fish left for your chosen meal of the day. Sometimes that might be a quick dish like a Fish Choka (see p114) or teamed up with a bunch of fresh produce to make a Fish Creole (see p117) for dinner.

A popular adage I've heard time and again over the years in the region regarding time wasting says: "*If you waste any more time, you're gonna dry up all the water on the beach*" and you certainly don't want to waste time with fish. In true Caribbean spirit, I tend to rinse mine with citrus and water before prepping it and then immediately bury it in green seasoning, which is reflected in the majority of recipes here.

CARITE
SALMON
REDFISH
RACKANDO
SHARK
SHRIMP
CARVALI
HERRING

CORN
FISH
FOR
SALE

Bake & "shark"

Most countries in the world have their own famous dish commonly associated with a certain place or region. In Trinidad, this renowned spot is Maracas Bay, the site for the lauded Bake & Shark (shown overleaf). While you can get this dish on almost every high street in Trinidad there's no substitute for a road trip up and down the northern range beneath the cover of canopies to Maracas Bay. Here, a golden-white sandy beach is lined with titan-tall tropical trees that cast shade on the numerous huts that have peddled the famous duo for nearly half a century. Big names on campus like Richard's and Vilma's, serve up the wondrous fried fish that nestles inside the fluffy but subtly crisp fried breads called "bakes". Overly hyped food trips can sometimes disappoint but the trade here far exceeds expectations, especially with the dizzying array of self-served add-ons (some listed below) that form as many combinations as the 26-letter alphabet has words. This is a toasted fish finger sandwich turned up to 11.

I put "shark" in quote marks because there seems to be a growing rumour that the cost of shark is now prohibitively high – vendors have sought alternatives like catfish and its many derivations for environmental reasons too. I've also never actually seen shark for sale in the UK nor have I really ever looked for it, so feel free to use any soft, filleted white fish.

Follow the recipe for fry bake and set aside in a bowl covered with a dish towel to keep warm or store in the oven on the lowest temperature until ready to serve.

If making the shado beni sauce, add all the ingredients to a food processor or blender and pulse until completely smooth. It will keep for a few days but preferably finish with the meal.

Follow the recipe for fry fish and keep warm.

Slice open your fried bake, line the bottom with some lettuce, add a piece of fried fish and then top with some cabbage and carrot, if using, and pineapple, tomato, cucumber and sauces of your choice to serve.

MAKES 8

8 Fry Bake (see p162)
Fry Fish (see p123)
200g (½lb) lettuce of choice
50g (¼ cup) white cabbage, shredded (optional)
1 carrot, grated (optional)
1 pineapple, topped, peeled and cut into 8 slices
2 tomatoes, sliced
¼ cucumber, sliced

FOR THE SHADO BENI SAUCE (OPTIONAL)

30g (1oz) fresh coriander (cilantro) or shado beni
3–5 garlic cloves, peeled
1 tsp hot sauce or ¼ Scotch bonnet pepper, deseeded
70ml (4½ tbsp) water
2 tbsp olive oil (optional)
¼ tsp sea salt
1 tbsp lime juice or citric juice of choice (optional)

TO SERVE

Lime and Pepper Sauce (see p235)
Tambran Sauce (see p230)
Mango Sour (see p232)
Tomato ketchup
Garlic mayonnaise

Saltfish buljol

For some reason, maybe growing up in London, I never thought too much about saltfish and by that, I mean thought about what it actually is. In my mind there was always just one type of saltfish, which I ate hundreds, maybe thousands, of times alongside Jamaican ackee. The markets in Guyana's Georgetown, such as Mon Repos and Bourda, were the first time I really saw an array of saltfish, not just salted cod but coras, copand, bangamary and more, all with their own taste and profile. But given that I grew up with cod, that's what I fall back on to make this saltfish *buljol* (a word said to derive from the French *brûlé* – burnt, and *gueule* meaning "muzzle") – a cooked or stewed saltfish combined with fresh vegetables.

Full accounts of the diets of those enslaved in the Southeastern Caribbean are hard to come by. Henry Gloster, a colonial administrator in Trinidad, reported in parliamentary testimony in 1830 that the plantation enslaved received 3½lb (1.5kg) of salted cod a week, supplemented by a rum or tobacco ration. This wasn't gospel though, one planter reported giving her enslaved less than what Gloster testified. Hence, for the longest time this dish and others that featured salted fish were considered the food of the underclass, so it's fascinating to see it now enjoyed by the patrons of the many luxurious hotels in the region.

It's no surprise that this dish is popular, as fully fledged salads are scarce to come by in any traditional Caribbean food, save a combination of lettuce, tomatoes and cucumber, which are often an afterthought. More time is spent either cooking produce down or preserving it using salt, fat, acid or heat. That being said, this is enjoyed as a weekend breakfast, usually stuffed into a fried bake (see p162) or in a sandwich with soft cloudy bread (see Plait Bread, p194).

Place the saltfish in a saucepan and cover with water. Boil over a high heat for 20 minutes. Drain the water, re-cover the saltfish with water and boil for 15 minutes. Drain the water again and set the saltfish aside for 5 minutes. When it's cool, use your hands to peel off any dark skin and remove any bones. Then either with your hands or a fork, mash the saltfish into flakes and set aside.

In a large pan, add the oil and heat over a medium heat. When hot, add the onion and sauté for a minute before adding the garlic, spring onions and thyme, if using. Continue to stir and sauté for another minute and

SERVES 4–8 AS A SIDE OR BAKE FILLING

400g (¾lb) saltfish
5 tbsp cooking oil of choice
1 red onion, chopped
3 garlic cloves, chopped (optional)
4–5 spring onions (scallions/green onions), finely chopped
1 sprig of thyme (optional)
1 tomato, cored and chopped
½ Scotch bonnet pepper, deseeded and chopped
½ red bell pepper, deseeded and chopped
½ yellow bell pepper, deseeded and chopped
all-purpose seasoning, to taste (optional)
¼ head iceberg lettuce, shredded (optional)
freshly ground black pepper

then add the tomato, scotch bonnet pepper and bell peppers. Stir to combine and then add the saltfish. Continue to sauté for another 2–3 minutes until the saltfish starts to turn slightly golden brown. Turn off the heat, sprinkle a dash of all-purpose seasoning and black pepper and stir again. Remove any thyme stems, fold in optional lettuce and serve.

Serve with Fry Bake (see p162), slices of avocado, hot sauce and Tambran Sauce (see p230).

NOTE *You can also desalinate your saltfish by soaking it overnight in water. Then you only need to boil it once for 20 minutes and drain.*

Fish choka

When discussing *chokas*, the likes of tomato and *baigan* (aubergine/eggplant) are usually the first to come to mind. That being said, pretty much any food can be made into a *choka* once you have a *choka* method down. Fish *choka* is less common at the takeout spots across Trinidad and Guyana, however, it makes an ample alternative to Saltfish Buljol (see p112). Where buljol is a lighter, fresher dish, this is more earthy, roasted and certainly hotter. You can have it with bakes (see p162, once you make bakes, you'll want any excuse to make and eat them) but as with most *choka* dishes it's most commonly eaten with Sada Roti (see p218).

There really is no single fish *choka* recipe given the vastness of how many types of fish there are, how many ways there are to cook them and the same is true for the added vegetables and so forth. Other fish *chokas* include smoked herring and saltfish, though any fresh fish works well. Feel free to use your imagination.

Clean and prepare the fish as you prefer and then add it to a bowl with marinade ingredients, cover and refrigerate for 30 minutes to a few hours. Alternatively, you can mix the fish and marinade and immediately move on to the next step.

Preheat the oven to 180°C (160°C fan/350°F/Gas 4).

Place the fish, tomato and Scotch bonnet pepper, and caraili, if using, in three distinct sections on a baking sheet lined with baking paper or foil. Cook for 20–25 minutes until the vegetables have started to slightly char. Remove from the oven, transfer eveything into a bowl, gently mash together and set aside.

To make the chounkay, heat the oil in a frying pan over a medium–high heat. When hot, add the onion and sauté for 2–3 minutes. Then add the garlic and spring onion and sauté for another 2 minutes. When the contents of the pan have started to brown, immediately take the pan off the heat and throw all the contents of the pan into the bowl of mashed vegetables.

Mix in the fresh coriander and serve with Sada Roti (see p218), bread or Fry Bakes (see p162).

SERVES 4

500g (1lb) cod fillets or fish of choice
1 large tomato, halved and cored
½–1 Scotch bonnet pepper, deseeded if you prefer (optional)
1 caraili (bitter melon), insides removed and chopped (optional)
1 tbsp finely chopped fresh coriander (cilantro)

FOR THE MARINADE

2 tbsp Green Seasoning (see pp26–27)
½ tsp sea salt
½ tsp freshly ground black pepper
½ tsp fish seasoning (optional)

FOR THE CHOUNKAY

5 tbsp cooking oil of choice
½ onion, chopped
5 garlic cloves, grated
1 spring onion (scallion/green onion), chopped

Fish Creole

The recipes of the 1988 Trinidadian benchmark classic *Naparima Girls' High School Jubilee Cookbook* don't feature any stories, however, the book itself is a fantastic snapshot of the blend of cultures not just in the country but the Caribbean as a whole. In the seafood chapter, the recipe for Mediterranean-style Fish "Kabobs" sits side by side with Indian-rooted fish curries like *Cascadura*, plus a likely Northern European-inspired Fish and Chips and a Fish Creole.

The Anglophone word "Creole" is said to bear an Iberian etymology – *criollo* in Spanish, *crioulo* in Portuguese (from the Latin root meaning "to raise" or "to bring up") – originally referring to a person of foreign descent born in the "New World", as distinct from the European or African born. Soon after it referred to anyone and anything born in the Americas. In 1783, when French planters were invited to settle in Trinidad, they came accompanied by their servants, the enslaved and freedmen from territories such as Martinique, Guadeloupe and Haiti. Soon after, the idea of Creole or Creolization essentially just meant anything consisting of a mixture. This recipe for "Fish Creole" is representative of that fusion ideology – fish cooked down in a mixture of varying herbs and spices to produce a dish very reminiscent of a bouillabaisse. It's a wholesome stew inoffensive to those less tolerant of spice and heat.

SERVES 4

500g (1lb) white fish, preferably filleted, cut into bite-sized chunks
2 tbsp Green Seasoning (see pp26–27 – optional)
4 tbsp cooking oil of choice
1 onion, chopped
3 garlic cloves, finely chopped
1 green bell pepper, deseeded and chopped
100g (¼lb) mushrooms, sliced or chopped (optional)
400g (14.5oz) can chopped tomatoes or 4 large tomatoes, chopped
1½ tsp dark brown sugar
1 tsp sea salt
½ tsp freshly ground black pepper
½ tsp Cajun seasoning
1 tbsp butter
1 tbsp white wine or sherry (optional)
1 Scotch bonnet pepper, whole, or pinch of dried chilli flakes (optional)

If using the green seasoning, place the prepared fish in a bowl and add the seasoning. Massage it in, cover and refrigerate for at least 30 minutes.

In a large frying pan, heat the oil over a medium–high heat. When hot, add the onion and sauté for 3 minutes before adding the garlic, bell pepper and mushrooms, if using. Sauté for an additional 2 minutes, then add the fish with any seasoning that clings on to it. Sauté for 1 minute, then add the tomatoes. Stir to combine and then add the sugar, salt, pepper and Cajun seasoning, if using.

Turn the heat down to low and at this point you can add the butter, white wine or sherry as well as the Scotch bonnet pepper or chilli flakes if you like. Simmer, uncovered, for 25–30 minutes.

Serve with plain white or brown rice.

Crossing the *kala pani*

In certain Hindu beliefs, the traversing of large expanses of water, the *kala pani* (or dark waters), was associated with cultural impurity as it was seen to lead to the dilution of a "purified" Hindu essence. In the Indian subcontinent, *kala pani* crossings were initially associated with the expatriation of convicts, low castes and other "undesirable" elements of society. Those who "voluntarily" crossed the kala pani were automatically thought to be compromising their Hinduness.

The disdain for cross-sea voyages may also have been rooted in the physical, tangible effects for those who set sail. For the *jahaji* ("ship-traveller"), these journeys, taking up to 13 weeks at sea, took place in cramped and unsanitary conditions. This aided the spread of many diseases which led to fatalities. By the 1850s, out of the dozen or so ships that had left India for the Caribbean, the average mortality rate was sometimes as high as 31 per cent, with an average of around 17 per cent. Those who left India were usually young adults in their twenties or thirties, sometimes part of family units and sometimes single. If they had children, the children travelled with them and could be expected to work when they reached the age of five. None of them ever knew if they would return "home".

The idea of not returning lingers in the memory of many brought to the Caribbean. The tragic folk tale entitled *Gang Gang Sarah flew over from Africa* tells of a bird (sometimes a witch) named Sarah (sometimes Sara or Sarie). Sarah was flying from her home in Africa one night, and was blown off course during a storm. She ended up at Les Coteaux (Tobago) where she met some acquaintances and stayed, but wished to return home in her old age. Sarah soon learned, however, that she had lost the art of flight through eating salt. She fell out of the tree which she climbed for take-off, never recovered and died soon after. For me, the stormy night represents the harrowing middle passage of the Atlantic Ocean, complete with the ailments which indentured Indians faced, plus the risks of torture and even suicide. It speaks to Sarah becoming a new person in the Caribbean and the impossibility of returning "home".

David Dabydeen, who has written extensively about the other Windrush, the under-represented diaspora of Caribbeans not from Jamaica or descending from indentured communities, talks of the complexities of crossing the *kala pani*: "*the physical and spiritual journey was justified by the dream of modernity – the prospect of a new beginning in new lands and promises of plenty*." Regardless of whether the hope of return was promised or imagined, upon arrival those in the Caribbean sought to fashion identities that contained homages to their motherland but simultaneously constructed something new, something unique and almost magical. This thread, to me, is what drives the fanhood of Caribbean nationality. You'll often read in the biographies of recipes that a dish may be known by one name in one place and another somewhere else, or that a certain dish has particular ingredients or techniques. These differences can be vehemently defended as "the right way" and when you account for the formation of new identities where people of all creeds believe they have a stake in the culture, this begins to make sense.

Author V. S. Naipaul, who was born in Trinidad and moved to England at a young age, speaks about being a double immigrant in his novel *The Enigma of Arrival*. The Windrush generation were again rooted in hope and promises that turned out to be half-truths. New identities had to be formed and new lives carved out. With this said, keeping memory and culture alive are things that our grandparents did, as did our ancestors. Memories live in the stories, the carnival revelry, songs, dance and, of course, food. So, if you ever wondered why Caribbeans take food so seriously, this surely is a fragment of the reason why.

Metemgee

When I tell people I have family from or that I am going to visit Guyana, the first retort is almost always "Ghana?" referring to the West African nation some 4,000 miles across the Atlantic Ocean. Most who make this error are seldom aware that the two nations are inextricably linked, with many of those working the Guyanese plantations of the transatlantic slave trade coming across that same ocean from Ghana. For me, food can tell these stories and *metemgee* (or *metem*), laden with ground provisions deeply rooted in the transplanted West African populace, is testament to this. Ghana and Guyana are among the few places I've seen fish, starch and boiled eggs combined on a plate (in garden egg stew and *waakye*, for example).

In a book of Guyanese proverbs and stories a tale is told of two villagers who, having not seen each other in a while, wax lyrical about Guyanese culture on the eve of the nation's independence from the British on 26 May 1966. I couldn't describe the essence of the dish better. She narrates *"The best way is to use all the local vegetables"*, as well as refraining from using Irish potatoes. She tells of her preference for a tasty dish that includes grated coconut and Pig-tails (locally manufactured, if available). For the provisions, she reels off a list of *"plantains, sweet potatoes, Eddoes and of course, Cassava"* that are bolstered by seasonings, *"Thyme and a piece of spice"*. All this to make the best Metemgee. And these golden tips remain the same today.

The end result is a dish thicker than a soup but a magnitude heartier than one. While some like to have the root vegetables slightly al dente, the joy for me is some hours to a day later when the liquid thickens and becomes one with stray bits of dissolved vegetables and the lightly salted *duff* – the puffy boiled dumplings that are a mandatory component of *metemgee* (at least for me anyway). The duff also seems to be a reimagined Caribbean version of the "swallows" of West Africa like *kenkey* or *fufu*, which always partner with meals there.

This is a dish that can easily hold its own as a vegan dish and feel free to use whatever ground provisions are available to you. However, for myself and many other *metemgee* evangelists, the meal is just a shadow of itself if there isn't a wedge of seasoned fried fish (see p123) sitting to the side.

DUFF Sift the dry ingredients into a large bowl, then slowly add 150ml (⅔ cup) water until the dough mixture comes together. This dough mixture does not need to be super tight and can be very loose and slightly sticky to the touch. Cover with cling film (plastic wrap) or a damp dish towel and leave to rest.

MAIN Keep the prepared vegetables for the ground provisions in a large bowl of water until ready to cook.

In a large pot or Dutch pot, heat the oil over a medium-high heat. When hot, add the onion and sauté for 2–3 minutes. Then add the garlic and ginger and sauté for a further two minutes. Next, add the ground provisions and stir to combine for 5 minutes. Add the seasoning ingredients and again stir to combine. Then add the coconut milk and 100ml (6½ tablespoons) water. Turn up the heat a notch and cook for a few minutes until boiling, then turn the heat back down to medium. Cover and cook for 25–30 minutes until the ground provisions are soft (when there's a hint of resistance as you pierce them, they're ready).

When done, add the plantain, corn and okra. Cover again and cook for 5–8 minutes.

Meanwhile, in a small saucepan, add one egg per two people eating (or one each if you are so inclined) and cover with water. Add a dash of salt and boil for 10 minutes. After this, discard the water, re-cover with cold water and leave for three minutes. When cool, take out each egg and slightly crack on a hard surface. Place back into the water and peel until the whole shell comes off. Repeat for all eggs and slice in half. The yolks should have hardened.

Fill a saucepan three-quarters full with water and bring to the boil. Gather your duff dough ball and tear into equal-sized pieces. Gently roll into oblongs with the palm of your hands and place into the water with a dash of salt. Cook for a minute, then nudge with a spatula or utensil if they are sticking to the bottom of the pan. After you've made sure that they aren't sticking, cook for 10 minutes until they start to float. Test the duff with a knife – they will be soft but still hold their shape. Place the duff into your main pot, cover and cook for a few minutes.

The dish is now ready to serve, however, you can leave it to simmer until the liquid is at your desired consistency.

Serve in a bowl or plate with a relatively deep base with halved eggs and fried fish, if you like.

NOTE *If you have a 4-hob cooker, you can cook all parts of this recipe at once. Skip boiling the duff in a separate pot and place it straight into the main pot to cook but be aware it can fall apart and dissolve easily.*

SERVES 6

1 onion, chopped
6–8 garlic cloves, chopped
2.5cm (1in) piece of fresh root ginger, peeled and finely chopped or grated
2 x 400ml (13.5fl oz) cans coconut milk
2 plantains (400g/¾lb), peeled and chopped
2 corn on the cob (ears of corn), silk and husks removed, sliced into 6 pieces
8–10 fingers okra, whole
Fry Fish (see opposite – optional)
3 eggs
sea salt

FOR THE DUFF

250g (2 cups) plain (all-purpose) flour
1 tsp sea salt
½ tsp baking powder
1 tsp granulated white sugar (optional)

FOR THE GROUND PROVISIONS

700g (1½lb) yellow or eddoe yams, peeled and chopped
300g (¾lb) sweet potato, peeled and chopped
1 cassava, peeled, deveined and chopped

FOR THE SEASONING

5 sprigs of fresh thyme
1 Scotch bonnet pepper, whole
1 tbsp Green Seasoning (see pp26–27 – optional)
1 tsp salt
1 tsp freshly ground black pepper
½ tsp ground cumin (optional)
½ tsp all-purpose seasoning (optional)

Fry fish

Unless it's an ingredient that can be fried with minimal amounts of oil or fat, you may notice a deficit of fried recipes in this book. As much of the recipes enjoyed in the Caribbean today are remnants of the underclass of years gone by, that is particularly true of fried food. Before oil was commercially available in the Caribbean in the 20th century, frying was a cooking method mainly reserved for the wealthy elites. Frying fish in oil was long-established in West Africa, however, but large amounts of cooking oil were not readily available on or near the plantations and so records of its consumption are few.

After oil for cooking became commercially available, frying seafood became one of the most popular means of cooking fish, especially as it could be preserved for some time by escovitching (preserving) it with peppers and vinegar. This fried fish recipe works wonders with almost any fish, marinating it in green seasoning for some time before dusting it with lightly seasoned flour. The same method that works here for regular uncut fish can also be used for fillets or fish cut into bite-sized chunks for Bake & "Shark" (see p108).

SERVES 4

4 fish of choice (1kg/2¼lb), such as snapper, kingfish, sea bass or tilapia, filleted shark or catfish, cut into bite-sized pieces (for Bake & "Shark", see p108)
10 tbsp plain (all-purpose) flour
2 tsp sea salt
250ml (1 cup) milk
300ml (1¼ cups) cooking oil of choice

FOR THE SEASONING

2 tbsp Green Seasoning (see pp26–27)
1 tsp sea salt
1 tsp freshly ground black or white pepper
1 tsp paprika (optional)
1 tsp Cajun seasoning (optional)
1 tsp fish seasoning (optional)

Clean and prepare your chosen fish as you prefer. If using whole fish, slice two or three diagonal slits on both sides of each fish and place them into a large bowl. Add the seasoning ingredients and thoroughly combine. Cover the bowl and refrigerate for 4 hours–overnight. Alternatively, you can mix the fish and seasoning ingredients and immediately move on to the next step.

Place the flour and salt in a flat dish, submerge the fish in the flour and let it sit for 10 minutes. Then dip the fish in the milk and dredge in the flour again.

Heat the oil in a large frying pan or heavy-based saucepan over a medium–high heat. When hot, take one fish from the flour, shake off any excess flour and place it gently in the oil. Cook on each side for 3–4 minutes until the coating is dark golden brown or the fillets are a light golden brown. Remove and drain on kitchen paper.

Serve with rice, Boil 'n' Fry Yam (see p44) or with Fry Bake (see p162) if using fish fillets.

NOTE *For Bake & "Shark" (see p108), you may wish to use large fillets that fit the size of one fry bake rather than fill the bake with a few smaller bite-sized chunks – this is fine, and the same instructions apply.*

Oil down

Coconut milk in curry is great but sometimes I don't think it captures the true potential and magic of the creamy texture like Metemgee (see p120) and Oil Down do. This recipe, the national dish of Grenada, the closest island north of Tobago, is enjoyed and known to some in other locales as "rundown". The name seems self-explanatory – when the coconut milk is cooked down and evaporated, then fused with this volume of slowly dissolving starchy vegetables and oily fish, the result is a concoction that moves slowly. As slow as a pedestrian in the heat of the Caribbean day, as slow as peak-hour Trinidad highway traffic, as slow as the tar of the La Brea Pitch Lake and as slow as the oil that revellers paint themselves in each year at carnival to remember the piping hot molasses that enslavers used to torture their enslaved. Oil Down, like Metemgee (essentially different versions of the same dish), is a real vestige of the West African ancestors of the Caribbean who fashioned new meals with what was available. The end result may not be the most photogenic, but these are truly the most beautiful dishes to me.

––––––

In a large heavy-based saucepan or Dutch pot, heat the oil over a medium heat until it crackles. Sauté the onion and garlic for 2–3 minutes until they begin to brown. Then add the chilli flakes, ginger, chives, thyme, fresh coriander and continue sautéing and stirring for 2 minutes. If it dries out, add a splash of water to loosen it up.

Now add the breadfruit, carrots, bell peppers and callaloo and cook, stirring, for 5 minutes. Then add the coconut milk, hot water and nutmeg and stir before adding the turmeric, which should change the colour of the dish. If you want to add fish, then add it now.

During cooking, use some force with your utensil to make sure nothing is sticking to the base of your pot. Add the salt, pepper and Scotch bonnet pepper and cook over a medium heat for 30 minutes, stirring occasionally. Add the green banana, turn the heat down to a simmer and cook over a low heat for another 20–30 minutes. There is no exact timing for oil down. After simmering you'll notice the amount of liquid continuing to reduce until you reach your desired consistency. As long as the starchy vegetables are cooked through, you are good to go.

Remove from heat and serve in a large bowl.

SERVES 6

5–6 tbsp cooking oil of choice
1 onion, sliced
3 garlic cloves, minced
1 tbsp dried chilli flakes
2.5cm (1in) piece of fresh root ginger, grated, or 1 tsp ground ginger
4 chives, chopped
2 tsp dried thyme or 2 sprigs of thyme
2 tbsp fresh coriander (cilantro)
400g (¾lb) breadfruit, cored and sliced or chopped (optional)
2 carrots, peeled and sliced
2 red or green bell peppers, deseeded and chopped
250g (½lb) callaloo (dasheen bush leaves) or flat-leaf spinach, stems removed
400ml (13.5fl oz) can coconut milk
200ml (scant 1 cup) hot water
½ tsp grated nutmeg
1 tsp ground turmeric
125g (¼lb) mackerel or fish fillet of choice (optional)
1 tsp sea salt or all-purpose seasoning
½ tsp freshly ground black pepper
1 Scotch bonnet pepper, whole
3 green bananas, peeled and halved and cut into bite-sized chunks if you like

Pepper shrimp

Driving along the coast from the North to the South of Trinidad on the way to San Fernando, we find a cluster of Chinese restaurants on the Guaracara–Tabaquite road frequented by those attending a local mosque. These moments – a Chinese restaurant, on a road named after Indigenous Amerindian geography, located in a Spanish-named city in a Spanish-named English-speaking country, frequented overwhelmingly by people of Indian heritage – remind us how truly diverse this corner of the Caribbean is, especially given the relatively small size of each country. Pepper shrimp is a staple on Chinese restaurant menus across the Caribbean, so it's evidently a favourite. Be they West African, North or South Indian or even Portuguese, all the hinterlands of the Caribbean people can be found to enjoy shrimp, so this makes sense. This pepper shrimp is not like the seasoned and sautéed version famed in Jamaica, but rather like the style you find in the Chinese province of Guangdong down to Hong Kong. These bite-sized shrimp traverse the line of peppery but not overly spicy in the way that only Southern Chinese food can. If possible, increase the amount of shrimp as these go fast!

If the prawns are whole, remove the upper body shells, leaving on the tails. Using the lime juice, devein the prawns and rinse with water. Pat dry and set aside.

In a large bowl or tray, add the cornflour and baking powder and stir to combine. Add the prawns and toss to coat completely.

In a deep frying pan or wok, heat the oil over a medium–high heat. When hot, in batches so as not to overcrowd the pan, add the prawns and fry for 2 minutes on each side until they have turned white-ish. Using a slotted spoon or metal tongs, remove the prawns and place on kitchen paper to drain.

Now, either discard all but 3 tablespoons of oil or take 3 tablespoons of oil from this pan and add to a wok or large frying pan. Heat this oil over a medium heat and add 1½ spring onions (reserving some green), the chilli, garlic powder and ginger and sauté for 2 minutes. Next, add the prawns and continue to sauté for 4 minutes. The prawns should have turned a golden colour. Turn off the heat, add the salt and pepper and stir.

Garnish with the remaining spring onions and the chilli flakes. Serve as a snack or with white rice.

SERVES 2–4

400g (1lb) raw tiger prawns (shrimp)
juice of 1 lime
5 tbsp cornflour (corn starch)
2 tsp baking powder
250ml (1 cup) cooking oil of choice
2 spring onions (scallions/green onions), finely sliced
1 red chilli, sliced
½ tsp garlic powder
½ tsp ground ginger
½ tsp sea salt
½ tsp freshly ground black or white pepper or Sichuan peppercorns
1 tsp dried chilli flakes

Roast fish

The Indigenous people of the Caribbean, such as the Caribs and Warrau, developed a diverse culinary tradition based on hunting, farming and fishing. They would use bows and arrows to hunt fish that they inebriated using tree bark and then dive to catch them aided by nets made of either palm fibre or cotton. The fish was then roasted on an open fire or sometimes wrapped in clay and placed directly in the fire. This technique of wrapping and insulating fish and meat has been followed by a plethora of cultures the world over, across generations too, be it using banana, lotus or grape leaves. Today we have the luxury of aluminium foil and ovens. These new technologies help continue the tradition of this roasted fish, though the recipe works just as well if you do have an open fire. Most of the recipes in this book are laden with an array of seasonings but this dish keeps it simple, using just garlic, vegetables and citrus to provide the flavour.

Clean and prepare your fish as you prefer, then slice a diagonal slit on each side of the fish and place them into a large bowl. Add the seasoning ingredients and rub into the fish, including the inside of the belly. Then place a garlic clove and a lemon slice inside the belly of each fish.

Preheat the oven to 180°C (160°C fan/350°F/Gas 4), line a tray with foil and lightly coat the foil with olive oil.

Place the fish on the tray and then top with the onion, bell peppers and carrots. Cook for 40 minutes. Remove from the oven and test the fish by slightly cutting into it – it should be white. Let cool and then serve with a rice dish of choice.

SERVES 3–4

3 medium or 1 large white fish (tilapia, snapper, kingfish), scaled
1 or 3 garlic cloves, peeled
1 or 3 slices of lemon
olive oil
½ onion, sliced
1 bell pepper of choice, deseeded and sliced into rings
⅓ carrot, peeled and thinly sliced

FOR THE SEASONING

3 tbsp Green Seasoning (see pp26–27)
1 tsp all-purpose seasoning
1 tsp freshly ground black pepper
1 tsp sea salt
1 tsp ground ginger
½ tsp chilli powder of choice
2 sprigs of thyme

NOSE -TO-TAIL

"The most famous preservation technique of the Arawak is barbecuing."

This chapter is amongst the shortest in the book and the reason is quite simple: meat consumption, especially fresh meat, was incredibly rare for most of the people of the Caribbean, as it was for the vast majority of underclasses around the world. The Indigenous people of the various countries hunted and ate what was native to where they lived. The Taino, for example, ate from the bird population, which remained abundant until European colonization. The indigenous birds were then subjected to a widespread onslaught and new species were quickly introduced by the Spanish. This onslaught included the people too, and the Indigenous tribes were constantly battling for their lives. As such, many of the early modes of meat consumption included some form of preservation.

Tasso, which Haitians may know as *tassot*, is reminiscent of jerky and used meat like wild pork and later bovine, which was sun-dried in the heat of the day as the savannah winds reduced it to a black, leathery appearance. Another tribe, the Arawaks, are credited for *cassareep*, a syrup made from cooked down cassava, which also preserved meat. This is seen in the Guyanese favourite Pepperpot (see p140), which historically featured any animal, from deer and rodents to marsupials. The most famous preservation technique of the Arawak though is barbecuing, said to derive from their term *babracot*, a kind of wooden grill consisting of a small stage of green sticks built two feet above an open fire. Meat was placed on top and smoked, then kept for a good many days. Early Spanish settlers observed Taino Indians from the island of Hispaniola using a similar wooden grill they called *barbacoa*, which the Spanish co-opted into BBQ (see p136).

The West Africans who were transported to the Caribbean were able to use vegetables and flour to fashion some of their traditional meals, but the same wasn't true for meat. With planters looking for the cheapest possible way to sustain their workers, meat was far from the top of the list. Unlike the pre-existing tribes, unless the enslaved ran away and settled in the rainforested hills (often termed as marooning) they couldn't hunt as they were not allowed to leave the plantations. In the early 1800s, a colonial commissioner wrote of the enslaved:

"We cannot imagine a more mischievous system or one more ruinous to the planter and to the slave ... to let these people loose in order that they may seek their weekly subsistence can only be an inducement to idle and profligate habits..."

Ordinances were ordered so that the enslaved across the Caribbean had some semblance of meat in their diets. This commonly came in the form of salted or corned pork and beef (up to 2kg/4½lb in some regions), as those in power were looking to cut costs to maximize profit and in the heat of the tropics there were no fridges or freezers. These meats were a luxury and became a favourite. Percy and Serena Braithwaite's collection *Guyanese Proverbs and Stories* illustrates the slang term "pork-knocker". It had several meanings but one explains:

"Salt-pork being his most expensive food item, he was chary in its use, so he always kept it tied to a piece of string so that when the rice was finished cooking and had imbibed the sweetness of the pork, he pulled the latter out of the pot, knocked it on the side of the pot to shake off any adhering rice grains, and put it back in his ration-box until required at the cooking of the next meal."

"Cow heel soup is a favourite among many, as are gizzard and liver, both cooked in various ways, such as stewed or boiled in soups."

In the original versions of many of the recipes in this book, such as Bhaji Rice and Cook-up Rice (see p57 and p62), salted pork was a staple ingredient. The fresh meat that the enslaved could access was generally the offcuts not favoured by the overclass. These were the innards, tails, heels and feet. The legacy of this is still apparent to this day. Cow heel soup is a favourite among many, as are gizzard and liver, both cooked in various ways, such as stewed or boiled in soups. The ancestors would wail at the current price of oxtail, which has become relished around the world. The comparatively less relished foot, particularly chicken foot, features in the European-turned-Caribbean Souse (see p150) another preserving dish, this time with pickle and black pudding, a European-imported favourite.

The situation remained like this until the people of the Caribbean became free. Subsequently, with the commercialization of chicken at "pens" around the Caribbean, freed people could easily rear and farm them at home, which meant that chicken emerged as one of the dominant meats. Brown Stew Chicken (see p138), an Afro-Caribbean reproduction of the Amerindian *cassareep* dishes, "Chinese" Fried Chicken (see p146) and the Jewish-inspired Pom (see p144) have all become national favourites in their respective locales. This fancy rears itself in a classic call and response Guyanese folk song "Small Days":

Rick chick chick chick (Congatay!)
I've been been to a dam (Congatay!)
I see Fowl Mama (Congatay!)
And she has ten fat chickens (Congatay!)
So I ask her for one (Congatay!)
And she says I can get' em (Congatay!)

"The sounds of roaming poultry wake you up in the morning, you cross paths with wandering flocks of goats on the way to school and cows sit in traffic, side by side with trucks."

That being said, pork still lingered on the tongue of many and it's a popular alternative for BBQ as well as a common bite seen in dishes like Jeera Pork (see p153). Another reason that this chapter is relatively short is that with the high proportion of Indian descendants among the population, pork was a no-go for religious reasons and secondly, the go-to use for meat in the Trini and Guyanese corner of the Caribbean is surely curry, which has its own separate chapter. Today, halal butchers and meat stalls line markets, high streets and highways all to service this. There's also a closer relationship to animals as the sounds of roaming poultry wake you up in the morning, you cross paths with wandering flocks of goats on the way to school and cows sit in traffic, side by side with trucks. Oil rigs on the highway are shoulder to shoulder with horse and donkey carriages, cows taking a leisurely break from their stroll frequently hold up traffic for some minutes, and chickens wake up and stroll around the village in their packs like a gang.

Historically, those of the Caribbean didn't eat much meat, not by choice, but through grit and strength managed to sustain countless resistances, rebellions and revolts with their diets. Today, out of choice, I don't eat meat often, so many of these recipes are special occasion dishes to me. Fortunately, I've omitted any use of wild meat, so every recipe should be accessible to anyone with access to a large supermarket or butchers.

BBQ chicken

The Caribbean is the only place in the world where you'll find people of African heritage running restaurants selling Chinese dishes like *Lo Mein*, neighbouring Chinese families offering Indian-style rotis and Indian families with barbecue joints complete with steel barbecue drums. OK, so you might find this somewhere else, but in the Caribbean the difference is that they all believe they are cooking food of their own national heritage. Although none of these groups can claim the creation of barbecue in the same way as those of the sadly dwindling Amerindian lineage, including the Arawaks, Caribs and Taino. We can credit the latter for the term barbecue, a derivative of the Taino word *"barbecoa"* (or *"barbekoa"*), which means a raised wooden structure used, amongst other things, to cure meats.

A common misconception, likely due to the dominance of Jamaicans in the diaspora, is that jerk chicken is Caribbean, when in fact it seems native to and a mainstream chart-topper only in Jamaica. Tourism influenced by the West is likely to credit for other islands adopting jerk. But almost everywhere else – from Cuba down to Guyana – "BBQ" reigns supreme. Barbecues are fashioned out of anything from old oil drums to repurposed car rims and engines. Their transportable nature means that the presence of barbecue at limes (see p42) is almost a given, with a few hands delegated to manning the grill all night and ensuring people are dealt with at varying levels of pace – such is the way of liming.

Barbecue, like jerk, most commonly comes in two forms: pork or chicken, though I rarely opt for the former. Unlike jerk, where a lot of emphasis is placed on both the seasoning and the intricate method of cooking which leads to a smoky, charred, peppery-hot finish, with barbecue the main takeaway is simply well-cooked meat accompanied by a sweet-ish sauce, where pepper can be added but is not a must-have.

Clean and prepare your meat as you prefer and then cut two diagonal slits onto the top of each chicken thigh. Place the chicken in a flat-bottomed bowl or casserole dish and thoroughly mix in the marinade ingredients. Rub into all the crevices of the chicken, cover with cling film (plastic wrap) and leave for at least 1 hour, better 4 hours, or overnight if possible.

Preheat the oven to 180°C (160°C fan/350°F/Gas 4) and prepare a grill rack and casserole dish.

Place the chicken on the rack (rub any clumped seasoning over the top) and keep the bowl with the marinade. Place the casserole dish below the grill rack to catch the falling juice/gravy from the meat. Cook for 30 minutes.

After 30 minutes, mix together the glaze ingredients and liberally brush over the chicken. Cook for another 30 minutes. Then flip over the chicken and cook for 20 minutes. Flip the chicken back over again and cook for another 10 minutes. Finally, if you would like some crisp or char to the chicken, turn up the heat to 200°C (180°C fan/400°F/Gas 6) and cook for a final 20 minutes.

Remove the chicken from the oven. Use a spoon and ladle the fallen juice from the casserole dish over the chicken and then liberally brush again with the remaining glaze and serve.

NOTE *If you don't have space to rack the chicken, you can cook it in a casserole dish, just ensure that intermittently you are throwing away the natural juice from the chicken otherwise it can become too moist.*

SERVES 3–4

3–4 chicken legs

FOR THE MARINADE

2 tbsp Green Seasoning (see pp26–27)
1 tsp onion powder
1 tsp garlic powder
1 tsp hot chilli powder or 1 Scotch bonnet pepper, deseeded and chopped
1 tsp sea salt or all-purpose seasoning
1 tsp freshly ground black pepper
½ tsp garam masala
1 tbsp Tambran Sauce (see p230/optional)

FOR THE GLAZE

5 tbsp BBQ sauce of choice
2 tbsp honey or Tambran Sauce (see p230)
1 tbsp hot sauce (optional)

Brown stew chicken

Stew Chicken is one of those dishes we take for granted. It's not flash, not quite Curry Chicken (see p90) and most definitely not jerk or BBQ (see p136). A constant, either in the oven ready when you came home from school or, if not, it arrived soon after your parents came home from work. Only afterwards, growing older and leaving home, do you realize the joys of a stew. Simple one-pot cooking, teeming with whatever flavour you can think of or access, which can last for days when accompanied by a big pot of rice.

We should be thankful for the stew. In one of Indo-Caribbean chutney folk singer Jairam Dindial's many legendary skit-songs, the lead character Ganpat is devastated that his wife Rosalin went to market to get rice and chicken for stew but instead came back with bread, butter and a crooked violin. Very understandable, as stew chicken here is not like any stew chicken elsewhere. The dish straddles spice and sweetness as the chicken is seared in a caramel made from heated jaggery or sugar, which combusts with flavour the second it's hit with the marinade mix. You may want to increase the amount of chicken as this will not last long!

In a large bowl, add the chicken and marinade ingredients and stir to combine. Marinate for a few hours to overnight, although you can also use straight away.

In a large frying pan, Dutch pot or heavy-based saucepan, heat the oil over a medium–high heat. When hot, add the sugar to the centre and cook for 2–3 minutes until it starts to bubble and the edges start to turn dark brown. Turn the heat down a notch to medium and add the contents of the chicken seasoning bowl and begin to stir and mix to coat and combine with the sugar. Continue to cook, stirring intermittently, for 10 minutes, at which point you should see some of the fat from the chicken. Add the hot water and optional vegetables, cover and cook for 10 minutes, then remove the lid, turn the heat down to medium–low and cook for a final 10 minutes, or until the gravy reaches your desired consistency. Remove the thyme sprigs, if used.

Serve with white rice, Bhaji Rice (see p57), Nasi (see p56) or Rice & Peas (see p59).

NOTE *When stirring the chicken, avoid touching or scraping the sugar with your utensil at the start or it may stick and be hard to shake off.*

SERVES 6

1.5kg (3lb 3oz) chicken, cut to desired size, or pieces of choice (I buy a whole chicken and skinless thighs)
5 tbsp cooking oil of choice
3 tbsp brown sugar of choice
200ml (scant 1 cup) hot water

FOR THE MARINADE

3 tbsp Green Seasoning (see pp26–27)
1 tsp sea salt
1 tsp freshly ground black pepper
1 onion, finely chopped
1 spring onion (scallion/green onion), finely chopped
½ Scotch bonnet pepper, deseeded and chopped
3 tbsp tomato ketchup
1 tsp dark soy sauce or Worcestershire sauce
2 sprigs of thyme (optional)

FOR THE VEGETABLES (OPTIONAL)

½ red bell pepper, deseeded and chopped
½ tomato, diced
½ carrot, peeled and sliced into rounds

Pepperpot

Though Indigenous tribes are documented as existing in every Caribbean region, due to generations of wars, invasions, genocide and diseases almost all traces of their existence have dwindled. The largest remaining population today is in Guyana where the legacies of tribes such as the Warrau, Arawak and Carib can still be seen. Of these legacies, the most famous is the cultivation and consumption of the cassava root vegetable.

I know from trying to make traditional *bammy*, a flatbread produced from coarse cassava flour, the endurance needed to manage an abundance of cassava. The rough bark starts to grate the skin, tiny barbs penetrate fingernails, and the errant liquid prunes the fingers. Given that, any way to preserve cassava after harvesting was sought after. The Arawak tribe developed a technique of changing the poisonous prussic acid of cassava juice into a kind of non-poisonous vinegar by cooking it. They called this *cassareep*, and *cassareep*, together with local spices and pepper, formed the basis of what is known in Guyana today as Pepperpot.

This pepperpot is quite different to the pepper pot that most other Caribbean islands like Jamaica know, or even the African–American version. The *cassareep* produces a deep, rich, slightly tangy sweetness coated in gentle pepper heat and a progressively thicker sauce over time, which sticks to bread like metal to magnets.

A neighbour in Guyana tells me that *"the pot is never done"*. Traditionally pepperpot isn't refrigerated, since *cassareep* is a preservative, rather you leave the pot on the fire and when you finish the meat you add more and cook it again. This is a concept seemingly familiar with my grandmother's idiom of "waste not want not". Traditionally, the dish was served with what the native peoples could catch, which included deer, hogs and even wild rodents such as labba, along with cassava bread. Today, even in Guyana, unless you venture deep into the interior,

you're more likely to find recognizable meats like beef, pork and oxtail, which are recommended for use.

While techniques like browning sugar were made to replicate *cassareep*, there's essentially no replacement for it. In London, I was able to find it with complete ease, though if not, since it is a preservative, it can be bought online. *Cassareep* can be an acquired taste to deal with, especially if it's your first time cooking with it. The less you use, the less thick and brown the dish will be, with the taste more dictated by the seasoning. The more you use, the thicker and deeper brown–black the sauce will be, with a heavy *cassareep* taste coming through.

Another saying popular in my family was *"the pot won't cook if you look at it"* and this is particularly true of the slow brewing process of this jet-black stew (shown on p143), which is usually reserved for Christmas time and paired with Plait Bread (see p194).

———

Place the meat in a large bowl. To season it, add the green seasoning and mix to marinade. Preferably leave to marinate for 4 hours to overnight but you can also use it immediately.

In a large heavy-based saucepan or Dutch pot, heat the oil over a medium heat. When hot, fry the meat (in batches) on all sides for about 4 minutes until it starts to turn brown. When done, set aside.

Next, discard the oil and add the 6 tablespoons of oil. Heat over a low–medium heat and, when hot, add the spring onions, garlic and ginger and sauté for 3 minutes. Next, add back in all the meat and stir to combine. Then add all the gravy ingredients and stir. The water should just about submerge all the meat.

Turn the heat up to high. When the liquid starts to boil, turn the heat down to medium, place the lid on and cook for 2 hours if cooking boneless meat like beef or pork, or 2½ hours if using pig foot, cow foot, oxtail or goat.

SERVES 4–6

1.5kg (3lb 3oz) mixed red meat
   and cuts of choice, such as beef,
   pork, mutton, oxtail
3 tbsp Green Seasoning (see
   pp26–27)
150ml (⅔ cup) cooking oil of
   choice, plus 6 tbsp
2 spring onions (scallions/green
   onions), finely chopped
3 garlic cloves, minced
2.5cm (1in) piece of fresh root
   ginger, peeled and minced
1 Scotch bonnet pepper (optional)
sea salt and freshly ground black
   pepper

FOR THE GRAVY

1.3 litres (5½ cups) water or beef
   stock
150–250ml (⅔–1 cup plus 1 tbsp)
   cassareep
3 tbsp brown sugar of choice
2 cinnamon sticks
6 cloves (optional)
7.5cm (3in) piece of orange peel
   (optional)
10 sprigs of thyme

Remove the lid, add the Scotch bonnet pepper, turn the heat down to a simmer and continue to cook for a further 30 minutes until the liquid has thickened to a thin syrup consistency. The colour will range from a deep brown to almost jet black depending on how much *cassareep* was used.

Add salt and pepper to taste and serve with white rice, Rice & Peas (see p59), Plait Bread (see p194) or roti (see pp204–219).

PRESSURE COOKER

To cut the time down, if you have access to a pressure cooker, follow the initial frying process and then follow the next part using a pressure cooker instead of a saucepan or Dutch pot. Pressure cook for 1 hour, then decant back into the original saucepan. Turn the heat up to high to bring to the boil, then turn the heat down to medium-low and simmer for 30 minutes.

NOTE *Pepperpot keeps for a few days and doesn't need to be kept in the fridge, however, it will set hard after some hours. Add a splash of water before reheating.*

Pomtajer

Only in talking to people outside of my family and friendship group and working with cooks from non-Caribbean backgrounds, did I learn that not everyone washes their meat before cooking. On one job, being told I didn't have to wash meat sent my mind into confusion. I simply could not imagine a scenario where I didn't gut open a lime or lemon, submerge the chicken into a bowl of water with vinegar and use that citrus fruit to clean down the meat. Though I frequently questioned why other people didn't do this, I never actually wondered why I and "we" do this.

A possible reason is located in the roots of Pom, the national dish of Suriname. The chicken casserole was thought to have been brought to the region by those of European Jewish heritage, who controlled around a quarter of the plantations in Suriname. Reminiscent of what some people know as Kugel, this dish was adapted to the tropics as potatoes were not readily available. Thus, they turned to the starchy arrowroot known as pomtajer. In preparing this dish, as was Jewish custom, raw chicken was doused with either lemon juice or vinegar and this practice was adopted by the Afro-Surinamese.

Coincidentally, the citric acid served the purpose of quelling the toxicity that the pom may have left inside it (as is the case with most tubers) and also giving the dish a tropical undertone, blurring the line between sweet and savoury. Think Caribbean Shepherd's Pie. Additionally, in a sort of funny diasporic musical chairs, with many of those Afro-Surinamese and Caribbean people now living in Europe and the USA, pomtajer is hard to find and so many revert back to the dish's original version using regular potatoes. Unless you live somewhere like Amsterdam where small shops sell pomtajer (mainly in frozen form), it's likely that this will be your course of action too.

In a large saucepan, add the potatoes and cover with water. Boil over a high heat for 25 minutes or until soft enough to easily pierce with a fork. When done, discard the water and put the potatoes into a large bowl. To this bowl, add the rest of the potato base ingredients and mash and stir to combine.

Next, in a large pan or Dutch pot, heat the oil over a medium–high heat. When hot, add the onion and sauté for 3 minutes before adding the garlic, tomatoes, Scotch

SERVES 6

5 tbsp cooking oil of choice
1 onion, finely diced
3 garlic cloves, minced
2 tomatoes, chopped
1 Scotch bonnet pepper or 1 tsp chilli powder of choice (optional)
2 tbsp tomato purée (tomato paste)
1kg (2¼lb) boneless chicken breasts or thighs, chopped into bite-sized pieces
1 tbsp lime juice
250ml (1 cup plus 1 tbsp) hot water or chicken stock
1 tbsp oil, unsalted butter or margarine
20g (¾oz) unsalted butter or margarine, cut into 6 pieces (optional)

FOR THE POTATO BASE

1kg (2¼lb) white potatoes, peeled and halved
1 tbsp lime juice
1–2 tsp sea salt (to taste)
½ tsp ground turmeric
½ tsp freshly ground black pepper
¼ tsp grated nutmeg
¼ tsp allspice (optional)
1 tbsp sugar of choice (optional)
2 eggs, beaten
juice of 1 orange
2 tbsp light soy sauce

bonnet pepper and tomato purée. Continue to sauté for 2 minutes, then add the chicken and sauté for another 5 minutes. Add the lime juice and stir before adding the hot water or stock. Stir to combine and cook for 10 minutes. Turn the heat down to medium–low, cover with a lid and cook for 5 minutes. Remove the lid and continue to sauté for 10 minutes until the liquid has thickened slightly.

Preheat the oven to 170°C (150°C fan/ 340°F/Gas 3½).

Line the base of a 30cm x 40cm x 5cm (12in x 16in x 2in) casserole dish with oil, butter or margarine and then apply a thick layer of the potato base using half the amount.

Ladle a few spoons of the chicken liquid onto the potato base and then spread the chicken out over the top. Next, cover the chicken with the other half of the potato base and use the back of a spoon to spread it out evenly. Again, you can splash over some of the chicken liquid and then place bits of butter evenly over the top if you wish.

Place the dish in the oven and cook for 1 hour 15 minutes, until the top is golden brown with some bits of slightly burnt brown. Remove the dish and let cool for 10 minutes before serving with rice and salad.

"Chinese" fried chicken

Documents of late 19th-century Chinese settlers in the Caribbean tell that in the multicultural atmosphere of the settlements, they found their "unusual" cooking style was much appreciated, with "Chinese chicken" emerging as a favourite for public consumption. Well, it's been a century since then and nothing has changed. Such is the enjoyment of this chicken dish that each country tries to claim it for itself, hence why you'll see "Guyanese chicken" touted at one place and "Trini chicken" at another. If Caribbean food from the likes of Guyana and Trinidad and Tobago are the hidden jewels of the food world, then Caribbean–Chinese food is like a chamber of secrets concealed below. It's hard to pinpoint exactly what makes this fusion food so good, and unfortunately outside of the Caribbean only large North American cities like Miami, Toronto and New York have Caribbean-Chinese restaurants. This crispy fried chicken recipe doused in sweet soy sauce is a great introduction.

If you want to make the chicken extra tender, place it in a large bowl with the salt and sugar, cover with water and leave it to brine for at least 30 minutes.

Next, in a large saucepan add all the boil ingredients and 1 litre (4⅓ cups) cold water, or to cover, and heat over a high heat until the liquid starts to bubble. Turn the heat down to medium-high and boil for 10 minutes. Discard the brine water and place the chicken into the boiling saucepan. You will probably have to boil one chicken half/2 thighs at a time, so follow the next step in batches. Turn the heat up to high until it starts to boil and, when it does, reduce to medium and boil for 10 minutes. Then turn the heat down to low, place on the lid and cook for 5 minutes. Remove the lid and simmer for a final 10 minutes, using a large spoon to ladle the liquid over the chicken if it is not fully submerged.

Remove the chicken from the saucepan, set the boil liquid aside and place the chicken on a rack or kitchen paper and leave to cool and dry for 30–45 minutes. After this time if the chicken is still not completely dry, then pat it down with a dish towel or kitchen paper.

Finally, add the oil to a wok, Dutch pot or heavy-based frying pan and heat over a medium–high heat. When the oil starts to bubble, add the chicken and fry. If the chicken is not completely submerged, use a large spoon to consistently ladle oil over the top. After 5 minutes, flip the chicken over and fry for another 3 minutes before turning

SERVES 4

2 medium chickens, halved, or
  4 chicken legs
1 tbsp sea salt (optional)
1 tbsp granulated white sugar
  (optional)
1 litre (4⅓ cups) sunflower oil

FOR THE BOIL

200ml (scant 1 cup) dark soy
  sauce
4 tbsp dark brown sugar
5 garlic cloves, peeled
7.5cm (3in) piece of fresh root
  ginger, peeled and sliced into
  strips
4 spring onions (scallions/green
  onions), roots removed
5 star anise
½ tsp Chinese five spice
½ tsp freshly ground black pepper

FOR THE BLACK SOY SAUCE

120ml (½ cup) Boil (see above)
60g (2oz) sugar of choice
pinch of sea salt

back for a final 2 minutes until the skin has turned brown and crispy. Remove the chicken from the oil, set on a rack or kitchen paper and let cool and dry.

For the black soy sauce, take 120ml (½ cup) of the boil liquid and pour it into a small saucepan with the sugar and salt. Boil over a medium–high heat for 10 minutes until the mixture starts to vividly bubble, expanding inside the saucepan. Turn the heat down to low and simmer for another 5 minutes and then take off the heat. The mixture should have a thick consistency.

Serve on top of Nasi (see p56) and pour the black soy sauce on top or put in a pot to the side.

NOTE *If you have a thermometer, a good temperature for the oil is around 150°C (300°F). Bear in mind that the chicken has already been boiling for some time, so an extended time frying is not necessary.*

Where are you from?

For the people who were transported to the Caribbean not only was their communal identity in limbo, so too was their individual sense of self. West Africans were given first names based on things like physical appearance or at the whim of traders, and their surnames often became those of their plantation owners. It's how my family had Scottish and English surnames like Bucchan, Simpson, Williams and Phillips without ever having stepped foot in Europe. For those from India, surnames were almost unknown among the lower class who travelled from Uttar Pradesh. In the list of emigrants on the first boat of 1845, printed in the *Indian Centenary Review of Trinidad*, every single name was without a surname.

It was similar when the Chinese stepped into the Caribbean. When registering upon arrival, the romanization of names was subject to interpretation by the Western ear and, even with the help of a translator, it was not uncommon for name order to be changed, its spelling to be twisted into familiar pronunciations, hard phonemes to be left out, or even for it to be changed to an English-sounding name. Such transformations can be seen in Guyana and Trinidad where Chinese honorifics such as "A" often became part of the official surname, such as Achong and Sue-A-Quan. In many cases, people acquiesced to these odd derivations to help facilitate their integration.

In addition to names, the other element of identity lost was language. Most of the Amerindian tribes were eradicated by European forces before any substantial accounts of their language could be recorded. The West Africans who arrived in the Caribbean were not uniform and spoke languages such as Akan (from Ghana) and Yoruba (from Nigeria) amongst many more. Colonial overseers forced English on them, which resulted in the Creole "broken" English and patois still spoken today. This marked another erasure of identity as the knowledge

of their mother tongue was soon lost. Also, once Indian and Chinese arrivals moved to the settlements, they were funnelled toward and spoke the Creole developed by the Africans who settled there before them.

When you travel anywhere in the Caribbean, if your clothes don't already give it away, as soon as you open your mouth and utter a word, people know you're not "from there". The layers of this run deep. Those of Caribbean descent who travel "back" to West Africa share the same fate, unable to speak Twi, Akan, Yoruba, Igbo and so forth. Not "from there" either. A driver of Indian descent tells of the loss he felt not being able to understand Urdu as his forefathers from Uttar Pradesh did, and how Bollywood DVDs and re-runs on TV with the subtitles turned on helped fill this void.

Likewise, my Uncle Sal, tells me how his mother, my Great-aunt Salima, while ethnically Indian, on arrival to Britain felt no kin with the Indians (from India) who she worked with, looked like and lived near, mainly because she was an outcast regarding understanding their subcontinental languages.

The importance of food to the people of the Caribbean and their identity is continually discussed in this book and it rears itself here. The question – where are you from? – is often wielded toward people of colour in the diaspora, with any answer constantly challenged. People of Caribbean descent, even having given so much to Britain, are rarely accepted as truly being British and no response or act can successfully retort. In the Caribbean, even if you are born in a certain country and have a local accent but moved overseas, you still can be seen as a foreigner and outsider. The one act that cements identity, status and positioning in the Caribbean beyond name and language is cooking. The ability to make a good batch of roti – yes; the ability to professionally wield a *karahi* to make a curry – yes. With the ability to make a crowd-pleasing Callaloo (see p38) or

Coconut Bake (see p164), I saw even the most cockney of Brits be told they're "Trini" now. Food again marks itself as one of the most important expressions of identity in the Caribbean. Over the years, for those who wanted to reconnect with their Caribbean heritage, there's no language to turn to and the erasure of names makes tracing lineage back further more difficult. I found over and over again that when many wanted to reconnect with their heritage, their first port of call was recipes, and hopefully the pages of this book can help with that.

Souse

While I frequently lament the world's current meat industry which seems to favour a handful of meats and cuts, leaving much of the rest sneered at, I can't pretend to be a fan of animal foot. Cow foot, chicken foot, and the likes of pig's foot favoured in places like the Dominican Republic, must be amongst the Marmite of meat cuts. There is no real in between; people seldom casually consume foot, either they love it, and it triggers waves of nostalgia, or the instant sight of it draws repulsion. These cuts, and thus any recipes attached to them, seem generationally linked and I fear may die out with the older generation. A swooning 1930s tune by Guyanese shanto singer Bill Rogers entitled "Jimmy Black Pudding and Souse" tells of a raucous crowd full of domestic servants, maids and butlers eager to buy the eponymous foods:

...Souse with seasoning,
Cucumbers and salad
The way how de ting so sweet
That all a dem Water street
Clerks and clerkess
Went there for their Saturday Night treat.

Souse, based on a European-imported pickle recipe, is a perfect illustration of a generation who had to make a lot with just a little and that little they did make, they endeavoured to make it glam in true Caribbean style. Perhaps this mentality of using a little to make a lot is what leant the word souse to the phrase *"to throw a souse"*, meaning a party or cookout done in the hopes of fundraising for a certain need or desire. Like almost every recipe, there are dozens of different ways of making it, including boiling everything at once, however, I prefer the less overpowering, easier to manipulate taste of this method.

SERVES 6

500g (1lb 2oz) chicken feet
3 tbsp Green Seasoning (see
    pp26–27 – optional)
3 garlic cloves, minced (optional)
1 tsp salt, plus extra to taste
1 corn on the cob (ear of corn), cut
    into 5–6 slices (optional)

FOR THE PICKLE

about 1 litre (4⅓ cups) warm
    water, to cover
60ml (4 tbsp) white vinegar
    (optional)
juice of 1 lime
¼ cucumber, sliced
½ onion, thinly sliced
1 spring onion (scallion/green
    onion), finely sliced
½ Scotch bonnet pepper, deseeded
    and finely chopped
15g (½oz) fresh coriander
    (cilantro), chopped
½ tsp freshly ground black pepper
sea salt, to taste

Clean the meat as you prefer and if the butcher hasn't
already done so, chop the nails off each digit. If you like,
you can marinate the chicken feet in a large bowl with the
green seasoning for a minimum of 4 hours, or overnight if
possible. Cover and refrigerate.

Add the chicken feet to a large pot, cover with
water, add the garlic, if using, and salt and boil for
40–45 minutes. After 30 minutes, add the sweetcorn,
if using. Alterntively, if using a pressure cooker, add the
chicken feet, garlic, salt and corn, if using, and cook for
about 10–15 minutes. Remove from the heat, drain off
the water and rinse with cold water and set aside.

In a glass bowl or casserole dish, add all the pickle
ingredients and stir. Add the drained chicken feet and
sweetcorn and stir. Cover and set aside at room
temperature for 2 hours, or overnight if possible.

Serve at room temperature in small bowls, large cups
or mugs.

Jeera pork

There is a joke that Europe colonized the world for its spices only to barely use them, and I think that there could be no better example than *jeera* – more commonly known as cumin. Mentions of it in Indian literature date back to 300BCE, though today it's often buried in a curry powder mixture amongst an array of other spices. Cumin can be quite overpowering, adding a teaspoon too much to a dish can mar it and, as such, few dishes lean on cumin as their primary ingredient.

What you may know as hors d'oeuvres or sliders are known in certain parts of the Caribbean as cutters. Cutters often feature toothpicks and come in many forms. In reality, anything chopped and diced small enough can be a cutter and jeera pork is amongst the most popular. Almost a *bunjal* (see p91) of sorts, this simultaneously arid but moist meat snack is perfect paired with a cold brew.

Put the pork in a bowl and add the marinade ingredients. Mix to combine and then cover and refrigerate for a minimum of 30 minutes.

In a Dutch pot or large saucepan, heat the oil over a medium heat. When hot, add the onion and sauté for 3 minutes before adding the garlic, spring onion and Scotch bonnet pepper. Sauté for a further 2 minutes. Add the ground cumin and garam masala and stir constantly for a minute. If the powder gets dry and starts to stick to the pan, then add the hot water.

Add all the contents of the pork bowl to the pan and cook for 10 minutes, stirring continuously and making sure nothing is sticking to the base of the pan. Add the salt and stir to combine. Turn the heat down to low, put on the lid and simmer for 20 minutes.

Remove the lid and if the gravy is adequate, you are done; if you'd like less, turn up the heat to medium–high and cook for a further 10 minutes. If you'd like more gravy, add hot water and stir. Finally, add the fresh coriander and gently stir in.

Serve with lime wedges and pierce each chunk with a toothpick.

SERVES 4–6

1kg (2¼lb) pork belly, shoulder and/or leg, cut into 2.5cm (1in) pieces
6 tbsp cooking oil of choice
½ onion, finely chopped
3 garlic cloves, finely chopped
1 spring onion (scallion/green onion), chopped
½ Scotch bonnet pepper, deseeded and finely chopped
1 tbsp ground cumin
½ tsp garam masala
60ml (4 tbsp) hot water (optional)
1 tsp sea salt
2 tbsp chopped fresh coriander (cilantro)
lime wedges, to serve

FOR THE MARINADE

2 tbsp Green Seasoning (see pp26–27)
1 tsp ground cumin
½ tsp garam masala

Bami

At every restaurant of South Asian heritage in Suriname wherever you see Nasi (see p56) for sale you'll most certainly see *bami* too. In short, *nasi* is fried rice and *bami* is fried noodles. Similarly, at Chinese restaurants throughout the Caribbean, wherever you find fried rice, you'll find a version of fried noodles, be it *chow mein* or *lo mein*. Their popularity is surely due to their versatility. The sweet and sourness can be manipulated, the heat can be scaled to suit and the number of vegetables added can take it from a quick bite to a full meal. Given that *bami* and *lo mein* are so similar in the base technique, you can tailor the recipe to your taste.

Add all the marinade ingredients to a small bowl and then add the chicken and mix well. Cover and refrigerate for 30 minutes. Alternatively, you can move on to the next step after 5 minutes if you are pressed for time.

Next, put all the sauce ingredients into a bowl and set aside.

Finally, prepare your noodles following the instructions on the packet and cook just under the recommended time. Drain and set aside.

Heat the oil in a large frying pan or wok over a medium heat. When hot, add the chicken and cook for 3–5 minutes. Turn the chicken a few times to ensure it cooks on both sides. When it's browned, remove to a plate.

Next, add half the spring onions, the garlic, ginger and Scotch bonnet pepper and sauté for 2 minutes. Now turn up the heat a notch and add your chosen vegetables and fry for 2–3 minutes. Then add the noodles and toss to combine before adding the sauce. Use a kitchen utensil to mix and combine all the ingredients and the sauce. Finally, add the chicken back in and mix to combine. Cook for a final 2 minutes and then turn off the heat.

Add a dash of salt and pepper to taste and serve. Garnish with the other half of spring onion.

NOTE *If you would like to serve more people, simply double the amount of meat and noodles used.*

SERVES 2

300g (10½oz) chicken breasts or thighs, cut into 1cm (½in) strips
200g (7oz) lo mein noodles, egg noodles or spaghetti
4 tbsp cooking oil of choice
2 spring onions (scallions/green onions), chopped
5 garlic cloves, minced
2.5cm (1in) piece of fresh root ginger, peeled and grated
¼ Scotch bonnet pepper, topped and finely chopped
sea salt and freshly ground black pepper

FOR THE MARINADE

1 tbsp rice wine or mirin
1 tsp dark soy sauce
1 tsp cornflour (corn starch)

FOR THE SAUCE

2 tbsp light soft brown sugar
1 tsp groundnut (peanut) or sesame oil
1 tbsp light soy sauce
1 tsp dark soy sauce
½ tsp oyster sauce

FOR THE VEGETABLES (OPTIONAL)

20g (¾oz) sugarsnap peas
30g (1oz) beansprouts
20g (¾oz) baby bok choi, leaves separated
1 carrot, peeled and julienned
½ bell pepper of choice, deseeded and julienned

FLOUR & WATER

"[Flour] has become a staple for almost every culture in some shape or form."

If, in some crazy event the Caribbean became devoid of wheat flour, I fear its countries may stop functioning for a time. Though not heavily consumed by any of the migrants to the Caribbean in their original homelands, it has become a staple for almost every culture in some shape or form. How did this happen? For the rest of this introduction I will refer to wheat flour as flour, though for thousands of years civilizations around the world, including West Africa and India, utilized all manner of local foodstuffs to make flour. In West Africa, the likes of corn, cassava, semolina and plantain were fermented or dried and milled to make foods like *fufu, kenkey* and pounded yam, which were a key part of the diet.

Again, as we've seen in other chapters, these foods were not readily available to the people who were transported across the oceans, and so their descendants sought to fashion new foods in the image of the old if they couldn't recreate them fully. According to Maureen Warner-Lewis in *Guinea's Other Suns*, in Trinidad, the West African Hausa were said to "*use young cotton leaves that they dried to a flour, boiled and swizzled to become slimy like ochro [okra]*." They did not eat much rice and preferred flour-based foods, possibly including Akara (see p176), similar to what they would have eaten back home. Those who came from India were, back in India, used to wheat flours like *maida* (white flour) as well as flours made from all manner of pulses, grains and produce from rice to chickpeas (gram flour), and coconut to amaranth.

Over the years, planters began to complain about the high cost of cultivating provisions to feed the labourers, and many sugar estates neglected the cultivation of provision crops. In fact, sometimes when they failed, the enslaved were allowed to starve to death. Planters, traders and ship crew had to continually devise ways, or were forced by government ordinances, to supplement the provision-ground foods the enslaved grew to sustain themselves (see p22) and to more cost effectively feed those they held. These supplements included varying amounts of wheat flour imported from Europe or the Americas, rationed according to the wealth of the planter and divided by the age and sometimes gender of the enslaved. Flour rations varied from 5kg (10lb) per week in Tobago to 20kg (40lb) in Guyana. This may sound like a good deal, but bear in mind the fractious nature of relying on ground produce all year round, especially in a tropical climate and without modern technology to refrigerate it. This, coupled with the fact that planters didn't always fulfil their legal obligations, meant that hunger and starvation were a reality for the field workers.

As a result, flour-based eats came to bolster West African stews and soups. Now instead of swallows (soft balls of fermented or boiled produce flours), like pounded yam and *amala*, there were fried and boiled dumplings (see p170 and p195), which accompanied Cornmeal Porridge (see p70) and Corn Soup (see p46) alike. After the abolition of slavery, West African descendants were left to fend for themselves, however, similar problems arose around the sustenance of indentured Indian labourers who were doing the same back-breaking, strenuous, exploitative work in the beating hot sun. Crossing the *kala pani* (see p118) on the ships departing from India, medical practitioners saw that the high mortality rate was not only caused by woefully unsanitary conditions but also the enforced change in diet. A Dr. Mouat, a professor of medicine appointed by the colonial government of Bengal, acknowledged that maintaining the emigrant's culinary habits and tastes would help them feel at home away from home. Amongst primarily rice and a small list of other ingredients, he recommended that flour be added to rations since he believed "chapatis" (roti) to be central to the diet of the people from Bihar, North India.

"Replicas of European baked goods like pasties and tarts emerged in the 20th century with an added Caribbean flavour twist."

As flour became more available, it worked its way into the heritage foods of those from India, as those of West African descent. Traditional Bengal *mithai* (sweets) like Kurma (see p180) and Jalebi (see p183) utilized imported flour and soon-to-be favourites like roti (see pp204–219) and Doubles (see p166) completely relied on it. Other snacks that once were made with split pea flour like Saheena (see p174) and Pholouri (see p172) were also made with regular flour.

Throughout this period, the European influence in the region displayed itself through baking. Replicas of European baked goods like pasties and tarts emerged in the 20th century with an added Caribbean flavour twist, ranging from cheese fused with chilli peppers (see Cheese Rolls on p186), coconut (Salara, see p185), dried fruit (Currants Roll, see p184) and fresh fruit (Pine Tarts, see p189). My love for all these isn't helped by the mobile bakeries that wheel around neighbourhoods and countryside lanes, blaring jingles and shouting their available wares out of the window, so just when you didn't think you needed a slice of salara or currants roll, now you do.

"Over the years, flour has woven itself into the fabric and identity of Caribbean food."

After labour exploitation was abolished, English soft bread (Plait Bread, see p194) became popular, although as the Caribbean remained in an impoverished and rural state, facilities such as large ovens to cook bread were still restricted to the elite class. It should also be noted that sanitary water was far from readily available too, which limited what could be baked. People looked to substitutes like fresh coconut milk to make alternative breads like Coconut Bake (see p164), which could be made in makeshift fireplaces or traditional *chulhas* (mud/clay fireplaces).

Nowadays, baking makes up just a small part of home cooking, with people opting for convenience and grabbing a bite from their local bakery or favourite street stall. Finding your baking oasis can take some years. This alone counts for the patriotism that people have for certain shops versus others, be it in San Fernando or South London, and bad customer service or convenience may be ignored when the food is so good.

Though we may praise the enslaved for being able to make do with what they had, that can sometimes strip their agency as fantastic cooks and purveyors of taste. It's not an accident that many of their recipes have stuck around for so long. Nowhere is this more apparent than in the combinations of flour and water. Over the years, flour has woven itself permanently into the fabric and identity of Caribbean food, providing the versatility which helped people from all backgrounds access some semblance of home.

NOTE *I am far from a good baker, so I always keep in mind the Caribbean adage "water more than flour" meaning "things are bad and the situation is a mess". So, if using water, always go slow and add in parts. The dough is half the battle after that, but the style of baking found in this chapter is very forgiving.*

Fry bake

OK, I don't want to confuse you but there are two bread snacks known throughout the Caribbean, especially Guyana and Trinidad, as bake. The irony is that this one, perhaps the more common bake, isn't actually baked, it's fried. The only way to really know which one is being spoken about is context. For example, Bake & Shark (see p108) would be referring to fry bake and rarely baked "bake". Similarly, references to having a slice or piece of bake would probably be referring to the likes of Coconut Bake (see p164). More confusingly, fry bake has a host of other names from float to johnny cakes, or even fry dumpling (though you can tell the latter apart as they are much smaller and more compact).

Their description in the *Dictionary of the English/Creole of Trinidad & Tobago* as a "fried yeast biscuit" from a "much thicker all-flour mixture that was leavened but not seasoned and fried" tells you what fried bakes are but does absolutely no justice to their wonders. When made well, the lightly crisp shell lets out a burst of steam when cut open, which reveals a bed of soft interior dough. Hints of salt and sugar come through but just barely, so as not to interfere with your filling, which can and tends to be anything. In both Guyana and Trinidad, beyond Bake & Shark I see menu boards peddling Bake & Shrimp, Bake & Chicken, Bake & Pork, Bake & Egg. A vibrant jazzy calypso song from 1935 called "The Tiger" mentions a man seeking "akra and float" and stuffing fish fritters with Akara (see p176) seems like it was very popular at one time. Other fillings included black pudding and most shops today sell it with my favourite pairing of Saltfish Buljol (see p112).

Fry bakes represent the essence of this chapter and the wider transformative nature of Caribbean cooking to me. Here, simple ingredients such as flour, water, salt and sugar are turned into something so heavenly you wonder how it can possibly be so good. These were the height of my late mum's breakfast and the thing I miss the most. The ability to have every single bake puff up like a balloon in the frying stage is something I haven't 100 per cent mastered yet, and for first-timers it can take some trial and error before you get a perfect batch, though really there's no failure here, as even flat bakes rolled with a tasty filling are just as sumptuous.

Sift the flour, baking powder, 2 teaspoons of sugar and salt into a bowl. In a separate cup or bowl, add the water, 1 teaspoon of sugar and yeast and let it sit for 5 minutes. Then slowly add the yeast water into the flour mixture and combine. Knead for 10 minutes while squeezing the dough and gently punching it in. Form it into a flat round ball, cover with 1 teaspoon of oil and cover it with cling film (plastic wrap). Ideally, leave to rest for at least 1 hour, or overnight if possible.

Divide the dough into 8 balls of roughly equal weight (about 65g/2¼oz each) and cover with a slightly damp dish towel while you work.

In a deep frying pan or Dutch pot, heat the oil over a medium–high heat. When hot, take a dough ball and shape it into a flat circle with your hands. Place on a dusted surface and roll out with a rolling pin into a circle 13–14cm (5–5½in) in diameter. Take the dough disc and gently place it into the oil. It should bubble immediately and after a few seconds it should start to puff up.

Depending on the heat of the oil and the thickness of your pan, fry the bake on each side for 30 seconds–1 minute. Check the underside and, when slightly golden, flip it over. It's normal that a few bakes in the batch won't expand while frying. When done, place into a large bowl or container lined with kitchen paper and cover with a lid or dish towel to keep warm. Repeat with the remaining dough balls.

Serve as part of Bake & "Shark" (see p108) or with Saltfish Buljol (see p112).

NOTE *You don't want to roll out the dough balls too thin or they won't puff up when frying and this will be difficult to cut into and slice open.*

MAKES 8

300g (2¼ cups) plain (all-purpose) flour, plus extra for dusting
2 tsp baking powder
3 tsp granulated sugar of choice
1 tsp sea salt
200ml (scant 1 cup) warm water
1 tsp dried active yeast
300ml (1¼ cups) cooking oil of choice, plus 1 tsp for oiling the dough

Coconut bake

When I reach Tobago, I'm told of a weekly fireside bread sale that can sell out quicker than the bread is put out. Either you put your name down and reserve or unfortunately you are found wanting. One of these breads is coconut bake, which I don't get to try at this particular sale, but the report illustrates to me how fond of it people across the sister islands are. In true Caribbean ingenuity, the excess coconuts have to be used somehow. Combining both coconut milk and the shredded dry meat makes a bread like no other. A bread made with two types of coconut is irresistible and when a loaf of bake arrives at the guesthouse it doesn't last an afternoon. The giving of a bake is a sign of affection I see multiple times. Be it someone's birthday, recovery from an illness or just reconnecting with an old acquaintance, almost any event calls for the making of a coconut bake wrapped in a dish towel to keep the loaf warm and moist. I will happily admit that some baked goods are better just bought from your local Caribbean bakery, however, this coconut bake is not one of them. Homely coconut bake is irreplaceable, and you need to devour it the moment it's fresh out of the oven and the second it's cool enough to slice and bite into.

Like fried bakes, coconut bakes can go with a wide array of accompaniments from eggs to saltfish or callaloo but for me just a timid spread of Golden Ray butter will do. Coconut bakes can be quite dense, so roll out the dough a bit thinner than you think is necessary and keep in mind that it will expand less than regular bread, though it will help if you use yeast.

Sift all the dry ingredients into a bowl. If the desiccated coconut doesn't sift, then when all the other ingredients have gone through the sieve simply add it in after. Mix the dry mixture with your hands and then add the butter. Use your hands to mix the butter into the dry ingredients until you have a sand-like mixture.

Slowly add your coconut milk into the bowl. Do not add it all in one go. Combine the mixture with your hands, kneading the dough. When the mix becomes a dough ball that doesn't stick to your hands or the bowl, it is ready.

Cover the ball with cling film (plastic wrap) or cover the bowl with a damp dish towel and leave to rest for at least 10 minutes.

Preheat the oven to 180°C (160°C fan/350°F/Gas 4).

Dust a surface with flour and roll out the dough into roughly 4cm (1½in) thick circle (the diameter is unimportant). Use a fork to pierce the surface of the dough all over. Next, place the dough onto a piece of greaseproof paper or foil and place in the oven. Bake for 20–25 minutes until golden brown. You can use a sharp knife to pierce the bake to see if it's done. If there is no residue on the knife, it is cooked on the inside.

Remove from the oven and leave it to cool for 10 minutes. It will keep for a few days, though it's better eaten immediately. Serve with a spread of butter. It also works as a side to Callaloo (see p38).

MAKES 1 MEDIUM LOAF

600g (4⅔ cups) plain (all-purpose) flour, plus extra for dusting

70g (2½oz) desiccated coconut

2 tbsp light soft brown sugar

1 tbsp instant yeast (optional)

4 tsp baking powder

½ tsp sea salt

2 tbsp unsalted butter (or vegan butter)

400ml (13.5fl oz) can coconut milk

Doubles

Trinidad and Guyana (and Suriname to a lesser extent) share a great deal of street food commonalities, but one huge difference is doubles. Doubles, in name, are overwhelmingly a Trini thing. Even though in other Caribbean countries you may see *"Bara and channa"* for sale it comes with much less fanfare, less extravagance and is harder to find. I've seen doubles described as a "sandwich", but that word seems almost offensive when speaking of doubles. Two *bara* (fried dough balls) are lathered with curried chickpeas (see p82), then scattered with an array of toppings which can take the snack in any taste direction (shown on pp168–169).

Doubles men (and women) line streets, corners, highways and hole-in-the-wall spots dishing out doubles with all your trimmings at a rapid pace, calculating the price, sorting change and having you on your way within a minute. I can't do justice to how amazing doubles are in words. The choices are laid out for you here, so adjust to your sweet or savoury preference, add as much spice as you can tolerate, and enjoy.

Sift the flour, turmeric, salt and cumin into a bowl. In a separate cup or bowl, add the water, sugar and yeast and let it sit for 5 minutes. Then slowly add the yeast water into the flour mix and combine. Knead for 5 minutes while squeezing the dough and gently punching it in. Form it into a flat round ball, coat with 1 tablespoon of oil and cover loosely with cling film (plastic wrap). Leave to rest for at least 1 hour, or overnight if possible.

Divide the dough into 16 equal pieces and cover with a damp dish towel while you work. Add the remaining 4 tablespoons of oil to a separate bowl and set aside.

In a frying pan or Dutch pot, heat the 300ml (1¼ cups) oil over a medium–high heat and line a bowl with kitchen paper. Now, dip the fingers of one hand into the bowl of oil and pick up a dough ball. Wipe the underside of the ball with oil and place it oil-side down on a flat surface. Using your fingertips, flatten out the dough into a circle about 9–10cm (3½–4in) in diameter. Don't worry if there's any holes from spreading it out too thin.

When the oil in the pan is hot, take the dough disc and place it in the oil. Let it sit for 3–5 seconds and you should see it puff immediately, flip it over with a pair of tongs and let it sit for 3–5 seconds. Turn again and sit for 3–5 seconds, then if you like you can flip once more for

MAKES 8

FOR THE BARA

300g (2¼ cups) plain (all-
   purpose) flour
½–1 tsp ground turmeric
1 tsp sea salt
½ tsp ground cumin
200ml (scant 1 cup) warm water
1 tsp light soft brown sugar
1 tsp dried active yeast
5 tbsp cooking oil of choice
300ml (1¼ cups) cooking oil of
   choice, for frying

FOR THE TOPPINGS

Curry Channa (see p82, cooked
   without the potatoes)
70g (2½oz) cucumber, shredded
   or grated, mixed with ½ tsp sea
   salt
Kuchela (see p229)
Tambran Sauce (see p230)
Lime and Pepper Sauce (see p235)
Shado Beni Sauce (see p108)
Mango Sour (see p232)

another 3 seconds until you achieve a golden, yellow colour, then place into the lined bowl and cover with a dish towel/ lid to keep warm.

Repeat with the remaining dough balls.

To serve, place one *bara* slightly overlapping another (like a Venn diagram) and top with 1 tablespoon of channa, 1 teaspoon of cucumber, 1 teaspoon of kuchela, 1 teaspoon of shado beni sauce, 1 teaspoon of mango sour or tambran sauce and a dash of hot sauce.

Aloo pie

Although I wax lyrical about Macaroni Pie on p192, in reality there is only one pie which so dominates the use of the noun that for a 100-odd mile stretch if you ask someone to pick you up "a pie" there will be only one outcome: Aloo Pie. Unlike any pie you've probably eaten, this soft and warm fried pastry houses a spiced potato mash so different that you will start to question if you've really eaten potatoes before.

At the takeout spots and the small vendors that line the roadsides at busy junctions, aloo pie and doubles are a duo as fierce as Manchester United's prime turn of the 21st century, Andy Cole and Dwight Yorke, coming at you like a one-two punch. If a roadside vendor doesn't sell both it's usually a nod to the fact that someone in very close proximity does, and does it better, though high-street shops will likely sell both. As with Doubles (see p166), you're often given the option to have the pie sliced open and filled with a hot pepper sauce (see p235), Tambran Sauce (see p230) and even Channa (see p82) but I find the potato filling alone is usually perfect.

Perhaps for convenience some vendors prefer to make the dough separately, then slice it open and add the potato, but this recipe favours the style of those who have a carousel of freshly enclosed pies hot out of the pot and stowed away in a heat-capturing box until, as always, they are sold out for the day.

MAKES 8

300g (2¼ cups) plain (all-purpose) flour, plus extra for dusting
2 tsp baking powder
½ tsp sea salt
½ tsp light soft brown sugar
2 tbsp butter or coconut oil
150ml (⅔ cup) warm water
600g (1lb 5oz) Russet potatoes, peeled and chopped
200ml (scant 1 cup) cooking oil of choice, for frying

FOR THE SEASONING

2 tbsp Green Seasoning (see pp26–27)
2 tbsp coconut oil or butter
1 tsp ground cumin
1 tsp sea salt
½ tsp freshly ground black pepper
3 garlic cloves, finely chopped, or 1 tbsp garlic powder (optional)
½ tsp all-purpose seasoning (optional)

Sift the flour, baking powder, salt and sugar into a bowl and mix lightly. Next, add the butter and use your hands to mix it together. Slowly add the water and knead for 5 minutes until it forms a dough ball that is slightly sticky to the touch but doesn't completely stick to the bowl.

Place a damp dish towel over the dough and leave it to rest for at least 30 minutes. Divide the dough into 8 equal dough balls (*loyas*) using the same method you would for roti (see p204). Cover again and leave the dough balls to rest for another 15 minutes.

Meanwhile, place the potatoes in a saucepan and cover with water. Boil for a minimum of 20 minutes until the potatoes are completely soft. You can test this by piercing them with a fork – they should break apart. Drain and let the potatoes cool for a couple of minutes. When cool, add all the seasoning ingredients and mix with a fork or potato masher until completely smooth.

Add some water to a small bowl and set aside. Heat the oil over a high heat, then reduce the heat to medium.

Dust a flat surface with flour, then take one dough ball and flatten it into a circle with your fingers, then roll it to a circle about 15cm (6in) in diameter. This does not need to be a perfect circle. Take 2 tablespoons of the potato mixture and place in the centre of the dough. Dip a finger into the bowl of water and run it around the edge of the dough circle. Next, fold the circle in half and gently press the edges together with your thumb and index finger to enclose the potato filling. Gently pat the pie to evenly spread out the potato mix on the inside. Flip it over and pat again, spreading out the potato.

Gently place the pie into the oil and spoon oil over the top. The temperature of your oil and how soft you like the pastry shell will determine how long you cook the pie. It should take 20–45 seconds each side before a final 15–20 seconds each side. When anywhere between light gold and golden orange in colour, remove and place on kitchen paper to cool. Repeat to make the remaining pies.

Serve with Tambran Sauce (see p230) and Lime & Pepper Sauce (see p235).

Pholouri

The classic Indian snack *pholouri* pronounced "phoolowrie" is a descendant of Bengali *fuluri*, and rears itself in an old Caribbean–Indian folklore tale called the "The bad seed". In this story, *pholouri* is used by a son to coax his bedridden father on a trip to a nearby forest. Here the son plans to "dispose of his father" as a means of pleasing his displeased spouse. *"Carry your father and put him in the forest,"* she says after he becomes too burdensome around the house. Some years later, the son, now a father himself, old and senile, is invited to the forest by his own son where flashbacks cause him to laugh, cry and reflect on his life ahead of his perceived fate, as he fears his son may do to him as he did to his own father. Fortunately, his son has no such ambitions and plans to love and care for him. While the moral of the story, as its name tells, is about nurturing, I can't help but overlook the role *pholouri* played in the initial coercion. It's no surprise as the soft split-pea-based dough balls often submerged and permeated with sweet, tangy Tambran Sauce (see p230) and hot pepper sauce (see p235) could tempt anyone. In Trinidad and Guyana, I would walk up the road a mile most days just to acquire a fresh bag. Here, large bowls of the dough are left to rise before being effortlessly scooped and squeezed between the base of the index finger and thumb, most commonly with a single hand, into a cauldron of oil. While this does produce the best, most uniform results, it's likely you may not have the decades of skill needed to caress *pholouri* batter into perfect little spheres and you probably won't have commercial amounts of oil at home either. Luckily, there are many wondrous workarounds, including oiled spoons, double spoons, ladles, ice-cream scoops and so on. For the latter, you can use a reserved amount of oil and fry each side at a time. All the aforementioned will produce errant, non-uniform *pholouri* and it is almost sacrilege to say, but it sort of doesn't matter when they all end up in the same place in a matter of minutes anyway.

Thoroughly rinse and drain the split peas and then soak them for at least 6 hours, or overnight if possible.

Drain, then add the peas to a blender along with 300ml (1¼ cups) water and pulse until completely smooth. Decant into a large mixing bowl. Next, sift in the dry ingredients and then add the optional ingredients if using and gently mix to combine. Do not overmix the batter.

MAKES 24

150g (¾ cup) dried split peas
200g (1½ cups) plain (all-purpose) flour
1 tsp baking powder
1 tsp ground turmeric
1 tsp sea salt
½ tsp ground cumin
½ tsp Green Seasoning (see pp26–27 – optional)
½ tsp dried active yeast (optional)
½ tsp garam masala (optional)
½ tsp hot sauce (optional)
400ml (1¾ cups) or 800ml (3½ cups) cooking oil of choice for frying, plus 60ml (¼ cup) oil for the spoons

Cover the bowl with a dish towel and leave to rise for at least 1 hour. After this time, the batter will have grown in volume, especially if you added the yeast.

In a heavy-based frying pan (skillet) or Dutch pot, add 400ml (1¾ cups) oil for shallow-frying or 800ml (3½ cups) for deep-frying, and heat over a medium–high heat. When hot, reduce the heat a notch to medium. Now, dip a spoon in the 60ml (¼ cup) oil, then scoop a medium heap of the batter and it should slide straight off the spoon into the cooking oil. Clean the spoon, dip it into the oil and repeat the process again. Ideally, cook the pholouri in batches of 6–7 so you don't overcrowd the pan.

If you're using 800ml (3½ cups) oil, deep-fry for 3 minutes. If you're using 400ml (1¾ cups) oil, fry one side for 3 minutes, then turn and cook the other side for 3 minutes until golden brown. After the first 3 minutes, the pholouri should float, which will indicate they are cooked on the inside. The colour will also depend on how much turmeric you use.

Remove with a slotted spoon or skimmer and place on kitchen paper to drain.

Serve with Mango Sour (see p232), Tambran Sauce (see p230) and hot sauce.

NOTE *You'll likely forget, but try to ensure that you coat the spoon with oil every time before scooping up the pholouri mixture. It will make it much easier to drop it into the oil.*

Saheena

The art of making a perfect traditional *saheena* is akin to constructing something like Japanese sushi. Seasoned split pea paste is smothered onto layers of dasheen bush leaves (see page38) and then expertly rolled, folded and tucked to stay neatly compact before being wrapped, steamed, sliced and then fried. Fortunately, for those with less finger dexterity, other forms of *saheena* were conceived, like this version, which aren't too dissimilar to fritters. Shredded (but not blitzed) green leaves are folded into a batter and then scooped into balls and fried.

Something about these snacks, perhaps their compactness, ease of creation or more evidently their brilliant taste, lingers on the tongue and in the memory. Just as *akara* fritters relocated everywhere with West African descendants, this dish was enjoyed across all corners of the Indian subcontinent before reaching the Caribbean. *Taikile Ambado* in the south, *maralva phodi* to the west – all translations of taro leaf fritter formed with the colocasia leaf. In the likes of Fiji, another recipient of indentured Indian labourers, you find *saina*, which is identical to the *saheena* primarily found in Trinidad and Tobago but also in Guyana and other Caribbean countries to a lesser degree. Where you find one style of *saheena*, you often find both – the rolled and sliced kind and the "chip-up" spherical fritter style. As fresh dasheen (callaloo) leaves can be very hard to find and as spinach, kale or even frozen dasheen leaves are more common, this recipe represents the (in my opinion) easier to fashion "chip-up" style.

MAKES ABOUT 20 OR 40,
depending on whether you scoop
with a teaspoon or tablespoon

400g (3 cups) plain (all-purpose)
   flour or 250g (2 cups) plain
   (all-purpose) flour and 150g
   (1 cup) split pea powder
½ tsp ground turmeric
2 tsp sea salt
1 tsp freshly ground black pepper
1 tsp ground cumin
1 tsp baking powder
3 garlic cloves, minced
200g (7oz) fresh spinach or 100g
   (3½oz) spinach and 100g
   (3½oz) kale, cut into thin strips
½ Scotch bonnet pepper, finely
   chopped, or ¼ tsp chilli powder
   of choice (optional)
300ml (1¼ cups) warm water
2 tsp dried active yeast
300ml (1¼ cups) cooking oil of
   choice, for frying

Sift the flour, turmeric, salt, black pepper, ground cumin and
baking powder into a large mixing bowl. Next, stir in the
garlic, spinach and Scotch bonnet pepper, if using, and then
add the water. Add the yeast and stir thoroughly to make a
batter. Cover the bowl and let it sit for at least 30 minutes.

In a large frying pan, Dutch pot or wok, heat the oil
over a medium heat. When hot, turn the heat down a
notch. Using either a teaspoon or tablespoon, scoop out a
heaped spoon of batter and drop it into the oil. Let it sit
for 2½ minutes until the underside has solidified. Now flip
and cook the other side for 2½ minutes. When done, use a
fork or slotted spoon and scoop out onto a plate lined with
kitchen paper to drain the oil. Cook in batches that your
pan will allow and don't overcrowd it. Repeat with the
remaining batter.

NOTE *If you chop the spinach too finely you will end up with
completely green fritters. You can dip your spoon in oil or
water after adding each spoonful to make dropping the batter
into the oil easier. If you can't find split pea powder, you can
make your own by simply blending split peas in a blender or
food processor. Just ensure the peas are completely dry.*

Akara

There can be no dish that looks less representative of how remarkably addictive and good it tastes than fritters. Fritters are quite simply a seasoned flour and water batter usually intertwined with a main ingredient, and wherever enslaved West Africans were displaced in the New World, we can find fritters. One of the fritters that has survived the test of time and seen many variations is *akara*, which some people may know as black-eyed peas fritters. Those familiar with Brazilian food may immediately draw a parallel to *akaraje*, as Brazil still has an extraordinarily high populace of West African descent.

In the likes of Trinidad, those of Hausa descent residing in Tunapuna surrounds during the late 19th– early 20th century were said to eat *akara* as the first course of a *sakara* (a feast taking place as part of a ceremony to pay respect to their ancestors in order to ensure future prosperity) and this was noted as being *"flour and water made into balls and fried"*. Generations before this, studies of the Yoruba descendants noted that they too consumed something called *àkàrà*, translated roughly as *bread* or *pastry* and *"composed of flour and ground beans, which is seasoned and made into a paste, and fried"*. In the Caribbean, this morphed into a food where a base of wheat flour was seasoned and to it was added pieces of cooked or salted fish. This was called *akara* (or *acra* or *accra*) and this centuries old description reads exactly like the "saltfish fritters" I eagerly anticipated my mum cooking on weekend mornings as a child.

A survey of barrack life in Trinidad included in the *Dictionary of the English/Creole of Trinidad & Tobago* notes: *"enterprising barrack-yard dwellers set-up their short-term 'frying stands' to catch the custom of workers going early to their respective duties"* of which one of the main wares was *akara*. Today, regardless of the *akara* form, this remains the case, be it in Trinidad, Jamaica, Brazil or back in West Africa, keeping that link and legacy alive.

MAKES 16

400g (14oz) saltfish
1 small onion, finely chopped
3 spring onions (scallions/green
    onions), finely chopped
½ red bell pepper, deseeded and
    finely chopped
170g (1⅓ cups) plain (all-purpose)
    flour
1 tsp freshly ground black pepper
1 tsp brown sugar of choice
2 tsp baking powder
½ tsp all-purpose seasoning
1 tsp Green Seasoning (see
    pp26–27)
250ml (1 cup plus 1 tbsp) cooking
    oil of choice, for frying

Place the saltfish in a saucepan and cover with water.
Boil over a high heat for 20 minutes. Drain and cover
with fresh water, then boil again for 15 minutes. Drain
the water again and leave the saltfish to the side for
5 minutes. When it's cool, use your hands to peel off any
dark skin and remove any bones. Then either with your
hands or a fork, mash the saltfish into flakes and set aside.

If you have a food processor or blender, pulse the
onion, spring onion and bell pepper to a fine mixture.
Decant into a bowl and fold in the saltfish. (Alternatively,
just mix the finely chopped vegetables with the saltfish.)

In a separate bowl, add the flour, black pepper, sugar
and baking powder, then mix to combine. Next, fold in the
saltfish and onion mixture. Add 200ml (scant 1 cup) water
and mix until the mixture resembles a batter. Add the
all-purpose seasoning and green seasoning and mix again.

In a small, deep frying pan, heat the oil over a medium
heat. When hot, use a tablespoon coated in oil and portion
a heaped tablespoon of the batter into the oil and slightly
flatten with the back of the spoon. Repeat twice more
until you have three akara in a pan. After about 30 seconds,
give the accara a nudge to ensure they have not stuck to
the pan. Fry for 3 minutes, then flip over. The fried side
should be golden orange. Fry on this side for 3 minutes
until it is a matching golden orange.

When done, use a slotted spoon to place the akara on
kitchen paper to drain the oil. Repeat with the remaining
batter, dipping your spoon in oil or water after adding
each spoonful to make dropping the batter into the oil
easier. Leave to cool for 5 minutes.

Serve with Tambran Sauce (see p230).

NOTE *You can use a large pan, however, you'll need to
add and use substantially more oil as the original
recommended amount may be too shallow in a large pan.*

Reaping revolution

When we are told the story of the decline of slavery in Britain it usually centres on a group of liberal, free-thinking British politicians who bravely challenged their peers and ushered in revolutionary change. What gets lost is where the seeds of upheaval were planted. In many cases this was the same place that the enslaved toiled each day – the plantation.

In Trinidad, the plantations were scattered primarily down the eastern half of the island. In Guyana, the land of the interior was unproductive, consisting of swamp and clay. As such, plantation production was focused on the coastal strip where 90 per cent of the country's population resides today. Like in the Caribbean, this production was focused on sugar. From the inception of the transatlantic slave trade, even before the middle passage ships were boarded, the enslaved were subject to abuse. This manifested over centuries, with constant dissension that led to increasingly brutal retaliations, both physical and mental. By the late 1700s this came to a head, and rebellions became more and more frequent. Regarding these freedom fighters, Jamaicans know the names of Nanny Maroon and Samuel Sharpe, Trinidadians may know of Sandy and Guyanese know of Coffey.

In 1673, Coffey, an Akan man (modern day Ghana) led a near 4,000-strong revolt against Dutch colonial forces. The revolt took place in the eastern Guyanese region of Berbice at the Lilienberg plantation and was a retaliation for the killing of a former crew of dissenters. Some years later in 1770, Sandy, a chief of the Koromantee (also in modern-day Ghana), a known clan with battle prowess, was flogged in Tobago. As retaliation he snuck into the house and room of the plantation co-owner and stabbed him to death. Revolt ensued. In both cases, halls were burned and plantations attacked with looted arms. Both men managed to escape but faced differing ends. Word spread to other plantations and other countries, including as far as Haiti. While these upheavals led to even harsher deterrents

from plantation owners, it was too late – the genie was out of the bottle.

Ultimately, it was arguably greed that caused the planters' downfall. Greed for the profits sugar and spices brought. The difference between the 1500s and the 1700s was that as the planters imported more workers, they became overwhelmingly outnumbered by those they enslaved, sometimes by 12 to 1 or more. Some plantation owners also governed in-absentia and barely even came to the Caribbean.

With the 1834 abolition of slavery, came the mass exodus of newly freed from the estates to the general population, leaving the plantations in desperate need of exploitative labour. John Gladstone (father of UK prime minister William Gladstone) wrote to the firm Gillanders, Arbuthnot and Company inquiring about the possibility of acquiring Indian immigrants for his estates, as other British planters had been doing in the East African colony of Mauritius. Thus, the indentured labour we know of today was initiated in Guyana in 1838, Trinidad in 1845, and a number of other Caribbean countries to a smaller degree. Gillanders suggested there would be no difficulty with these replacements, writing that they have "*few wants beyond eating, sleeping and drinking*", referring to the "*hill coolies of India*" as "*more akin to the monkey than the man.*"

The conditions the indentured Indians faced mirrored those which had just been abolished because the intention was always exploitative labour and prior consent didn't change the reality of the system. Like the West Africans before them, it was not surprising that they began to defy the systems under which they operated almost as soon as they arrived. They displayed far from the benign ambivalence they had been tagged with. Grievances included wage disputes, violent managers and the sexual abuse of immigrant women by the overseers. Sites like Cedar Hill Plantation and Jordan Hill Plantation in

Trinidad, and Plantation Leonora and Non Pariel in Guyana, all witnessed such rebellion. After some decades, the Indian government abolished support for Indentureship in 1917, effectively cutting off the labour supply. By then hundreds of thousands of Indians had journeyed to the Caribbean. The plantation, however, remained the same as it ever was, a European-created institution designed to form the basis of brutal colonial exploitation.

In the song "The Slave", famous Trini calypso singer Mighty Sparrow pays tribute to this legacy: "*We had to chant and design to express our feelings/ To dat wicked and cruel man/ That was the only medicine to make him listen*". Though when singing didn't work, revolt did.

Today we consume sugar, spices and rum directly from these plantations, often ignorant of their vivid history. We drive by fields unaware of what occurred there. Black and white photos might make us think this is ancient history, but these stories are just a conversation or two away – our grandparents talking to their grandparents. They are more present than we think, as many enslavers were still compensated for the loss of the enslaved up until the mid-2010s. Food for thought.

Mithai

The history of the elaborate, vibrant sweet treats of India could, and probably has, warranted its own encyclopedia. Depending on family ties or geography, *mithai* (or *mittai*) is a catch-all term for these sweets. On special occasions like *Diwali* and *Phagwah* (see p240), as well as after the closing of *puja* ceremonies, plates and boxes are decked with the likes of *gulab jamoon*, *ladoo*, milk *barfi*, fudge, *prasad* and *roat* – the mastery of which can take a lifetime. Given this, most people do tend to head to the local "sweet shop".

The first of these sweets most commonly sold at stores, famed candy kiosks in Tobago and takeout spots outside of celebratory events, and snacked on by many, is *kurma* (sometimes also confusingly known as *mithai*). These sweet breadsticks are fused with cinnamon and then coated in spiced sugar to produce an obsessive crunch. The second are the fluorescent syrup-dunked swirls of *jalebi* often seen in stacks clinging to each other. Made traditionally with curd, the mix partially ferments, which produces a soft crunch that manages to simultaneously ooze and sponge.

These recipes have both paired down the usual amount of sugar as knowing how to make your own mithai can be a slippery slope, especially if there's no one at home to share them with!

Kurma

Sift the flour, cinnamon, nutmeg, salt and allspice, if using, into a large bowl. Add the butter and work it into the dough with your hands until the mixture resembles sand. Next, add the vanilla extract and condensed milk or sugar, if using, then slowly pour in the water and begin kneading into a dough ball. You want a dry, stiff dough so don't add extra water, rather keep using your strength to work the ingredients together until they form a dough ball. Cover the dough ball with a damp dish towel or wrap in cling film (plastic wrap) and leave to rest for at least 30 minutes.

Cut the dough ball in half. Take one half and roll it out to about 1cm (½in) thick. Use a knife to score the flattened dough into 1.5cm (⅝in) wide strips and then divide those strips into lengths of 7–10cm (2¾–4in).

Heat the oil in a large wok, Dutch pot or frying pan over a medium heat. Fry in batches of 12–15 pieces for

MAKES ABOUT 50 STICKS

400g (3 cups) plain (all-purpose) flour
1 tsp ground cinnamon
½ tsp ground nutmeg
¼ tsp sea salt
¼ tsp allspice (optional)
100g (6½ tbsp) unsalted butter, coconut oil or margarine
½ tsp vanilla extract
2 tbsp condensed milk or sugar (optional)
180ml (¾ cup) water or coconut milk
600ml (2½ cups) cooking oil of choice

FOR THE SYRUP

250g (1¼ cups) granulated white sugar
2.5cm (1in) piece of fresh root ginger, peeled and whole
1 star anise

10 minutes or until golden brown and hard. Use a slotted spoon to remove and place on kitchen paper to drain the oil. Repeat the process with the second half of the dough. When all are cooked, place into a large bowl and set aside.

To make the syrup, add 200ml (scant 1 cup) water and all the syrup ingredients to a medium saucepan and cook over a medium-high heat for 15 minutes, stirring continuously. The liquid should start vividly bubbling and you'll see thick liquid start to gather on the inner sides of the pan. Also note the liquid will turn a slightly yellow hue. Remove the ginger and star anise from the pan, then take the pan

off the heat and immediately pour half over the *kurma* in the bowl. Use a large utensil (not your hands!) to stir to ensure the syrup is coating as many of the *kurma* as possible. When done, repeat with the remaining syrup.

Store in an airtight container and preferably eat immediately or within 2 days.

NOTE *As soon as you take the syrup off the heat you'll have to move with some pace as it can set and become hard quickly.*

Jalebi

MAKES ABOUT 40

80ml (5 tbsp) warm water

1 tsp granulated white sugar

1 tsp dried active yeast

80g (½ cup plus 1 tbsp) plain (all-purpose) flour

1 tbsp cornflour (corn starch)

¼ tsp bicarbonate of soda (baking soda)

pinch of–1 tsp ground turmeric or yellow, orange or red food colouring

3 tbsp full-fat yogurt

1 tsp cooking oil of choice or melted ghee

200ml (scant 1 cup) cooking oil of choice, for frying

FOR THE SYRUP

150g (¾ cup) granulated white sugar

3 cardamom pods or ¼ tsp green ground cardamom

1 tsp lemon or lime juice

In a large cup, add the water, sugar and yeast and stir. Leave the mixture for 15–20 minutes until the yeast starts to gather and bubble to the surface.

Sift the flour, cornflour and bicarbonate of soda into a large bowl and mix to combine. Add the turmeric or colouring, yogurt and teaspoon of oil, then slowly add the yeast water while whisking for 2 minutes to make a runny batter. Decant the batter into a cake icing syringe or a repurposed squeezy sauce bottle.

To make the syrup, add 200ml (scant 1 cup) water, sugar and cardamom to a small saucepan. Bring to the boil over a medium–high heat until the pan starts to bubble and then turn the heat down to medium. Let it boil and bubble for 10 minutes and then turn the heat down to low and simmer for 5–7 minutes. Stir in the lemon juice and leave to cool on the lowest heat setting.

Next, add the oil for frying to a small flat-bottomed frying pan and heat over a medium–high heat. When hot, turn the heat down to medium and squeeze a spiral circle (I put a dot in the imaginary middle and then count 3 spaced circles outward) or pretzel of batter into the oil and fry for 2 minutes. You can tell it is ready to flip by gently prodding and feeling hard resistance. Flip and fry for another 2 minutes until the colour deepens and then use a slotted spoon or fork to place it on kitchen paper to drain. Continue in batches that fit the pan but ensure there is space between them (usually 3 per batch).

While you are doing this, take three pieces that have cooled on the kitchen paper and submerge them into the warm syrup for a few seconds or up to a minute, depending on your preference. Use a fork to remove them from the syrup and place on a tray lined with foil or baking paper. Let cool and dry, then eat.

Store in an airtight container and preferably eat immediately or within 2 days.

NOTE *The syrup doesn't need to be super thick, just sticky enough that it coats and sticks to the jalebi. The syrup must be kept warm otherwise it will immediately start to set. The amount of food colouring depends on your visual preference. You can use double or triple the amount of oil and a bigger frying pan to fry in bigger batches to reduce the cooking time.*

Currants roll

Sift the flour, sugar and salt into a bowl and add the butter. I find that grating is a good way to get cold butter pliable enough to mix without the need for a food processor. Mix together and slowly add enough water to bring the dough together. It's unlikely you will need the whole amount.

When the dough has come together in a relatively dry ball, wrap it in cling film (plastic wrap) or cover with a damp dish towel and place it in the fridge or freezer for 20 minutes.

Meanwhile, add all the ingredients for the currant mix to a bowl, combine with a fork, then set aside.

Preheat the oven to 180°C (160°C fan/350°F/Gas 4).

Flour a surface and roll out the dough ball into a 30cm (12in) square. It doesn't need to be perfectly shaped. Take the currant mix and spread it over the dough, leaving a border around the currants of about 3cm (1¼in). Next, take one side and roll it tightly down over the currants. When you reach the other side, fold it up and pinch the dough to combine it with the edge, then roll it over so the flap is on the base of the roll. If it helps, you can dip your finger in water or milk to help seal the flap. Tuck the edges inside to seal and close.

Place the roll on a tray lined with baking paper. Before putting in the oven you may find it helps to gently cut incisions into the top of the roll at a 45° angle, spaced about 4cm (1½in) apart. These will also be the guide for when to help slice the roll later, after it is baked. Be careful not to slice too deeply as the sugar and currants may erupt out during baking.

Bake for 20 minutes, then brush the top with milk and continue to bake for another 20 minutes. Remove from the oven and leave to cool for 10 minutes before eating. Use a serrated knife and slice to serve as you would a loaf of bread.

MAKES 1 ROLL

300g (2¼ cups) plain (all-purpose) flour, plus extra for dusting
2 tbsp light soft brown sugar
½ tsp sea salt
120g (1 stick plus 1 tbsp) unsalted butter, frozen
100ml (6½ tbsp) cold or ice-cold water
30ml (2 tbsp) milk of choice (optional)

FOR THE CURRANT MIX

200g (7oz) currants (or chopped raisins)
2 tbsp coconut oil or unsalted butter, melted
2–3 tbsp light soft brown sugar
¼ tsp sea salt
¼ tsp ground cinnamon
¼ tsp grated nutmeg
¼ tsp vanilla extract

Salara

MAKES 1 ROLL

300g (2¼ cups) plain (all-purpose) flour
2 tbsp light soft brown sugar
1 tsp dried active yeast
½ tsp sea salt (optional)
2 tbsp butter, melted
200ml (scant 1 cup) milk of choice, warmed, plus 10ml (2 tsp) for washing

FOR THE FILLING

100g (3½oz) desiccated coconut
60g (¼ cup) light soft brown sugar
2 tbsp coconut oil or unsalted butter
1cm (½in) piece of fresh root ginger, peeled and grated
1 tsp ground cinnamon
1 tsp vanilla extract
½ tsp grated nutmeg
½ tsp allspice (optional)
½ tsp sea salt
1½ tsp pink or red food colouring

Sift all the dry ingredients into a bowl and add the butter. Mix with your hands, then slowly pour in the warm milk. Knead until you have a smooth dough ball that doesn't stick. Cover the ball with cling film (plastic wrap) or a damp dish towel and leave to rest for 30 minutes.

Meanwhile, add all the filling ingredients to a bowl and stir to combine with a spoon. The mixture will turn deep red. Preheat the oven to 180°C (160°C fan/350°F/ Gas 4).

Take the dough and roll it out into a large rectangle about 40cm x 30cm (16in x 12in). Use a spoon to portion out the filling across the dough, leaving a 4cm (1½in) border around the edge. Then, from the long side, tightly tuck and roll the dough. When you reach the other side, fold it up and pinch the dough to combine it with the edge, then roll it over so the flap is on the base of the roll. If it helps, you can dip your finger in water or milk to help seal the flap. Tuck the edges inside the roll to seal close.

Place the roll on a baking tray lined with baking paper. Brush the top with milk and bake for 25–30 minutes. Remove from the oven and leave to cool for 10 minutes. Use a serrated knife to slice and serve as you would a loaf of bread.

If you like your roll a darker colour, you can brush it with milk a second time halfway through baking.

Cheese rolls and pine tarts

European influence is perhaps seen nowhere more prominently than in the baked treats of the Caribbean. Fully-fledged bakeries and small one-person mobile stalls sell all manner of baked snacks that look like they wouldn't be out of place in the British West Country. Selecting which ones to choose is tough, but I opt for a savoury and sweet duo to satisfy both cravings. Savoury cheese rolls are like sausage rolls but lined with a peppery-cheese spread. The sweet pine tarts are similar to the strawberry tarts we had as kids but filled with a spiced pineapple jam and enclosed in even more alluring pastry. But this doesn't do the taste and joy of Caribbean-inspired baking justice. The only way is for you to bake a batch of each to enjoy yourself.

Cheese rolls

Sift the flour and turmeric into a bowl and add the margarine. Combine with your hands until the mixture resembles fine sand. Slowly add the water and knead for a few minutes to combine into a ball. Wrap in cling film (plastic wrap) or cover with a damp dish towel and chill for 30 minutes.

Dust a flat surface with flour and roll out the dough into a rough large square. With the short edge facing you, fold one third into the centre and then another third over the top (like a letter going into an envelope). Fold once widthways and roll it out. Fold in half, then half again, then wrap the dough with cling film (plastic wrap) or cover with a damp dish towel and refrigerate for 30 minutes.

While the dough is resting, mix all the filling ingredients together in a bowl and set aside. Preheat the oven to 180°C (160°C fan/350°F/Gas 4) and line a large baking tray with baking paper.

Dust a flat surface with flour, cut the dough in half, then make 4 cuts across horizontally to get 10 squares. One by one, roll out into 15cm (6in) squares. Place a big pinch of the filling in the centre of a square and spread it out flat, leaving a border of a few centimetres. Dip your finger in water and run it around the edge of the square. Next, fold it like a letter going into an envelope. Use a fork to crimp both edges and make 3 holes in the top. Brush the top with egg white and place on the baking tray. Repeat with the remaining dough and filling. Bake for 15–20 minutes. Leave to cool before eating.

MAKES 10

450g (3½ cups) plain (all-purpose) flour, plus 100g (¾ cup) for dusting
¼ tsp ground turmeric
150g (9 tbsp) margarine, cold
200ml (scant 1 cup) cold water
1 egg white

FOR THE FILLING

280g (9½oz) mature Cheddar cheese, grated
1 tbsp margarine
1 tsp hot sauce
1 tsp sea salt
1 tsp freshly ground black pepper

Pine tarts

Sift the flour, sugar and turmeric into a bowl and add the margarine. Combine with your hands until the mixture resembles fine sand. Slowly add the water and knead for a few minutes and combine into a dough ball. Wrap the dough ball with cling film (plastic wrap) or cover with a damp dish towel and refrigerate for 30 minutes.

Next, dust a flat surface with flour and roll out the dough ball into a rough large rectangle. With the short edge facing you, fold one third into the centre and then another third over the top (like a letter going into an envelope). Then fold in half lengthways and roll it out. Fold in half, then in half again and wrap the dough with cling film (plastic wrap) or cover with a damp dish towel and refrigerate for 30 minutes.

While the dough is resting, place all the filling ingredients into a saucepan and heat over a medium-high heat. Stir to combine and when it starts to boil, turn down the heat to medium and cook for 30 minutes until thick and the colour turns a darker yellow.

Preheat the oven to 180°C (160°C fan/350°F/Gas 4) and line a large baking tray with baking paper.

Dust a flat surface with flour and place the dough on to it. Roll out the dough to a thickness of about 5mm (¼in). Using a bowl or plate 11–12cm (4¼–4½in) in diameter, cut out 13–15 circles. Spoon 1 scant tablespoon of the filling into the centre of a circle and then use the back of the spoon to spread it out, ensuring there is a border of a few centimetres. Dip your finger in water and then run it around the edge of a circle. Fold over three flaps to enclose the filling, making a triangle-shaped tart. Finally, brush the top with egg white and place the tart on the baking tray. Repeat with the remaining dough circles and filling.

Bake for 15–20 minutes. Remove from the oven and leave to cool before eating.

NOTE *If you have limited space, you can cut the dough in half and roll it out in batches. It is important to use margarine for the Cheese Rolls and Pine Tarts as it stays colder and is easier to work with than butter.*

MAKES 13–15

450g (3½ cups) plain (all-purpose) flour, plus 100g (¾ cup) for dusting
2 tsp granulated white sugar
¼ tsp ground turmeric
150g (9 tbsp) margarine, cold
200ml (scant 1 cup) cold water
1 egg white

FOR THE FILLING

432g (15oz) can pineapple in juice, pulsed or blended until smooth
2 tbsp dark brown sugar
¼ tsp ground nutmeg
¼ tsp ground cinnamon
1 tsp vanilla extract
½ tsp sea salt

Egg balls

It's interesting how some remnants of ancestral heritage rear themselves in a new land and some don't. In Jamaica, which has a high number of West African descendants, it's rare to see any egg-based street food. In Guyana, the egg balls peddled look like they were plucked straight off a Lagos highway in Nigeria with the "egg rolls" enjoyed there. These egg bites, reminiscent of Scotch eggs, were originally made with flour but as flour wasn't always plentiful in the Caribbean, African descendants turned to cassava and rather than turn it into flour, they essentially mirrored the technique used with pork but with the starchy cassava inner instead. This is protein in protein, and amidst the hustle and bustle of tropical cities it's no surprise that it's a daily go-to.

Top and tail the cassava, cut lengthways down the middle and remove the thin inner vein (it is inedible), then chop it into large chunks. Peel off the bark and repeat until all the pieces are done.

Place all the cassava in a saucepan and cover with water. Boil over a high heat for 20 minutes. When done, you should be able to mash the cassava with relative ease. Discard the water and place the cassava in a large bowl. Add the salt, pepper and any of the optional ingredients and mash to combine.

Place 5 of the eggs in a saucepan and cover with water. Boil over a high heat with a dash of salt for 10 minutes. Drain the hot water and fill with cold water. When cool, take out an egg and crack gently on a hard surface. Place the egg back in the water and slowly peel away the shell. Repeat for all the eggs.

In a small bowl, crack open the sixth egg and beat. In another small bowl, add the flour. Next, take a handful of the mashed cassava mix and roll into a ball, then flatten out with a slight curvature. Place an egg in there, then take another handful of the mix, flatten it and while slightly cupping your hand enclose the egg with the mashed cassava. Cupping your hands, attempt to enclose the egg and gently smooth over any rough edges to resemble a Scotch egg. If there are any gaps, take a pinch of the mashed cassava and patch them up.

When fully covered, dunk all sides of the egg ball in the beaten egg, shake off any excess and then coat in the flour. Set aside and repeat with the remaining eggs.

In a Dutch pot or frying pan, heat the oil over a medium-high heat. When hot, place a ball in the oil (or two if you

MAKES 5

650g (1lb 7oz) cassava
½ tsp sea salt
½ tsp freshly ground black pepper
1 garlic clove, grated, or 1 tsp garlic powder (optional)
1 tbsp chopped fresh coriander (cilantro) (optional)
1 tsp hot sauce (optional), plus extra to serve
1 tbsp unsalted butter (optional)
6 eggs
200g (scant 1½ cups) plain (all-purpose) flour
700ml (2¾ cups) cooking oil of choice, for frying
Mango Sour (see p232), to serve

have space). Use a spoon to ladle oil over any parts of the ball that aren't submerged. Cook on each side for 8 minutes until golden and then use a slotted spoon to place the ball on a plate lined with kitchen paper to drain. Serve with any hot sauce and Mango Sour as a dip.

NOTE *You can use half the amount of oil though you'll have to cook each side separately, which increases the chance of splitting. This does happen, so don't worry too much.*

Macaroni pie

Sometimes you see a building and stare in awe, wondering how it stands, about the foundation, the structure and so on. I often thought the same way about the Macaroni Pie that I would see at the table of distant family members from time to time. Different from the silky mac 'n' cheese that I was used to, like a plinth, this pie stood upright without stabilization when sliced. After years of wonderment, I probe and find out that the difference is due to a combination of egg and the wildly unexpected addition of condensed milk. I have no idea what the genesis of the latter is, and while we often love to canonize the past and assume a deeper meaning for everything that came before us, I like to think maybe someone residing in a tropical climate simply had the end-of-world-proof cans of condensed milk handy.

This recipe is certainly not a definitive version of macaroni pie; just use it as a starting block and adjust it to your preference. Change the cheese amount in either direction, mix cheeses, try your luck with vegan cheeses and perhaps nutritional yeast, use plant-based milk, gluten-free flour, fresh seasoning rather than powders. If really pressed, you can use any short pasta as a replacement for the macaroni. The combinations, as with macaroni and cheese recipes, are limitless and only you will know what will satisfy you. Like our condensed milk scientist, perhaps you'll even discover a new addition that will affect a generation.

Preheat the oven to 180°C (160°C fan/350°F/Gas 4).

Boil the macaroni following the instructions on the packet. Drain into a bowl and set aside.

In a small saucepan, heat butter, milk and flour over a medium heat. Whisk to combine and after 5 minutes turn off the heat. Add half of the grated cheese and combine until the cheese mostly melts into the mix. Next, add the seasoning ingredients and mix until combined. Pour the contents of the saucepan into the bowl of macaroni and mix. Add half the remaining cheese and stir to combine.

Decant the mixture into a 25cm x 13cm x 8cm (10in x 5in x 3¼in) greased baking dish, then cover the top with the remaining cheese. Place in the middle of the oven and set to distribute heat from the bottom and top evenly if possible, otherwise grill mode will suffice. Cook for 25–30 minutes until the top layer is a deep orange. You can continue cooking for a bit longer until protruding bits of macaroni are browning and almost burnt as many like the top layer of their macaroni pie crispy and crunchy.

SERVES 4–6 AS A SIDE

400g (14oz) elbow macaroni
2 tbsp salted butter
250ml (1 cup plus 1 tbsp) condensed milk or milk of choice
2 tbsp plain (all-purpose) flour
400g (14oz) Cheddar cheese, grated

FOR THE SEASONING

1 tsp sea salt
½ tsp onion powder
½ tsp garlic powder
½ tsp freshly ground black pepper
½ tsp all-purpose seasoning (optional)

Plait bread

Hefezopf to the Germans, *Kolach* to the Ukranians, *Vánočka* to the Czechs, *Kozunak* to the Bulgarians and Macedonians, *Challah* to those of the Jewish faith, while for others it's simply Plait Bread. In Guyana, it's often called Guyanese bread or Guyanese-style Plait Bread. Whatever its name, wherever it's situated, particularly in Europe, plait bread is associated with religious holidays such as Easter and Christmas. In Guyana particularly, the bread, which tastes a few eggs shy of brioche, is enjoyed during the winter holidays, especially paired with Pepperpot (see p140 for recipe and photo of both on pp142–143). The Guyanese style is a refined simple one, requiring minimal ingredients but creating a gloriously soft bread. When eaten with any stew, but particularly Pepperpot, the liquid seeps into the bread like a sponge.

Plait bread comes in many complex threads and styles. The breads can range from 6–12 plaits threaded together in all manner of shapes, which are then blasted by the baking furnace. Even though I've been lucky to watch many Caribbean bakers in action, particularly at Mixed Blessings in South London, I'm nowhere near this baking artisanship, so I keep it simple with a three-strand plait. Really this bread shouldn't be restricted to one week of the year, as it makes for a top loaf to keep in the kitchen on the weekend and throughout the following week.

MAKES 1 LOAF

300ml (1¼ cups) warm water
50g (¼ cup) white granulated sugar
1 tbsp dried active yeast
500g (3¾ cups) plain (all-purpose) flour
½ tsp coarse sea salt
50g (4 tbsp) unsalted butter, melted
10ml (2 tsp) whole milk, egg white or melted butter

In a small bowl, add the water, sugar and yeast and stir. Leave the mixture for 15–20 minutes until the yeast starts to gather and bubble to the surface.

In a large bowl, sift 450g (3¼ cups) of the flour and the salt and then add the butter and mix with your hands or a mixer to combine. Slowly add the yeast mixture while you combine with your hands. The mix will be quite wet at this point. Add the remaining flour and continue to mix and knead. As you continue, the dough will become smoother. Keep going for about 10 minutes until the dough is smooth. It will still stick somewhat to the bowl but this is OK. Cover the bowl with a dish towel and leave it to rest for 30 minutes.

Knead the bread again and you can leave it to rest again for 30 minutes or continue on to divide it into 3 pieces of equal weight. Roll out each piece into a length of 40cm (16in) and then place them on a baking tray lined with baking paper. You then need to plait them. The easiest way I remember to do this is to form a /|\ then tuck the right roll over the centre on (the right now becomes the centre), then the left roll over the centre (the left now becomes the centre) and repeat in that order until fully plaited. Tuck both ends under. Cover with a dish towel or cling film (plastic wrap) and leave to rest for a final 30 minutes.

Preheat the oven to 180°C (160°C fan/ 350°F/Gas 4).

Brush the bread with milk, egg white or butter, then bake in the oven for 25 minutes. When done the top will be a golden brown colour. Leave to cool on a rack for 30 minutes before serving. Keep in a bread bin or airtight container for up to 3 days.

NOTE *The plait may split open while baking, giving a ripped look down the middle of the bread. This is completely normal and perfect breadmaking is a skill that takes decades.*

Coconut boil dumplings

Boiled dumplings are one of the simplest foods in this book – representative of this chapter and the food of the Caribbean as a whole as they turned what was available into sustenance. Flour was rationed out to enslaved and indentured workers alike, so was used in creative ways to bolster meals. I can see how the legacy trickled down to my family's table, with them looking to bolster dishes for a broad family too. For me though, these dumplings do more than the sum of their parts. Somehow, they add a magical dimension to soups and stews that I can't get enough of, and I often delve into the soup pot like a diver when nobody is looking, hoping to salvage one more.

I grew up primarily with thick, hockey puck-shaped boiled dumplings as a side, or finger-sized "spinners" in soups, however, after living in Trinidad, my head has been turned and I can't look back. Here, thinner dumplings that often fold over like a flap in the boiling process are the default "boiled dumplings" and find themselves in soups and curries alike. Like most foods of the Caribbean, there are endless combinations and varieties, which change as many times as there are houses on a given street. My favourites include cutting the flour with desiccated coconut (as seen here) or using coconut flour; however, cornmeal and cassava are common variations, as is adding grated vegetables like pumpkin into the mix. Sometimes milk is used too, though I prefer this addition in Fry Bakes (see page 162).

Sift all the dry ingredients into a bowl. Slowly pour in 150ml (⅔ cup) water and combine until the dough is tight and dense. If the dough is still wet to the touch, add 1 tablespoon of flour and combine. Wrap the dough ball in cling film (plastic wrap) or cover in a bowl with a damp dish towel and leave to rest for 20–30 minutes.

Divide the dough into 7 roughly equal balls and roll each out into 10–12cm (4–4½in) circles. You can cut each circle into 3 pieces either now or after cooking.

Bring a saucepan of water to the boil over a high heat and, when hot, add in a dash of salt and 3 dumplings. Boil for 10–12 minutes. Sometime during this process, the dumplings will begin to float and some of them may start to naturally curl inward like a dog's ear. When done, you will be able to pierce them with a fork or knife but feel some resistance. Drain and repeat with the remaining dumplings. Serve in Corn Soup (see p46), Oil Down (see p124) or Crab & Dumplings (see p101).

MAKES 7

170g (1⅓ cups) plain (all-purpose) flour or wholemeal (whole wheat) flour
30g (1oz) desiccated coconut or coconut flour
1 tsp baking powder
1 tsp sea salt
½ tsp light soft brown sugar (optional)

Bakabana

Sometimes when shop psychology works you just have to applaud and say "You got me". As I discuss with *kurma*, in many takeaway spots in Suriname, directly beside the hole to order at eye level is a beaming cabinet of golden fried and baked goods. These are always expertly priced to round off a whole note. Small meals like Nasi (see p56) or Bami (see p154) cost 80SRD (Suriname dollars) and the treats are priced at 10–20SRD – so your 100SRD (currently equalling $3US) note is a write-off. One of these treats that I simply cannot bypass is *bakabana* – banana or plantain in a fried batter. This alone is already a guaranteed sale. Anything with the keywords "fried" and "plantain" in the same sentence is for me. However, *bakabana* usually comes with an added partner of peanut sauce perfectly umami-fied with a hint of some form of soy sauce and reminiscent of satay. The *bakabana* are placed in a small plastic bag and followed by a few dollops of the sauce, which seep into the batter over the time it takes you to eat whichever main you wolf down.

For those in Suriname descending from West Africa, the likelihood of their forefathers snacking on the same combo of plantain and peanuts, as in dishes like *kelewele*, which are enjoyed in Ghana today, helps explain why it's a hit across the region. This seems no coincidence given that the Dutch shipped in excess of 600,000 enslaved to the northeast corner of South America. On mentioning this dish to a friend they tell me it also sounds very familiar to *pisang goreng*, a Southeast Asian treat, which makes sense considering the influence of the region in Suriname, as seen with *bami* and *nasi*. Even though *bakabana* seems like a simple concoction, plantain can sometimes be hard to work with, so the best advice is don't overheat the oil and employ patience when dealing with the plantain, which can be easier said than done.

SERVES 2

200ml (scant 1 cup) cooking oil
  of choice, for frying
3 overripe plantains, peeled and
  cut diagonally into 5mm (¼in)
  thick slices

FOR THE BATTER

80g self-raising flour (⅔ cup
  all-purpose flour plus 1 tsp
  baking powder)
100ml (6½ tbsp) sparkling water
  or warm water
pinch of sea salt

FOR THE SAUCE

2 tbsp smooth peanut butter
1 tbsp light soy sauce
½ tbsp granulated sugar of choice

Place all the batter ingredients into a small bowl and whisk or stir until smooth.

Heat the oil in a large wok, Dutch pot or frying pan over a medium heat. When hot, turn the heat down a notch. Place about five slices of plantain in the batter, if space permits, coating both sides. Use a fork to scoop out a slice one by one, drain/shake off any excess batter and then place straight into the oil. Fry for 5–6 minutes on each side and when ready the outer should be golden brown. Line a large bowl with kitchen paper, add the fried plantain and drain on the kitchen paper. Cover the bowl with a dish towel to keep warm. Repeat with the remaining slices of plantain and batter.

To make the sauce, add all the ingredients to a small bowl with 75ml (5 tablespoons) and mix until smooth.

Serve the plantain with the sauce drizzled on top or in a small bowl to use as a dip.

ROTI

"Roti, by way of its ancestral journeying around the world, is one of those foods that's on the cusp of being a global staple."

No matter how much I love certain Caribbean food, there is always somewhere my ancestors have professed their love of the same dish more effectively, be it poetry, folklore or song. In the case of roti, in his 1985 song "Buss up shut" (a type of roti), legendary Trinidadian calypso singer Baron narrates the tale of Millicent who came to town for *Phagwah* (see p240) down in Penal. When the roti started to be shared she ate so ravenously that other people began to stare, but she didn't care, she simply sang: *"Buss up Shut, Buss up Shut OYE!! / How I love this thing so. Only I alone know."*

I can relate. At school there were two times you really didn't want to cross paths with your high-school crush, the first was tucking into a piping hot, flaky Jamaican patty and the other was with a steamy, gravy-filled roti with errant dhal or roti skin tucked into your burgeoning facial hair and school uniform. In those moments I chose to satiate my taste buds and belly first. I've been eating roti since I was born, with torn pieces of flatbread put on my plate to be eaten with whatever else was cooking. The odd thing about this is that I grew up in a predominantly Jamaican household and due to the comparatively low number of Indians who reached Jamaica, the food developments which happened in Trinidad and Tobago, Guyana and Suriname did not occur there. As such, the foods that were mainstream in those countries did not become so in Jamaica (and most other English and ex-colonies).

As well as its Indian heritage, roti also represents a new layer of Creolization, one that didn't take place in the Caribbean but that occurred in the diasporas of the UK, US and Canada, where Caribbean people were all grouped under the same umbrella. My mum's oldest sister married into an Indo-Guyanese family, her best friend's mum who hailed from Grenada took her under her wing, and a number of "aunts" and "uncles" who frequently came to lime (see p42) were from Trinidad and Tobago. I know that many other people growing up Caribbean in the West have very similar stories. As such, foods like roti became part of our lives. Due to the demands of the London rat race, few people ever had time to make their own roti, so we sourced them from the Hosein family of Horizon Foods, who've gone on to be the largest suppliers in the UK.

Across the vast reaches of India, roti is remarkably varied in recipe, shape and size. Dating back to the 1600s, roti was made with rice, sorghum, millet and corn. Other, sweeter kinds were stuffed with coconut shreds, dates, raisins, cardamom-flavoured sucrose and concoctions of mango juice and coconut milk. These "flat soft breads" often "wrapped around a filling" were typical of the cuisine consumed by the lower classes in Northern India. In the same way that religious elements of Indian culture morphed into something unique in the Caribbean, so too did roti. Northern Indians who came to the Caribbean brought memories and recipes with them. From their arrival, when pulses may not have been readily available, what was accessible in increasing quantities was imported wheat flour.

"Roti is an inherently communal activity due to the amount made in a single batch."

A number of rotis influenced in name but visually quite different to those seen back in India, emerged in the Caribbean. For many in the Caribbean, the word "roti" thus usually conjures up one of those in particular. For some roti means Sada (see p218), others Paratha (see p204), but for me it's Dhal Puri (see p210) – dhal being the split peas and *puri* (or *poori*) meaning puffed up bread. Here, soft blankets of gently saline flatbread provide sanctity to a slender layer of garlicky, spiced, blended split peas. There are many different joys here, meat or fish curries and vegetables wrapped in tight and snug, where the bread and runaway split peas soak up the flavours and colours, or slightly warm and straight up plain just like when I was a kid.

The technique (shown on p209) of securing those ground split peas, or potato if making Aloo Roti (see p212), into the dough is one that can seem daunting, but after a while you get the hang of it. So don't fret, it's a technique that has been harnessed over centuries, if not millennia.

Roti, by way of its ancestral journeying around the world, is one of those foods that is on the cusp of truly being a global staple. The original name of *paratha* is one that many know from their ventures to Malay, Indonesian, Himalayan and regional Indian restaurants. While they share similarity in the method of making, being all made from layered, wrapped and twisted dough (shown on p208), the version in this chapter, made without egg, gets its flaky demeanour from being clapped either with a pair of *dablas* or hands. This gave it its Creole names "clap roti" and "buss-up shut (shirt/shot) roti", so named due to its resemblance to a busted, torn shirt. The streaking of this roti lends well to tearing, canoodling a grip of meat or veg inside it and devouring.

The loss of many Indigenous Caribbean languages to the colonial dominance of English means we not only lost words but Indigenous modes of expressions. Expressions that simply don't exist in the blunt literalness of English. This, of course, extends to food. There's no more beautiful moniker for food I've found recently than Dosti Roti (see p217). The term *dosti*, as described in Hindi and Urdu dictionaries, translates as both "friendship" and "to befriend". Here, two plain rotis form a friendship as they are joined together in a sumptuous marriage. It's apt that the term also means to befriend as surely anyone you want to will succumb to receiving a lovely warm batch of soft, silky roti.

For the indentured workers, these roti formed part of a late-day meal, usually accompanied by curry and black tea. More weighty rotis, like Pepper Roti (very reminiscent of a Turkish gözleme, see p207) stuffed with a spicy, cheesy potato mix, satisfied hunger built up after a long day's work. Sada Roti (see p218) dominated the early day, as the quick flatbread was a common breakfast choice. When travelling to Guyana or Trinidad you see it touted on every high street and roadway, paired with light but gratifying vegetable or fish *chokas* (see p114).

Roti is an inherently communal activity due to the amount made in a single batch. Even if only one person participates in making it, you can be sure a lot more will be eating it. Apart from perhaps sada roti, I've never heard of or seen anyone make a single roti – it doesn't make sense. Rather, make at least ten and then freeze any leftovers, which can be reheated on a *tawa*, hot plate, non-stick pan or placed with kitchen paper underneath and microwaved.

Making roti is thought to be a full-day or even multiple-day affair, so I envy folks like Ms Asha and Patsy in Trinidad, who when tutoring me in the ways of roti-making, effortlessly make huge batches while simultaneously parenting and conducting any other number of chores. They have an end product after an hour or so. I'm probably a few decades shy of such roti-making astuteness. Since my grandmother passed away, I always have a soft spot for the idioms and adages offered by elderly Caribbean folk. In passing, a local Moruga acquaintance, Cliff, tells me "It's better to try and fail, then fail to try", and I can't think of any food in this book to which that is more applicable than roti. Even if it doesn't look like what you see in shops, it will still taste great.

Given the time constraints of the modern world, many people buy roti and support local businesses so they can focus on making curries and stews. That being said, there are few greater joys than the first time you make your own batch. I've eaten roti everywhere, from Fort Lauderdale in Florida to Queens in NYC, from Scarborough in Toronto to Clapham in South London, and I worked at my favourite Roti Stop in Hackney, Northeast London for a year. This has all taught me that there's no right or wrong roti. The only way to get to know how you like roti, and with which of the endless combinations, is through trial and error. The best tips are to apply low–medium heat, don't rush and be patient.

While the Trini and Guyanese argue over who does roti the best, I must say that Suriname, quietly in the corner minding its own business, may be right up there with them. For those not able to get to the tricky-to-reach country, Amsterdam has a sizable Surinamese community.

A QUICK NOTE *Some words crop up when dealing with roti.* Loyas *are the individual dough balls, which are then* baelay-ed *(rolled out), preferably with a* baelna *(belna/balana) and on a* chowki *– a round wooden board. These are cooked on a* tawa *baking plate, flipped with a* dabla *– a long wooden spatula and clapped with two* dablas. *The* chowki, dabla *and* baelna *can all be replaced but the* tawa *I'm not so sure about (see pp214–215).*

"...rved Daily..."

"...ROTI"

- DHALPOURIE &
- BUSS-UP-SHUT

~ with ~

- CHICKEN GOAT
- DUCK SHRIMP...

etc.

Buss-up shot roti (Paratha)

MAKES 8–10

650g (scant 5 cups) plain
   (all-purpose) flour, plus
   100g (¾ cup) for dusting
2 tsp baking powder
2 tsp sea salt
1 tsp granulated brown sugar
   (optional)
400ml (1¾ cups) warm water
180ml (¾ cup) cooking oil of choice

In a large bowl, sift 650g (scant 5 cups) of the flour, the baking powder, salt and sugar, if using. Slowly add the water and knead until the mixture comes together in a dough. Don't fold the dough, rather roll it around the bowl while squeezing and pressing it. Roll it around the edges so it wipes up all the flour. The dough should be slightly moist to the touch and for this recipe it's fine if the dough is sticking to the bowl a tiny bit.

Separate the dough into equal-sized chunks (*loyas*) and cover the ones you aren't shaping straight away. Eight equal parts should weigh about 120g (4¼oz) each; 10 equal parts should be about 100g (3½oz). Weights will fluctuate, so feel free to eyeball it. Slightly round each of them, place them on a lightly floured flat surface and cover with cling film (plastic wrap), damp kitchen paper or a damp dish towel. Let them sit for 10 minutes–1 hour.

Put the oil into a small bowl and the remaining 100g (¾ cup) flour in a bowl. Take one dough ball and lie it on a lightly floured flat surface, then flatten it out into a circle with your fingers and roll it into a circle about 20cm (8in) in diameter with a rolling pin. This does not need to be a perfect circle. Dip the fingertips of one hand in the oil (or use a basting brush) and rub onto the entire face of the flattened-out dough circle. Next, sprinkle a dash of flour onto the dough.

Now, take a knife and cut an incision as per Step 1 on page 208. Fold the inside out (as per Step 2 on page 208), then from one edge roll over in a clockwise or anti-clockwise motion, tucking any outer bits inside the middle (as per Step 3 on page 208). Just before you have completely rolled the dough, stand it up, wrap the last bit of dough around and tuck it into the middle. Press in the middle so it is snug, then use your palm to slightly flatten it (as per Step 4 on page 208). Turn it upside down and use your palm to flatten it again. The dough should resist and spring up as you flatten it. Cover the dough ball with a dish towel and repeat with the remaining dough.

Take out a dough ball, slightly flatten with your palm and then dip both sides into your small bowl of flour. Next, roll out the dough ball into a circle reminiscent of a pizza base with a rolling pin. The thickness of this is personal preference and will affect the diameter. A minimum diameter of 25cm (10in) is recommended. Since this roti will be "buss'd up", a perfect round circle isn't necessary.

When ready to cook, heat a *tawa* or non-stick frying pan (skillet) over a medium heat. Test your pan with a splash of water and if it immediately sizzles and evaporates, it is hot enough to cook on. Next, take a brush, kitchen paper or traditionally the bottom of a metallic cup, dip it into the remaining oil and lightly oil the pan. Take one roti and drape it over your hand and with pace slap it down onto the pan. (If the dough happens to fold over on itself or not make it to the pan perfectly, wait a few seconds and use a *dabla* or flat kitchen utensil to scoop underneath and flatten out.) Using the tool you used to dip it into the oil, do so again, and lightly coat the

roti. After 45 seconds, check the underside and you should see light browning. Use a *dabla*, any thin flat kitchen utensil or your hands and flip. Lightly coat again with oil in the same way and cook for 45 seconds.

The "bussin' up" or "clapping" process can be done in a few ways. When still on the *tawa* or pan you can use the handles of two *dablas* or any kitchen utensils, or your hands, and, in an outside-in motion, lift up and clap the roti together with strength. Rotate it, then clap again until it flakes up. Alternatively, when the roti is cooked, fold it in half and place on a plate lined with kitchen paper. Let it cool for a minute, then pick up with your hands and clap the roti between your palms.

When done, store in an airtight container lined with kitchen paper. Repeat until all the roti are cooked.

Serve with any curry (see pp82–101), plant-based recipe (see pp26–47), Oil Down (see p124) or Pepperpot (see p140).

Pepper roti

Follow the instructions for making the dough balls (*loyas*) for the Buss-up Shot Roti on p204.

To prepare the stuffing, add the potatoes to a large saucepan, cover with water and a dash of salt and then boil for 25–30 minutes until soft (when a fork can easily pierce them).

When the potatoes are cooked, drain and add them to a large bowl along with all the remaining ingredients, except the cheese. Use a large fork or masher to combine to a smooth mix and set aside.

Add the remaining 100g (¾ cup) flour and 100ml (6½ tablespoons) cooking oil to two separate small bowls and keep nearby. Place the grated cheese in a third bowl.

One by one, take out a dough ball (*loya*), slightly flatten with your palm and then dip both sides into your small bowl of flour. When you have two coated in flour, roll them out to the same size – roughly 25cm (10in) in diameter.

Heat a *tawa* or large non-stick frying pan over a medium heat. Take a brush, kitchen paper or traditionally the bottom of a metallic cup, dip it into the remaining oil and lightly oil the *tawa*. Place one *loya* on the hot *tawa* and then sprinkle a large pinch of cheese on it. Immediately take 2–3 tablespoons of the potato mixture and place it on top of the cheese, then use the back of the spoon to spread out the mixture flat. Sprinkle on cheese again, leaving a 1cm (½in) gap around the edge. Wet the edge with a pastry brush and water and then sit the second *loya* on top. To help the two *loya* stick together, use a fork to crimp the rim. Finally, brush the top with oil and use a *dabla* or super-flat utensil to scoop under the roti and flip it. This process of building the pepper roti should take about 2 minutes when you have the hang of it but it helps to keep the heat down so it doesn't burn. When you flip the roti it should have light brown marks across it. Brush the new face-up side with oil and cook for 2–3 minutes, then flip again and cook for a further minute.

Remove the roti from the *tawa* and place on a board, slice into quarters and keep warm in a large bowl or tray covered with a dish towel.

Repeat the process, including oiling the *tawa* before starting a new roti, with the remaining dough and filling.

MAKES 4–5

FOR THE DOUGH

650g (scant 5 cups) plain (all-purpose) flour, plus 100g (¾ cup) for dusting
2 tsp baking powder
2 tsp sea salt
1 tsp granulated brown sugar (optional)
400ml (1¾ cups) warm water
180ml (¾ cup) cooking oil of choice

FOR THE STUFFING

500g (1lb 2oz) potatoes of choice, peeled and chopped
3 tbsp finely chopped fresh coriander (cilantro)
½ onion, minced
2 spring onions (scallions/green onions), finely chopped (optional)
3 garlic cloves, minced
½ bell pepper of choice, deseeded and finely chopped
½ Scotch bonnet pepper, deseeded and finely chopped
1 tsp ground cumin
1 tsp sea salt
½ tsp freshly ground black pepper
1 carrot, peeled and grated
1 tbsp butter or coconut oil
300g (10oz) mature Cheddar cheese, grated

Roti technique

1. Cut an incision from the bottom centre of the roti almost to the top.

2. Fold over the inside edges of the flap (like a jacket lapel).

3. From one end, start rolling up the roti until just before you reach the end.

4. Stand the dough up and tuck in the ends to the centre. Then use your palm to flatten it. Turn it upside down and flatten again.

Filled roti technique

1. Take the flattened *loya* in your palm and add the filling.

2. Raise the edges up and around the filling.

3. Use the inside of your index finder and thumb to continue until the filling is covered.

4. When the filling is covered, gently pinch and twist the dough to seal.

Dhal puri

MAKES 8

650g (scant 5 cups) plain
   (all-purpose) flour, plus 100g
   (¾ cup) for dusting
2 tsp baking powder
2 tsp sea salt
½ tsp ground turmeric
1 tsp granulated brown sugar
   (optional)
400ml (1¾ cups) warm water
80ml (⅓ cup) cooking oil of choice

**FOR THE SPLIT PEA
FILLING**

250g (9oz) yellow split peas
6 garlic cloves, peeled
½ tsp garam masala (optional)
½ tsp ground cumin (optional)
½ Scotch bonnet pepper,
   deseeded
1 tbsp chopped fresh coriander
   (cilantro)

In a large bowl, sift 650g (scant 5 cups) of the flour, the baking powder, salt, turmeric and sugar, if using. Slowly add the warm water and knead until the mixture comes together in a dough. Don't fold the dough – instead roll it around the bowl while squeezing and pressing it. Roll it around the edges so it wipes up all the flour. The dough should be slightly moist to the touch but not sticking to the bowl. Baste the dough with 1 tablespoon of oil, cover and leave to rest for at least 1 hour or overnight.

Separate the dough into 8 equal-sized chunks (*loyas*) weighing about 120g (4¼oz) each. Weights will fluctuate, so feel free to eyeball it. Slightly round each of them, place on a lightly floured flat surface and cover with cling film (plastic wrap) or damp kitchen paper.

Wash and rinse the split peas at least three times, discarding any debris, and then put the peas into a large saucepan and cover with water. As a benchmark, the space between the top of the peas and the water should be the same as the distance between the top of your finger and the line of your first finger joint. Boil the peas over a high heat for 20–30 minutes. At the 20-minute mark, begin checking that the peas aren't getting too soft. You should be able to crush them between your thumb and index finger with some force but not with ease. As soon as you can do this, remove the pot from the heat and drain the peas into a bowl. Leave them to dry and cool for 1 hour.

Using either a mill, food processor or large pestle and mortar, grind the peas with the remaining ingredients for the split pea filling. If your food processor isn't big enough to process the full amount, you can do it in batches. Some people prefer a paste-like consistency, others a sand-like consistency. A good rule of thumb is that you can clench your fist with the peas in your hand and the peas naturally clump together but are easily separated. When done, cover and set aside.

One by one, take a *loya* and flatten it with your palm, then use your fingers to spin it into a disc. Place it on a lightly floured flat surface and use your fingers to spread it out into a circle about 14cm (5½in) in diameter. Place the dough circle in one hand and with the other take a full pinch of the split pea mixture and place into the centre of the dough (see Step 1 on page 209). Bring up the sides of the dough and pinch them together while rotating the dough ball until the split peas are completely enclosed (see Step 2 on page 209). Using the inner part of your thumb and the lower part of your index finger, softly grip the raised and centred sides and rotate the dough ball with your palm, this will smooth the ball so the peas don't escape or burst out (see Step 3 on page 209). Repeat with the remaining dough balls and filling, and loosely cover each under a damp dish towel when done.

Put the remaining 100g (¾ cup) flour in a bowl. One by one, take a dough ball and slightly flatten with your palm, then dip both

sides into the flour. Next, carefully flatten the filled ball with your hands so the filling remains inside, then roll out with a rolling pin. The thickness is personal preference and will affect the diameter. A minimum diameter of 25cm (10in) is recommended. If rolled out too thin, the roti may burst and the edges crisp up.

When ready to cook, heat a *tawa* or non-stick frying pan over a medium heat. Test your pan with a splash of water and if it immediately sizzles and evaporates, you are ready to cook. Place the oil into a bowl. Next, take a brush, kitchen paper or traditionally the bottom of a metallic cup, dip this into the oil and lightly oil the *tawa*. Take one rolled out dough and drape it over your hand and with pace slap it down onto the pan. (If the dough happens to fold over on itself or not make it to the pan perfectly, wait a few seconds and use a

dabla or flat kitchen utensil to scoop underneath and flatten out.) Using the tool you used to dip it into the oil, do so again and lightly coat the roti. After 45 seconds, check the underside and you should see light browning. Use a *dabla*, any thin flat kitchen utensil or your hands to flip. Coat again with oil in the same way and cook for 45 seconds. Flip back onto the other side and cook for a further 30 seconds. Remove from the pan, fold in half, then fold again and place in a large bowl or container and cover to keep warm. Repeat with the remaining dough.

Serve with any curry (see pp82–101), plant-based recipe (see pp26–47), Oil Down (see p124) or Pepperpot (see p140).

NOTE *You can cook over a higher heat and turn the roti over sooner (after 20–30 seconds).*

Aloo roti

In a large bowl, sift 650g (scant 5 cups) of the flour, the baking powder, salt and sugar, if using. Slowly add the warm water and knead until the mixture comes together in a dough. Don't fold the dough, rather roll it around the bowl while squeezing and pressing it. Roll it around the edges so it wipes up all the flour. The dough should be slightly moist to the touch but not sticking to the bowl. Baste the dough with 1 tablespoon of oil, cover and leave to rest for at least 1 hour or overnight.

Separate the dough into 8 equal-sized chunks (*loyas*) weighing about 120g (4¼oz). Weights will fluctuate, so feel free to eyeball it. Slightly round each of them, place them on a lightly floured flat surface and cover with cling film (plastic wrap), damp kitchen paper or a damp dish towel.

Place the potatoes in a saucepan and cover with water. Bring to the boil over a medium–high heat and add a dash of salt. Place on the lid and boil for 25 minutes until the potatoes are completely soft. You can test this by piercing with a knife or fork. Drain and place potatoes in a bowl. Add the remaining filling ingredients and mash with a fork or potato masher until completely smooth.

Take one *loya* and flatten it with your palm, then use your fingers to spin it into a disc. Place it on a lightly floured flat surface and use your fingers to spread it out into a circle about 14cm (5½in) in diameter. Place the dough circle in one hand and with the other take a full pinch of the potato filling and place into the centre of the dough. Bring up the sides of the dough and pinch them together while rotating the dough ball until the potatoes are completely enclosed. Using the inner part of your thumb and the lower part of your index finger, softly grip the raised and centred sides and rotate the dough ball with your palm to smooth the entire surface of the ball, so the filling doesn't escape or burst out during cooking. Repeat with the remaining dough balls and filling, and cover with a damp dish towel.

Put the remaining 100g (¾ cup) flour in a bowl. Take one dough ball (*loya*) and slightly flatten with your palm, then dip both sides into the small bowl of flour. Next, carefully flatten the filled ball with your hands so the filling remains inside, then roll out with a rolling pin. The thickness is personal preference and will affect the diameter. A minimum diameter of 25cm (10in) is recommended. If rolled out too thin, the roti may burst and the edges crisp up.

MAKES 8

650g (scant 5 cups) plain (all-purpose) flour, plus 100g (¾ cup) for dusting
2 tsp baking powder
2 tsp sea salt
1 tsp granulated brown sugar (optional)
400ml (1¾ cups) warm water
80ml (⅓ cup) cooking oil of choice, plus 1 tbsp for basting

FOR THE FILLING

300g (10oz) potatoes of choice, peeled and chopped
3 garlic cloves, finely chopped
2 tbsp unsalted butter, ghee or coconut oil
1 tbsp Green Seasoning (see pp26–27)
1 tsp sea salt
1 tsp ground cumin
½ tsp freshly ground black pepper
½ tsp all-purpose seasoning (optional)
½ Scotch bonnet pepper, deseeded and finely chopped (optional)

When you are ready to cook, heat a *tawa* or non-stick frying pan over a medium heat. Test your pan with a splash of water and if it immediately sizzles and evaporates, it's hot enough to cook on. Place the remaining oil into a bowl. Next, take a brush, kitchen paper or traditionally the bottom of a metallic cup, dip this into the oil and lightly oil the *tawa*. Take one roti and drape it over your hand and, with pace, slap it down onto the pan. (If the dough happens to fold over, wait a few seconds and use a *dabla* or flat kitchen utensil to scoop underneath and flatten out.) Using the tool you used to dip it into the oil, do so again and lightly coat the roti. After 45 seconds, check the underside and you should see light browning. Use a *dabla*, any thin flat kitchen utensil or your hands to flip. Coat again with oil in the same way and cook for 45 seconds. Flip back on to the other side and cook for a further 30 seconds. Remove from the pan, fold in half, then fold again and place in a large bowl or container and cover to keep warm. Repeat with the remaining dough.

Serve with any curry (see pp82–101), plant-based recipe (see pp26–47), Oil Down (see p124) or Pepperpot (see p140).

NOTE *You can cook over a higher heat and turn the roti over sooner (after 20–30 seconds).*

Tawa bridge

There are a number of traditional tools mentioned in this book, most replaceable with some kind of modern appliance if I'm being honest, but one I see time and again, resistant to the winds of time, is the *tawa* (or *tava/tawah/thavā*). A *tawa* is a flat, circular metal griddle akin to a baking stone, which was and is used in India for all manner of things, from cooking *dosas* to dry-roasting pulses and nuts. However, in the Caribbean, it serves one broad purpose: cooking roti. I admire the many *tawas* I come across in the same way some people appreciate cars, from the small 20cm (8in) versions to the industrial ones a metre (40in) wide. I see them everywhere, some perched against a wall, some with a designated spot secured by a nail, some kept inside, others outside. Some chipped, scratched and dented, others completely smooth.

In Fifth Company, a small town in South Trinidad, an incredible vendor works with powertools, efficiently churning out Dutch pots, *karahis* and cast-iron *tawas* on a near-industrial scale. I'm told that I should "break" my *tawa* before use. This is done by washing it with hot water and performing an exfoliating scrub of sorts with oil and salt. In doing this and basking in its luminescent metallic glory, I wonder about the journey these pans go on to become their inevitable seasoned, wrinkled, stubbly, darker versions.

All the utensils I use for cooking foods from the Caribbean are hand-me-downs from my mum – stacks of Dutch pots and wooden spatulas all older than me. My first *tawa* was also the first Caribbean kitchen mainstay I acquired myself. So this *tawa* is like a reflection of me; each added scratch and black mark are akin to noticing a new strand of grey hair or wrinkle. Like the flour and oil that seeps into the fabric of the *tawa*, the cosmetic changes are irreversible. Perhaps like Oscar Wilde's Dorian Gray, I can trap the essence of my youth into this relic and keep it hidden in my attic.

Just as with Dutch pots, everything cooked on a *tawa* simply tastes better. Especially those aged like fine wine. As well as roti, I make regular flatbread, short pancakes and even taco tortillas to great effect. (I also use mine on an electric hob just fine.) I worked at roti shops where the same handful of *tawas*, always on the fire, have been used for decades and the thought of using new *tawas* is laughed off. I also learned the hard way that *tawas* don't talk. By this I mean that they stay silent; save for the cackle of a low heat there's little audio or visual tell that a *tawa* is absolutely raging hot, especially once they evolve to their final blackened form. If you get tempted to nudge it a bit when it's slightly off-centre or you want to shift a roti without the *tawa* budging, you will find out this hellish sensation the hard way. Hopefully I went through this so you don't have to. Always keep a cloth or dish towel handy when dealing with a *tawa*, even up to half an hour after you've finished your roti duty. If you want to test its hotness when you're starting or finishing, simply splash a tiny bit of water on it and it will immediately fizz and evaporate if hot or do nothing if cold.

Where to buy: Local Indian stores in the diaspora may be able to point you to regionalized or modernized versions of the *tawa*, mostly thin plates with protruding plastic or wooden handles. Online is the best bet for the thick, rounded-with-handle types common in the Caribbean and seen in this book. (Note, if you try to bring one back from the islands, you can't carry it in hand luggage.) You can try to make roti with a large, ideally heavy-bottomed, non-stick frying pan, but this comes with extremely variable results. Hot plates of the *tawa* kind have been found in Indus Valley excavations dating back thousands of years BCE and since then, for all the modern inventions that have come along, nothing yet has successfully challenged the *tawa*.

Dosti roti

MAKES 8–10

750g (5¾ cups) plain (all-
purpose) flour, plus extra
for dusting
2 tsp baking powder
1 tsp sea salt
2 tsp granulated brown sugar
(optional)
400ml (1¾ cups) warm water
4 tbsp unsalted soft butter or
cooking oil of choice
80ml (⅓ cup) cooking oil of choice

In a large bowl, sift the flour, baking powder, salt and sugar, if using. Slowly add the warm water and knead until the mixture comes together in a dough. Don't fold the dough, rather roll it around the bowl while squeezing and pressing it. Roll it around the edges so it wipes up all the flour. The dough should be slightly moist to the touch and for this recipe it's fine if the dough is sticking to the bowl a tiny bit. Cover with cling film (plastic wrap) or a damp dish towel and leave to rest for at least 15 minutes.

Separate the dough into 8–10 equal-sized chunks (*loyas*), weighing about 120–130g (4¼–4½oz) each and cover the ones you aren't shaping. Flour a flat surface and then take two dough balls and flatten them out with your fingers. Roll out each one into a circle about 20cm (8in) in diameter. Take one disc and brush with 1 tablespoon of butter or oil, then sprinkle over a dash of flour. Next, take the second disc and place on top of the first like a sandwich. Gently align and press down around the edges. Roll out into a circle about 25–30cm (10–12in) in diameter.

When you are ready to cook, heat your *tawa* or non-stick frying pan over a medium heat. Test your pan with a splash of water and if it immediately sizzles and evaporates, you are ready to cook. Place the 80ml (⅓ cup) oil into a bowl. Next, take a brush, kitchen paper or traditionally the bottom of a metallic cup, dip this into the oil and lightly oil the *tawa*. Take one roti and drape it over your hand and with pace slap it down onto the pan. (If the dough happens to fold over on itself or not make it to the pan perfectly, wait a few seconds and use a *dabla* or flat kitchen utensil to scoop underneath and flatten out.) Using the tool you used to dip it into the oil, do so again and lightly coat the face of the dough. After 25 seconds the roti should start to bubble. Use a *dabla*, any thin flat kitchen utensil or your hands to flip, being mindful not to burn yourself on the pan. Coat again with oil and cook for 25 seconds. Flip back on to the other side and cook for a further 20 seconds. Remove from the pan and place in a large bowl or container and cover to keep warm. Repeat with the remaining dough.

Split the roti open with a knife and peel apart the two skins. Serve with any curry (see pp82–101), plant-based recipe (see pp26–47), Oil Down (see p124) or Pepperpot (see p140).

Sada roti

Sift the flour, baking powder, yeast, if using, and salt into a bowl and slowly add the warm water. Mix to combine, add the butter or oil if you like, then knead for 5 minutes, squeezing but not folding the dough. When it forms a soft ball that is slightly sticky, cover the dough with a damp dish towel and leave for 30 minutes.

Divide the dough into 8 roughly equal-sized dough balls (*loyas*). Round and smooth the chunks into balls and place on a lightly floured flat surface and cover for a further 20 minutes if you have time.

Dust a surface with flour and take one of the dough balls. Flatten it out with your palm and then roll out into a circle 18–20cm (7–8in) in diameter. Preheat a *tawa* (or baking stone, non-stick frying pan) over a medium heat (not too hot). Test your pan with a splash of water and if it immediately sizzles and evaporates, you are ready to cook. Place the dough disc on the *tawa* and cook for 40 seconds until you see bubbles rising. Then flip the roti and cook the other side for 40 seconds. Each layer should have specks of light brown across it.

Place the cooked roti in a bowl, stacked on top of each other and cover tightly with a dish towel. Repeat with the remaining dough.

When ready to serve, use a knife, if needed, to cut an incision and pull the roti apart. Serve with Bodhi, Bhaji and Pumpkin Talkari (see pp34–35).

MAKES 8

600g (4⅔ cups) plain (all-purpose) flour, plus extra for dusting
2 tbsp baking powder
1 tsp instant yeast (optional)
1 tsp sea salt
300ml (1¼ cups) warm water
1 tbsp unsalted butter or cooking oil of choice (optional)

PRESERVES
& JUICES

"Every culture that makes up the vivid fabric of the Caribbean has its own long history of fermentation and preservation."

Many of the fermentation and preservation techniques seen in the Caribbean today can trace some kind of root to the Indigenous tribes of the region. As discussed in the Nose-to-tail chapter, much of this was done as a means of survival. Meat was not an everyday occurrence and without ample salt to cure it, something had to be done to preserve meat in the tropical climate. This can be seen in the use of cassava to make *cassareep*, which helped keep meat, as well as the original barbecuing technique. Over time we also see the emergence of what we would recognize as beers in the form of *masato*, made from arrowroot, and *chica*, a fermented beer made from maize. We also see breads made from cassava, which Jamaicans will recognize as *bammy*.

We tend to focus on means of survival as the inspiration behind these preservation techniques as that's what we can theorize easily. We know the Indigenous tribal people didn't have fridges, we know they were often on the move, we know food could be hard to come by. What's less discussed in relation to the fermentations and preserves of days gone by are the other reasons they may have been enjoyed – like sensation and taste. In his book *Food of the Gods*, American ethnobiologist and writer Terence McKenna posits, *"The shaman who gorges himself on chilli peppers to raise inner heat is hardly in a less altered state than the nitrous oxide enthusiast after a long inhalation."* In layman's terms, getting high. I've never partaken in the consumption of any oxides, but I can confirm that eating chillies native to the Caribbean, freshly plucked off the branch, is an out of body experience. One that with the burning sensation brings instant regret but can't be that bad because in a few days we forget that tongue-numbing pain and do it all over again. The Moruga Scorpion (see p236) and Mother-in-law Pepper Sauce (see p239) are testament to this, as well as the comparatively more tolerable Lime & Pepper Sauce (see p235). Getting high has negative connotations, but after eating these chilli condiments there's some element of this sensation that must be baked into the reasons (beyond taste) that people have consumed them for generations.

Another use of preserved and fermented foods was medicinal. Much of this was rooted in some form of West African theology and religion. The breadfruit plant, for example, which grows plentifully on trees across Trinidad, Guyana and beyond, was highly regarded by the Igbo people of Nigeria. The pods, leaves and roots were used in traditional medicine and the preservation of the stem bark using extraction is said to have been used as a cough remedy. On the plantation, the enslaved experienced all manner of ailments and illnesses, from respiratory problems, to chronic and joint pain, lacerations, orifice infections and so on. With planters constantly cutting costs, medical care was scarce. As such, the enslaved turned to the resources of their own communities. Local fruits, weeds, leaves and plants were dried, sometimes juiced and turned into powders to help cure people, with many levels of documented success.

"Something in these recipes has meant they have been continually passed down from generation to generation and stayed in the public consciousness."

Every culture that makes up the vivid fabric of the Caribbean has its own long history of fermentation and preservation. In Ghana, where the Akan people originated from, *Gari* was a daily staple which was made by peeling fresh roots, then grating them into mash before putting them into sacks for fermentation. Kenkey was another daily staple made from fermenting white cornmeal. Alcoholic drinks were a central product of fermentation too, with wines made by fermenting palm sap into palm wine. In India, there is evidence of brewing and the fermentation of wines utilizing fruits, barleys and sugar dating back thousands of years. The coincidence is that most of the global human transportation described in this book was based on fermentation and preservation. The cane fields of the Caribbean were chopped and hacked in the extreme heat, amidst rodents, snakes and mosquitoes, to preserve the essence of the cane into sugar and molasses. Much of this molasses was then fermented into rum using the knowledge of the enslaved, which ushered in astronomical profits for the planters, traders, and royalty and governments of the colonizers.

Something in these recipes has meant they have been continually passed down from generation to generation and stayed in the public consciousness. The varying demographic make-up of each Caribbean nation and sub-region means that some dishes are popular in some places and others are not. In the countries with a high Indo-Caribbean presence, many of their culinary preserving traditions like kuchela and mango sour are now commonplace. In Jamaica, even with its abundance of mangoes, you would actually be hard pressed to find Kuchela (see p229) and Mango Sour (see p232). On the other side of the Caribbean, however, you can't go to a shop without being offered them as a topping. In Trini homes I visited for the first time, I could guarantee there would be Tambran Sauce (see p230) and Coconut Chutney (see p227), utilizing local produce and stored in all manner of repurposed jars, as those who came generations before them would have done. The Javanese hailing from Indonesia also brought with them incredibly vivid sauces, including sambal (see p228), while the indentured Portuguese workers from Madeira brought Garlic Pork (see p242), which has become a festive favourite in Trinidad and Guyana.

"All of [the recipes] happen to be incredibly moreish – in my house they end up being finished in days."

Some of these recipes involve an element of graft, like peeling and grating mangoes or busting open and grating coconuts, which can take time. I find these tasks quite relaxing, though I understand domestic circumstances aren't the same for everyone. Most of these recipes can be purchased in ready-made form and, if you've never tried them before, that may be a good starting point, though as I frequently say, there's nothing better than home-made. All of them happen to be incredibly moreish – in my house they end up being finished in days. With the stories of these recipes I hope to restore some agency to the ancestors for preserving not just food, but an incredible array of tastes.

STERILIZING JARS

Many of the recipes in this chapter call for a sterilized jar or bottle. To do this, wash the jar in hot, soapy water and when still wet place upside-down in an oven preheated to 180°C (160°C fan/350°F/Gas 4) for 10–15 minutes, until dry. Alternatively, sterilize your jar in a pan of boiling water for 10 minutes. Leave to dry upside down on a clean dish towel. When ready, ladle or pour your hot preserve into the still-warm jar, almost to the top and then screw on the lid tightly (it's always a good idea to use new lids), then leave to cool.

Coconut chutney

Coconut chutney is not what you may imagine a chutney to be (a savoury jam with a tinge of sweetness). This coconut chutney eaten alongside Indo-Caribbean food is rather a grated coconut *choka* (see p28). When dealing with the hardened flesh of coconuts, most people either eat it in chunks or blend it with water to make fresh coconut milk. This relish goes in a completely different direction, roasting grated coconut until charred, then combining it with minced hot chillies and balancing it with fresh coriander (cilantro) before giving it that subtle hot, spiced touch only a mustard and cumin-seasoned chounkay can. Even though this chutney has a hint of heat in it, when devouring a hot curry, it still provides respite and when served with an array of plant-based dishes like Bhaji and Pumpkin Talkari (see p34), it adds another level of flavour to the plate.

———

Preheat the oven to 200°C (180°C fan/400°F/Gas 6).

Place the coconut, garlic and Scotch bonnet pepper on a baking tray, lined with parchment paper and roast for 30 minutes until the coconut turns brown. Remove from the oven and leave to cool for 10 minutes. Alternatively, if you have a grill or BBQ, you can grill the coconut, garlic and Scotch bonnet pepper for 5–10 minutes until the outer turns black. Scrape off some of the black char and continue as below.

Break the coconut into manageable-sized chunks for your food processor and place them all in with the garlic, Scotch bonnet pepper and fresh coriander, then pulse into a fine mix. This mixture should be dry and not a slushy blend. Decant into a bowl and set aside.

If making the chounkay, in a small frying pan, heat the oil over a medium heat. When hot, add the remaining chounkay ingredients and fry until they start to turn brown. Decant the oil (without the seeds) into the coconut mixture, add the salt and stir.

Store in an airtight container and use within 2 weeks. Serve with rice and curry (see pp82–101).

NOTE *If you are serving a smaller amount of people just use a single coconut.*

MAKES 300G (10OZ)

300g (10oz) hard coconut flesh
(2 small brown coconuts)
5 garlic cloves, peeled
½ Scotch bonnet pepper,
deseeded if you prefer
4 tbsp chopped fresh coriander
(cilantro)
1 tsp sea salt

FOR THE CHOUNKAY (OPTIONAL)

4 tbsp cooking oil of choice
¼ tsp mustard seeds
¼ tsp cumin seeds
pinch of asafoetida

Bami sambal

Preservation is usually portrayed as a means of savouring foods for sustenance and longevity. Little discussed is how prior generations preserved foods because they loved the flavour. As many of our ancestors didn't have access to writing or were even literate, it's hard to know. I mention this because every culture I find that utilizes dried shrimp, has a secret sauce or condiment using it which they know and love but that is an enigma to the wider world. In West Africa, in countries like Ghana, said condiment is *shito* and throughout Asia you find shrimp sauces and satays.

In Indonesia, you have sambal, which found its way to Suriname by way of the Dutch and from the first bite I'm hooked. Every sense of the tongue is touched with the sugar, the salt, the soy, the heat and the shrimp essence, all seeped in fresh tomatoes. You'll usually find *bami sambal* or *nasi sambal*, which are used for the base of those dishes, however, the taste is so unique and exciting that I find myself putting a dollop beside pretty much any meal I have.

If you prefer, you can soak the dried shrimp in a bowl of water for 30 minutes, then drain.

In a large frying pan, wok or Dutch pot, heat the oil over a medium–high heat. When hot, add the onion and sauté for 3 minutes before adding the garlic and galangal or ginger and bay leaf, and continue to sauté for 2 minutes until the onion is translucent. Add the shrimp and stir for a minute. Next, add the Scotch bonnet peppers and tomatoes and continue to stir. Now add the salt and sugar and continue to mix for another 3 minutes.

Add the water and wait until it starts to bubble. When it does, turn the heat down a notch to medium, place the lid on and cook for 10 minutes. Remove the lid, turn the heat back up a notch and let the liquid thicken by cooking for another 5–10 minutes. During this time, use a utensil to gently mash the ingredients while you stir. They should already be quite pliable by now. When it resembles a tomato sauce, it is ready. Take off the heat, leave to cool and then decant into a sterilized jar.

Store in the fridge and use within a month. Serve on the side of Bami (see p154) or Nasi (see p56).

MAKES 300ML (1¼ CUPS)

80–100g (2¾–3½oz) dried shrimp or 3 tbsp shrimp paste
100ml (6½ tbsp) cooking oil of choice
1 onion, finely chopped
5 garlic cloves, minced
2 x 5cm (2in) pieces of galangal root or 1 tsp ground galangal or galangal paste, or 2 x 5cm (2in) pieces of fresh root ginger or 1 tsp ground ginger
1 bay leaf
5–10 Scotch bonnet peppers, chopped
2–3 tomatoes, finely chopped
½ tsp sea salt
2 tbsp dark brown sugar
125ml (½ cup) boiling water

Kuchela

Unless you've eaten fresh mangoes in a tropical province, I don't think you've ever really eaten mangoes. Such is the divinity of mangoes that old Indian scriptures suggest some Hindus believe them to be a worldly reincarnation of the creator god Prajapthai. Buddhists too consider the fruit sacred, as the Buddha himself was apparently known to rest in a mango grove. Mangoes of all shapes and kinds are utilized in every way from juicing to cooking, to turning into sweets, so it seems obvious that people would seek ways to preserve their wonders. There are a number of mango preserves and pickles available but the star for me is Kuchela.

This condiment (sometimes known as mango *achar*) takes a pile of grated and dried green mango and laces it with a strand of hot pepper that knits its way through the smokiness of the masala spice mix and mustard-seed-flavoured oil. This nicely plays off the sour sweetness of the fruit. The condiment works with nearly any dish, regardless of whether it's Caribbean or Indian. After trying it your only issue will be how to grate more mangoes quicker.

Grate the peeled mangoes on the largest hole of your grater, discard the stone and set aside. Place the grated mango into a clean cheesecloth and squeeze out as much juice as possible. (Keep the juice and drink it.)

Spread out the grated mango flat on a tray and sun-dry over the course of a day or place in the oven at the lowest possible temperature with the door open for 3–4 hours until dry but not crispy.

When dry (a tiny bit of moisture is OK), place in a bowl and add the salt and amchar masala and stir to combine. In a small bowl or pestle and mortar, add the Scotch bonnet pepper, garlic and green seasoning and mash until smooth (or use a food processor). Combine this with the mango mixture and set aside.

In a frying pan, heat the oil over a high heat and add the mustard and fenugreek seeds. After 2 minutes or so, when the mustard seeds start to pop and the fenugreek seeds turn dark, scoop them out of the pan and pour the oil (minus the seeds) over the mango mix. Decant into a sterilized jar with every last bit of oil. You want the mix to be submerged by the oil as it will dry out otherwise. If you need more oil, simply repeat the previous step. Cool and keep for 1 month. Serve with any savoury dish.

MAKES 300ML (1¹/₄ CUPS)

5 large hard green mangoes (1.75kg/3lb 11oz), peeled
1 tsp sea salt
3–4 tbsp amchar masala
1–2 Scotch bonnet peppers, finely chopped
6 garlic cloves, finely chopped
1 tbsp Green Seasoning (see pp26–27)
150–200ml (²/₃–¾ cup) oil of choice (avocado oil and extra virgin rapeseed oil recommended)
½ tsp mustard seeds
½ tsp fenugreek seeds

Tambran sauce

Shaking the tamarind or "tambran" tree is a collective affair. Five or six people are summoned, all taking different angles with long bamboo sticks, then the more experienced folk disappear into the canopy, to ensure every last pod is collected. I'm sure there is some industrial shaker that can do a much more efficient job, but it would be a lot less fun, less social and much more expensive. The tamarind pods then have to be collected by sifting through the leaves and rubble, while trying to avoid the stinging red ants and even the odd miniscule scorpion. On the day I join in, the pods are lugged to the boot of a car on the way to the masterful Giselle Granger's domain, whose tamarind sauce can be seen across the supermarkets and roadside stalls of southern Trinidad.

Apart from Green Seasoning (see pp26–27) and one hot sauce, this is the other recipe I would say is near mandatory in any kitchen (pictured front centre opposite). A few drops add a new flavour dimension to any meal and it rarely lasts longer than a fortnight before I have to make another batch.

Boxes of in-shell tamarind usually come in weights of 300–400g (10–14oz), while the concentrated blocks come in packs of about 200g (7oz). When shelled, the former usually produces about the same amount as in this recipe. Deseeded paste is also common in many shops and can be used following the instructions on the packet. This recipe favours using the concentrated blocks of tamarind rather than fresh, which can be hard to come by in certain locales.

Heat 400ml (1¾ cups) of water in a saucepan over a high heat, then turn down to medium. Add the tamarind and stir with a wooden spoon. After 5 minutes the block will start to break down. Continue stirring until it has completely dissolved, and the mixture is thick.

Place a colander or sieve over a bowl and decant the tamarind mixture into the colander. Pour 100ml (6½ tablespoons) water over the mixture and use a fork or utensil to squeeze through the mix, just leaving behind the seeds and pith.

Place the tamarind mixture back into the saucepan over a medium heat. Add the remaining ingredients and stir. Continue to stir for a further 5 minutes until dissolved and combined. Decant into a sterilized jar and leave to cool. When cool, put on the lid. Refrigerate for up to 1 month. Add a generous dollop on any lunch or dinner dish as you would ketchup.

MAKES 500ML (GENEROUS 2 CUPS)

200g (7oz) concentrated tamarind block
1 tbsp Green Seasoning (see pp26–27) or 1 tsp each garlic and ginger powder
1 tsp amchar masala or ground cumin
4 tbsp dark brown sugar
½ tsp sea salt
½–1 Scotch bonnet pepper, finely chopped, or 1 tsp chilli powder of choice
½ tsp freshly ground black pepper

RIGHT *Kuchela* (left), *Tambran Sauce* (centre) *and Bami Sambal* (right).

Mango sour

Even though I just raved about mangoes in the recipe for Kuchela (see p229), the mango's supremacy means that one mango condiment wasn't enough and there are different mango condiments for different taste preferences. Mango sour, possibly the most popular mango condiment depending on where you are, says what it does on the tin (see photo on p191). This brilliant yellow sour mango relish accompanies nearly anything you can think of and often works to quell the fire of a locally made hot pepper sauce. In Guyana, asking *"You want sour with that?"* is almost an automated response after any purchase. If desired, bags of pholouri (see p172) are doused with it, curries are dotted with it, doubles (see pp166–167) are spooned with it, rotis are lined with it and egg balls (see pp190–191) are dunked in it. All this crams a taste of mango in every and anywhere possible. Mango sour can get really sour, like screw face sour, so it's fine to manipulate the recipe to suit your tolerance, whether it's altering the amount of salt or sugar content.

Place all the ingredients in a saucepan with 500ml (generous 2 cups) water and bring to the boil over a high heat, then turn the heat down to medium–high, cover and cook for 10 minutes. Remove the lid, stir, then cook for another 5 minutes. The mangoes should be soft and begin to mush if pressed. Remove the mangoes from the water and, using a fork, strip the flesh and place back into the pan (discarding the stone).

Remove from heat and use a fork to mash all the ingredients. You can remove the Scotch bonnet pepper now or after the next step. If you would like the consistency thicker, you can continue to cook for another 5 minutes. Decant into a sterilized jar.

Refrigerate for up to 2 months. Add a generous dollop to rice, roti (see pp204–219) and curries (see pp82–101).

MAKES 500ML (GENEROUS 2 CUPS)

600g (1lb 5oz) unripe/raw green mangoes, peeled
4 garlic cloves, peeled
1 Scotch bonnet pepper, stem removed
2 tbsp apple cider vinegar or white vinegar
1–2 tsp sea salt
1 tsp granulated white sugar (optional)

Mango chow

The kids of the small village of Moruga in South Trinidad argue fiercely about any and every thing. Who is the fastest, who has the fastest bike, who can swim or dive the furthest, who's seen the biggest scorpion and so on. One thing, however, like the flick of a light switch, appears to suspend all debate and bacchanal and that is the announcement that chow is on the agenda. Bikes are dropped, footballs kicked aside, and all focus is on ensuring that the chow is made with haste. This snack hits all the senses with sweet and tangy fruits mixed with salt and (a varying level of) hot sauce. One kid takes the lead and quarterbacks the situation delegating one colleague to get salt from their kitchen, another to get a little dollar bag of hot sauce from the shop down the road and one to get the knife with which the fruit will be peeled and cut into enough slices to satiate the entire group.

This day's order is a freshly picked fruit called pommecy, also known as golden apple, a local fruit gathered from a nearby tree up the hill. Chow, however, is also commonly made with Portugal oranges and known as Portugal or "Pottugal" chow, or with either green or unripe crunchy mango as in this recipe. Blink and you miss it though, some of the kids are distraught at the fact they didn't hear the call that chow was being made, though not me because I was shamelessly at the front of the queue tussling with five- and seven-year-olds for my share.

No chow will beat that made with freshly picked fruit and home-made hot sauce (see p235), though with organic store-bought fruit and the hot sauce recipes in this book you can come close. As for the quantities, it really does depend how much you want to make or how many mouths you'd like to feed, so adjust and multiply the ratios as you see fit.

SERVES 2

1 mango, peeled, pitted and
   chopped into slices, or
   1 pineapple, peeled and diced,
   or 2 large oranges, peeled and
   segmented
½ tsp sea salt
1–2 tsp hot pepper sauce
sprinkle of chopped fresh
   coriander (cilantro)
½ lime, cut into segments

Put the prepared fruit in a bowl, add the salt, hot pepper sauce and fresh coriander and gently mix to combine. Serve with the lime.

Lime & pepper sauce

While not the hottest pepper in the world, there surely can't be a more deceptive pepper than the Wiri Wiri variety, which is almost synonymous with the word pepper in Guyana. Even looking at them it seems odd to accuse them of being peppers, as they look more like a savoury sibling of a cherry. Diminutive, colourful and without the curled, wrinkled facade that makes peppers look so offensive. However, this friendly charm is lost as soon as you attempt to taste one and all regular chilli pepper rules apply.

While other pepper sauces load up with bulbs and vegetables, this sauce keeps it minimal and allows the taste of the peppers to come through. Nature has a funny way of using all our senses to know what category a food falls into and with the use of deep orange and red peppers this sauce looks almost cartoonishly radioactively hot. Fundamentally though, since there are not many additions to dilute the heat, this sauce is hot, but the addition of the lime juice provides a delicate undertone and is surprisingly refreshing, which seems odd to say about a hot sauce.

Note, you can spend time deseeding the majority or all of the peppers, though I can't imagine this sauce without the luminescent seeds shining through.

Place the lime in a small saucepan, cover with water, add a dash of salt and bring to the boil. When hot, let it bubble for 30–60 seconds and then turn off the heat. Remove the lime, drain and wait for a few minutes for it to cool before juicing and zesting.

Before you begin to handle this number of peppers, it is recommended you wear disposable kitchen gloves. Slice the peppers in half and add to a blender or food processor along with the garlic, if using, salt, lime juice and zest, and vinegar. Secure your blender or processor and pulse until completely smooth.

Decant into a sterilized jar and keep in a cool, dark place or in the fridge for about 2 months. Shake thoroughly before use. Add a few drops to enhance any savoury dish.

NOTE *Wear gloves when handling this number of peppers and also handle the jar with care and wash your hands after handling the jar.*

MAKES 250–300ML (1 CUP PLUS 1 TBSP–1¼ CUPS)

1 lime
10 Scotch bonnet peppers or Wiri Wiri peppers, tops removed, deseeded if you prefer
10 garlic cloves, peeled (optional)
1 tbsp sea salt
80ml (⅓ cup) white vinegar

Moruga scorpion

Before embarking on my last trip to Trinidad, Bernard, head honcho of North London's Roti Stop, where I used to work, insists that I should always tap my shoes before putting them on. The reason being that the stab of a wandering scorpion could be paralyzing or even worse. Given this, the Moruga Scorpion pepper is aptly named. The debilitating force of the scorpion contained in such a miniature body is often vastly underestimated, as is that contained in these chilli peppers, which are grown across the Caribbean, but for some reason specifically in this region of Southern Trinidad.

The Scorpion pepper is frequently named amongst or as the hottest pepper in the world according to the New Mexico State University's Chile Pepper Institute (which sounds like one of the most fun places to work in the world), alongside others such as North America's Carolina Reaper and Northern India's Ghost (Bhut) pepper. For those who've never eaten these chilli peppers before it is akin to handing the keys of a supercar to someone who has only driven a milkcart.

The Scorpion pepper tots up a score of 1.2–2 million Scoville heat units (SHU). For comparison, a regular store-bought jalapeño pepper is 2,500–8,000 SHU and the Scotch bonnet and Wiri Wiri peppers many have become accustomed to are around 350,000 SHU. Given this, Scorpion peppers are anything from four to two hundred times hotter than anything you've probably experienced before. On top of this, with this *choka*-like recipe, the roasting of the peppers unleashes a ferocious dragon, a final boss of hotness. This is hard to describe but instant regret comes to mind, the same regret as a youthfully ill-fated bicycle trick or swimming pool dive that you immediately know you messed up a split second in – that moment of no turning back. In the chilli world, most mistakes can be eradicated with water or some dairy liquid, but not here in Moruga, neither can quell the flame, the numbing, the bright lights, shortness of breath or the sweats. For the uninitiated, the only cure is time – time well spent with your thoughts about the mistake you just made.

It's likely that unless you are in certain parts of North America or the Caribbean you may not be able to source these peppers, in which case Scotch bonnets will suffice and are what I've used in this recipe, probably for the best.

**MAKES 1 SMALL JAR
(ABOUT 100G/3¹/₂OZ)**

7 Scotch bonnet peppers, tops removed
3 jalapeño peppers or 1 red bell pepper, deseeded and top removed (optional)
2 garlic cloves, peeled (optional)
1 tsp chopped fresh coriander (cilantro)

Put on disposable plastic gloves or kitchen gloves before you continue to avoid any mishaps.

If you wish, you can deseed the Scotch bonnet peppers to reduce the heat. Then wash and dry the Scotch bonnet and jalapeño peppers and garlic, if using, wrap in foil and place over a low-medium flame for 15–20 minutes until the peppers begin to char and turn black in some parts. Turn off the heat, remove and leave to cool for 5 minutes. Remove from the foil and place into a pestle and mortar or mini food processor with 2 tablespoons water, fresh coriander and blend for a couple seconds. This is not meant to resemble a sauce or paste.

Store in a small jar or airtight container for up to a fortnight and apply with caution – as in ¼–½ teaspoon per serving with any savoury dish.

NOTE *If you aren't doing this on an outdoor grill, immediately open all possible windows, though if you ever want to deter people from coming into the kitchen and sneakily nibbling at roti or bakes, feel free to keep them all closed.*

Mother-in-law pepper sauce

I'm not sure exactly whose mother-in-law inspired this moniker, but if my own mother, aunties and grandmother set any precedent, then I can only begin to imagine the wrath of the Caribbean woman who did. Caribbean folklore hailing from India to Africa is rife with fearsome women who are not to be crossed by any means.

The Soucouyant is probably the most popular figure in Afro-Caribbean folklore, shedding her skin to become a vampiric fire spirit that sucks the life from the living at night. Additionally, the La Diablese (or Lajables and pronounced "La-Jah-Bless") is a devil woman who hides her cloven hoof beneath a sea of petticoats, enticing men to their doom, while Mama D'leau is a beautiful woman with long flowing hair who hides the lower half of her body in water concealing the fact that she has the lower half of a giant snake. Similarly, the Indo-Caribbean legend of Saapin tells of a strikingly beautiful long-haired woman with a cobra tattooed on her back. She releases the snake at night to seek out her victims.

So this recipe almost lives on in the legacy of this folklore, especially those that are fooled by its salad-like appearance and the fact that unlike most store-bought hot sauces, which come with a miniscule opening, this is usually kept in deceiving containers, from coffee jars to jam jars, repurposed fizzy drink bottles, empty butter pots and so on. Like most people in the Caribbean, as Patrice Roberts sings, "I like it HOT!"

It should be mentioned, however, that this won't be like other sauces you are accustomed to as it's mainly composed of very finely chopped vegetables and herbs rather than blended to a liquid. There is also no real definitive recipe, so adjust and adapt to your desired taste and heat.

MAKES 500G (1LB 2OZ)

3–6 Scotch bonnet peppers, deseeded and chopped
1 rib of celery (leaves included), or 1 caraili (bitter melon), deseeded and chopped (or use both)
1 large carrot, peeled and grated
1 onion, chopped
4 garlic cloves, chopped
juice of 1 lemon or 2 limes
5g (⅛oz) fresh coriander (cilantro)
sea salt and sugar, to taste

Add all the ingredients to a food processor or blender and pulse until it reaches your desired consistency. I prefer it not to be completely blended to a paste as the texture makes a nice difference from a regular hot sauce. If you don't have a blender or processor, you can finely chop, then grate each ingredient and mix or mash together with a pestle and mortar.

Store in an airtight jar in the fridge for up to 2 months.

Carnival

Living and feeling alive are two completely different things. The latter, for Caribbean people, reaches an apex each year at carnival. The pulsating soca beat permeating the concrete of the road, the calypso steel pans caressing the ear drums, the pageantry of the outfits, the whining (wining), the dancing – all life's ills are temporarily submerged for those days of joy. As Trinidadian writer Earl Lovelace colourfully puts it in one of his novels, *The Dragon Can't Dance*, centred around the country's annual festivities, "*the music insists that you dance*". Whether you are mourning the neighbour or dealing with family issues – dancing is the cure. "*Dance to the hurt!*" Regardless of what trouble you are in, if your spouse has taken all your money and eloped with another, then dancing is the cure. As he puts it: "*It is dancing that you ward off evil. Dancing is a chant that cuts off the power from the devil.*"

The irony of such lively action is that the origins of the carnivals we know today are arguably tributes to the deceased of the day and days past. As we saw with the crossing of the *kala pani* (see p118), ties were severed with old homes for those who arrived in the Caribbean. In the case of West Africans, a book on Guyanese proverbs and stories details that with the decline of the original songs and the broken periods in the links of culture, as well as tribal elements of dances of the Africans (which arguably live on today), new elements arose and gave birth to an admixture of ideas and fancies.

Carnival, like Cook-up Rice (see p62), Callaloo (see p38) and many of the other recipes in this book, represents this melange of cultures in the region. The impetus for the carnivals seen today seems to be a continuation of the tradition of the orisha festivals of Yorubaland, where the Yoruba people (from modern day Nigeria) honoured their deities. Moreso, the events helped sustain a legacy of Yoruba culture through costume, dance and music.

The week before Ash Wednesday each year, revellers "*playing mas [masquerade]*" parade in costumes mirroring those found in West Africa; vibrant strips of multilayered fabric reminiscent of Yoruba Egungun costumes found in the festivals of Benin and Nigeria. Displays of wealth were a key tenet of the carnivals, hence the mimicking of the elite European classes. Additionally, feathers were considered among the Yoruba to be powerful in invoking positive energy (*ase*) and wealth, inspiring the costumes you see today. Particularly amongst the French enslaved, who were not permitted to masquerade, early descriptions of Black celebrants reveal an emphasis on King, Queen and regal English costumes (known as mummer costumes), as well as military outfits and those similar to the masked balls of Versailles. Another mode of mimicking was almost dark comedy, as revellers imitated the way their ancestors had been punished and tortured. This is seen commonly then and today with the covering of oneself with oil as a nod to the boiling hot molasses that ancestors were burned with.

With the arrival of indentured Indians in the 19th century, the festivities had an entirely new element added to them. Historians illustrate that the West Africans were drawn to the Islamic celebrational festivities of *Hosay* and *Tadja* commemorated by their new compatriots. For those for whom the festivals had no religious significance, it is thought that the attraction was the carnival revelry which accompanied the procession, as they felt at home with the carnivalesque and street theatre. This was arguably also the case for the Hindu tradition of *Holi* (or *Phagwah*), the spring festival of colours that features carnivalesque revelry coated in a kaleidoscope of coloured powder. African enslaved, freedmen, Indian and Chinese indentured labourers, all brought to the region cultural traditions that the Europeans considered exotic, pagan and subhuman. Today, these disparate traditions blend in Carnival, a Creolization of traditions.

Those who lament an overbearing police presence at and negative media coverage of today's Notting Hill Carnival, can rest assured that this also dates back centuries. Historic colonial accounts and newspapers were far from impartial and were actively hostile, contemptuous and disapproving of carnival. They saw savagery in the African theatrical acts, and abhorred the flaunting of pagan rites and promoting of Indian culture in a Christian country by uncultured "Coolies". Police abused 1830s "Obeah" laws and convicts of *obeah* (anything culturally African) were sentenced to six months in jail and thirty-six lashes with whips. In the 1880s, laws were passed aimed at repressing "unruly" lower-class activity. These laws made the playing of drums, gongs and various bamboo percussion illegal between 10pm and 6am without obtaining prior police licensing. At every juncture this suppression led to riots and protests. These are to name just a few ordinances, and every Caribbean region had scores of their own.

Whether it's the roads of Port of Spain or the side streets of Notting Hill, if you ever wondered why Caribbean people take carnival so seriously, this is why. It's not just a way of honouring their ancient ancestors but also the more recent relatives who fought to have free time and then found their joy policed at every turn. Carnival is a time to finally be free.

Garlic pork

On the tail end of the beautiful winding highway from East coast Demerara to Berbice, one of the frequent town-name signs I spot reads "Portuguese Quarters". With Brazil neighbouring Guyana, I knew of their role in this part of the world. Portugal's colonial activity primarily focused on Brazil, where a handful of African nations transported and possessed the highest number of enslaved anywhere during the transatlantic trade era – more than all other European colonies combined.

That being said, I didn't know that part of the desperate search to replace the labour of the freed West Africans was a small cohort of Portuguese totalling in the few thousands, primarily from the then poverty-stricken island of Madeira, where exploitative cane cultivation had been occurring. These workers followed in the same path as those from India, believing they were leaving destitution in the hope of a comparatively better life. Like the Indian population, many of these Portuguese didn't return home but stayed and became part of the tapestry of Caribbean life. People in Trinidad and Guyana may be familiar with the term *dougla*, referring colloquially to someone of both African and Indian heritage, but it was also used to refer to those of African and Portuguese heritage.

Every group of people who came to the Caribbean brought with them a custom that has become commonplace in the general population. For the Madeirans it was the Christmas holiday tradition of Garlic Pork. Known in Portuguese as *Carne de vinha d'alhos* (or *vina dosh*) and translated as "meat in garlic", this recipe was created as a light snack to sustain the Roman Catholic community the evening before they gathered for Christmas Day midnight mass and a large meal afterwards.

For Garlic Pork, cuts of pork are chopped into bite-sized chunks and seasoned with ample amounts of garlic cloves, chilli peppers and a select few other herbs and then submerged with vinegar. They sit in a jar for at least a week before being cooked in their own fat and preserved juices. The end result is an addictive munch that most certainly will keep vampires at bay. Although the dish is traditionally reserved for Christmas, it has become so popular it's not odd to see it as a cutter (like Jeera Pork, see p153) throughout the year.

**MAKES 1.2 LITRES
(5 CUPS)/SERVES 6**

1kg (2¼lb) pork belly or shoulder,
    cut into 3cm (1¼in) cubes
1 tbsp sea salt
1 tbsp brown sugar of choice
10–15 garlic cloves, finely chopped
5–10 Scotch bonnet peppers,
    stems removed and finely
    chopped
15 sprigs of thyme
600ml (2½ cups) apple cider
    vinegar or white vinegar

In a large bowl, add the pork, salt, sugar, garlic, Scotch bonnet peppers and thyme and mix to combine. Add a splash of vinegar to the base of a sterilized jar and then layer in the pork and all the other ingredients except the vinegar. When you've filled the pork and dry ingredients to the top, pour in the vinegar to submerge everything (you may not need all the vinegar). Store in a cool, dark place (not the fridge) for a minimum of 5 days and up to a fortnight or month.

Drain the pork in a sieve and pat down with kitchen paper (discard the seasoning ingredients). When dry, heat a dry frying pan (without oil) and then fry the garlic pork in batches for 10–15 minutes at a time until dark brown and seared.

Serve as a snack.

Juices

Those carrying ice-cold bags of fresh juice appear like the mirage of a tropical oasis in the heart of a desert on a hot day in the Caribbean, and hope overrides all other emotions. For some reason, food and drink just tastes a bit different when you see it made before your eyes. In the sleepy town of Melanie, east of Georgetown, my neighbour frequently invites me over to lime (see p42) under the perfect shade-abundant canopy of his front yard to escape the onset of the relenting midday heat. Here, mangoes and passion fruit drop like English autumn conkers and if not then can be easily snagged with the wiggle of a long wooden rod. Whatever the fruit, a small knife is used to carve out all useful parts, which are then pulsed and combined with water and any necessary aid to take the juice to that perfect taste sweet spot. The whole process embodies all facets of the joy of the Caribbean, an experience that no amount of money can make any better.

Lemon, lime, ginger & turmeric juice

MAKES 1.2 LITRES (5 CUPS)

100g (3½oz) fresh root ginger,
    peeled and chopped
juice of ½ lemon
juice of 2 limes
1 tsp ground turmeric
4 tsp sugar of choice

———

Add the ginger to a heavy-based saucepan or Dutch pot, then add 1.2 litres (5 cups) water. Turn the heat up to medium, then add the lemon and lime juice and stir. When the mixture has come to a slight boil (bubbles forming), stir in the turmeric and then turn down the heat and simmer for 15 minutes. Take the pot off the heat and let the liquid cool to room temperature.

Pour the liquid through a sieve. Discard the excess ginger. Add the sugar and stir until it dissolves. Funnel the bowl contents into an airtight bottle and refrigerate for 1 hour before drinking. Store in the fridge for a few days.

Mango & passion fruit juice

MAKES 1.2 LITRES (5 CUPS)

1 mango (preferably overripe/
    soft), peeled and pitted
pulp of 5 passion fruit
4 tsp sugar of choice

———

Place all the ingredients and 1 litre (4⅓ cups) water into a juicer and pulse. If using a blender, blend until completely smooth, then sieve into a bowl to remove any excess pith. Preferably, cool in the fridge for 1 hour before drinking. It will keep in the fridge for a few days.

Bibliography

INTRODUCTION

Page 9: Hinds, D., "Small Islan' Complex" in Salkay, A., *Island Voices: Stories from the West Indies* (Liveright Publishing Corporation, 1970), p66

Page 9: New Musical Express, *NME Guide to Rock and Roll*, 1978. Accessed at https://history-is-made-at-night.blogspot.com/2012/05/nme-guide-to-rock-roll-london-1979.html?m=1

Page 10: Caribbean Development Bank, "Tourism Industry Reform: Strategies for enhanced Economic Impact", 2017

Page 12: https://www.bbc.co.uk/news/uk-43808007

Page 13: Thompson, A., "Symbolic legacies of slavery in Guyana", *NWIG: New West Indian Guide / Nieuwe West-Indische Gids* (Vol. 80, no. 3/4, 2006), pp191–220

Page 13: Central Intelligence Agency, 2020 *World Fact Book* of the United States Central Intelligence Agency

Page 13: Vaneker, K., "Discovering Pom's Potential" in Finnis, E. (ed.), *Reimagining Marginalized Foods: Global Processes, Local Places* (University of Arizona Press, 2012), p91

Page 13: Tinker, H., *A New System of Slavery: The Export of Indian Labour Overseas: 1830-1920* (OUP, 1974)

Page 13: Winer, L., "Indic Lexicon in the English/Creole Of Trinidad." *NWIG: New West Indian Guide / Nieuwe West-Indische Gids* (79, no. 1/2, 2005), pp7–30

PLANT-BASED

Page 21: Balkaran, L., *Dictionary of the Guyanese Amerindia: And Other South American Native Terms: An A-Z Guide to Their Anthropology, Exploration, History, Geography, Legend, Folklore and Myth* (LBA Publications, 2002), p63

Page 21: Brett, W. H., *Legends and Myths of the Aboriginal Indians of British Guiana* (1880), p105

Page 21: Arnaiz-Villena, A., Parga-Lozano, C., Moreno, E., Areces, C., Rey, D. and Gomez-Prieto, P., "The Origin of Amerindians and the Peopling of the Americas According to HLA Genes: Admixture with Asian and Pacific People", *Current genomics* 11(2), pp103–114

Page 21: Brett, W. H., *Legends and Myths of the Aboriginal Indians of British Guiana* (1880), p8

Page 22: Balkaran, L., *Dictionary of the Guyanese Amerindians: And Other South American Native Terms: An A-Z Guide to Their Anthropology, Exploration, History, Geography, Legend, Folklore and Myth* (LBA Publications, 2002), pxii

Page 22: Odie-Alie, S., "Women in Agriculture: The Case of Guyana", *Social and Economic Studies* (35, no. 2, 1986). http://www.jstor.org/stable/27862835.

Page 22: Woodville Marshall, K., "Provision ground and plantation labour in four windward islands: Competition for resources during slavery", *Slavery & Abolition* (Vol. 12, 1991), p51

Page 22: Friedman, G. C., "The Heights of Slaves in Trinidad", *Social Science History* 6 (no. 4, 1982), pp482–515

Page 23: Debysingh, M., "Cultural change and adaptation as reflected in The Meat-eating habits of the Trinidad Indian population", *Caribbean Quarterly* 32 (no. 3/4, 1986), pp66–77. http://www.jstor.org/stable/40653665

Page 34: Pariag, P., *The Eating Habits of the Lower Class East Indian in Trinidad* (Unpublished paper, University of the West Indies, St. Augustine, 1975), p24

Page 34: Mahabir, N. K., *Medicinal and Edible Plants Used by East Indians of Trinidad and Tobago* (Chakra, 1991), p152

Page 38: Khan, A., *Callaloo Nation: Metaphors of Race and Religious Identity among South Asians in Trinidad* (Duke University Press, 2004), p8

Page 38: Esposito, E., "Callaloo or Pelau? Food, Identity and Politics in Trinidad and Tobago", *Food Across Cultures: Linguistic Insights in Transcultural Tastes* (Springer International Publishing, 2019), p54

Page 38: Minshall, P., *The Use of Traditional Figures in Carnival Art* (Paper presented at the First National Conference on the Performing Arts, Port of Spain, Trinidad, 25 July 1985), p24

Page 42: McNeal, K. E., *Trance and Modernity in the Southern Caribbean: African and Hindu Popular Religions in Trinidad and Tobago* (University Press of Florida, 2011), p30

Page 42: Burton, R. D. E., *Afro-Creole: Power, Opposition, and Play in the Caribbean* (Cornell University Press, 1997), p41

Page 42: McNeal, K. E., *Trance and Modernity in the Southern Caribbean: African and Hindu Popular Religions in Trinidad and Tobago* (University Press of Florida, 2011), p30

Page 42: Winer, L., *Dictionary of the English/Creole of Trinidad & Tobago: On Historical Principles* (McGill-Queen's University Press, 2009), p532

Page 42: Alleyne-Forte, L., *Jokers on the Abyss' Edge: A Collection of Short Stories* (Printex Converters, 1994), p68

Page 42: Winer, L., *Dictionary of the English/Creole of Trinidad & Tobago: On Historical Principles* (McGill-Queen's University Press, 2009), p532

SEEDS & PULSES

Page 49: McGowan, W., Rose, J. G. and Granger, D. A. (ed.s), *Themes in African-Guyanese History* (Hansib, 2009), p8

Page 49: Woodville Marshall, K., "Provision ground and plantation labour in four windward islands: Competition for resources during slavery", *Slavery & Abolition* (Volume 12, 1991), pp48–67

Page 49: Ottley, C. R., *Tall Tales of Trinidad and Tobago* (Horsford Printerie, 1972), pp27–31

Page 49: "Anansi and the Pot of Beans" accessed at https://archive.org/details/anansipotofbeans00norf

Page 50: Warner-Lewis, M., *Guinea's Other Suns* (Second edition, University of West Indies Press, 2015), p35

Page 50: Higman, B. W., *Jamaican Food: History, Biology, Culture* (University of the West Indies Press, 2008), p12

Page 50: Kumar, A., "Feeding the *Girmitiya*: Food and Drink on Indentured Ships to the Sugar Colonies", *Gastronomica* (16, no. 1, 2016), p44

Page 50: "*How the 19th-century flow of indentured workers shapes the Caribbean*" (The Economist, 4 May 2023). Retrieved from https://www.economist.com/the-americas/2017/03/11/how-the-19th-century-flow-of-indentured-workers-shapes-the-caribbean

Page 50: Younger, P., *New Homelands: Hindu Communities in Mauritius, Guyana, Trinidad, South Africa, Fiji, and East Africa* (Oxford University Press, 2010), p98

Page 50: Younger, P., *New Homelands: Hindu Communities in Mauritius, Guyana, Trinidad, South Africa, Fiji, and East Africa* (Oxford University Press, 2010), p58

Page 62: Clarke, A., *Pig Tails 'n' Breadfruit* (New Press, 2014), pp60 and 63

Page 62: Mühleisen, S., *Genre in World Englishes: Case Studies from the Caribbean* (John Benjamins Publishing Company, 2022), p22

Page 62: Esposito, E., "Callaloo or Pelau? Food, Identity and Politics in Trinidad and Tobago", *Food Across Cultures: Linguistic Insights in Transcultural Tastes* (Springer International Publishing, 2019), pp14–17

Page 68: McMillan, M., *The Front Room: Migrant Aesthetics in the Home* (Black Dog, 2009), p29

Page 68: Saunders, G., "Aspects of Traditional African-Bahamian in the late 19th and early 20th century," *Journal of the Bahamas Historical Society* (17, October 1995), p2

Page 68: McMillan, M., *The Front Room: Migrant Aesthetics in the Home* (Black Dog, 2009), p29

Page 68: McMillan, M., *The Front Room: Migrant Aesthetics in the Home* (Black Dog, 2009), p19

Page 68: Brathwaite, P. A. and Brathwaite, Serena, *Guyanese Proverbs and Stories* (Forum Printery, 1967), pp19–20

Page 72: Younger, P., *New Homelands: Hindu Communities in Mauritius, Guyana, Trinidad, South Africa, Fiji, and East Africa* (Oxford University Press, 2010), p98

Page 72: Winer, L., *Dictionary of the English/Creole of Trinidad & Tobago: On Historical Principles* (McGill-Queen's University Press, 2009), p212

Page 72: Bahri, H., *Rajpal Pocket Hindi English Dictionary* (Rajpal & Sons, 2005), p126

CURRY?

Page 77: Davidson, A., *The Oxford Companion to Food* (Oxford University Press, 2014), p240

Page 77: Achaya, K. T., *A Historical Dictionary of Indian Food* (Oxford: Oxford University Press, 1998), p51

Page 77: Achaya, K. T., *A Historical Dictionary of Indian Food* (Oxford: Oxford University Press, 1998), p51

Page 78: Mishra, V., *The Literature of the Indian Diaspora: Theorizing the Diasporic Imaginary* (Routledge, 2007), p91

Page 78: Black, J. K., *Area Handbook for Trinidad and Tobago* (U.S. Government Printing Office, 1976), p113

Page 78: Richards-Greaves, G., "The Intersections of

'Guyanese Food' and Constructions of Gender, Race, and Nationhood", *Food and Identity in the Caribbean* (Bloomsbury Academic, 2013), p83
Page 88: Gounder, F., Brereton, B., Egger, J. and Neus, H. (eds.), *Collective Memory, Identity and the Legacies of Slavery and Indenture* (Taylor & Francis, 2022), chapter 1 by Primnath Gooptar
Page 88: Younger, P., *New Homelands: Hindu Communities in Mauritius, Guyana, Trinidad, South Africa, Fiji, and East Africa* (Oxford University Press, 2010), p100

SEAFOOD

Page 103: Macmillan, A., *The West Indies, Illustrated: Historical and Descriptive, Commercial and Industrial Facts, Figures, & Resources* (W. H. & L. Collingridge, 1909), p25
Pages 103–104: Lewis, M. G., *Journal of a West India Proprietor 1815-1817.* Edited by Mona Wilson (Houghton-Mifflin Co., 1929), p54
Page 104: Adams, J. E., "Fish Lovers of the Caribbean", *Caribbean Studies* (25, no. 1/2, 1992), pp1–10 http://www.jstor.org/stable/25613055.
Page 104: Carmichael, A. C., *Domestic manners and social condition of the white, coloured and negro population of the West Indies* (Whittaker, 1834), p179
Page 104: Younger, Paul, *New Homelands: Hindu Communities in Mauritius, Guyana, Trinidad, South Africa, Fiji, and East Africa* (Oxford University Press, 2010), p88
Page 104: Brett, W. H., *Legends and Myths of the Aboriginal Indians of British Guiana* (1880), p52
Page 118: Mehta, B., *Diasporic (Dis)locations: Indo-Caribbean Women Writers Negotiate the Kala Pani* (University of West Indies Press), p5
Page 118: Carpi, D. and Stierstorfer, K. (eds.), *Diaspora, Law and Literature* (De Gruyter, 2016)
Page 118: Ottley, C. R., *Tall Tales of Trinidad and Tobago* (Horsford Printerie, 1972), p24
Page 118: Ottley, C. R., *Tall Tales of Trinidad and Tobago* (Horsford Printerie, 1972), pp29–30
Page 118: Dabydeen, D., *India in the Caribbean* (Hansib, 1987), p9

NOSE-TO-TAIL

Page 131: Higman, B. W., *Jamaican Food: History, Biology, Culture* (University of the West Indies Press, 2008), p330
Page 131: Balkaran, L., *Dictionary of the Guyanese Amerindians: And Other South American Native Terms: An A-Z Guide to Their Anthropology, Exploration, History, Geography, Legend, Folklore and Myth* (LBA Publications, 2002), p45
Page 131: *Papers and Correspondence: One Volume: Relating to New South Wales Magistrates; The West Indies: Liberated Africans; Colonial and Slave Population; Slaves; the Slave Trade &c*, Session 2 February to 31 May 1826, Vol XXVI
Page 132: Bryans, R., *Trinidad and Tobago: Isles of the Immortelles* (Faber, 1967), p242
Page 132: Brathwaite, P. A. and Brathwaite, Serena, *Guyanese Proverbs and Stories* (Forum Printery, 1967), p42
Page 132: Richards-Greaves, G., *Rediasporization: African-Guyanese Kweh-Kweh* (University Press of Mississippi, 2020), p38
Page 132: Henry, E. A., *The Guyanese Slang Alphabet* (DORRANCE Publishing Company Incorporated, 2022), p26
Page 148: Jha, J. C. and Anand, R. P., "Indian Heritage in Trinidad", *India Quarterly* (28, 1972), pp364–379
Page 148: Chee-Beng, T., *Routledge Handbook of the Chinese Diaspora* (Taylor & Francis, 2013), p364
Page 148: Younger, P., *New Homelands: Hindu Communities in Mauritius, Guyana, Trinidad, South Africa, Fiji, and East Africa* (Oxford University Press, 2010), p58

FLOUR & WATER

Page 157: Warner-Lewis, M., *Guinea's Other Suns* (Second edition, University of West Indies Press, 2015), p107
Page 157: Higman, B. W., *Slave Populations of the British Caribbean, 1807-1834* (University of the West Indies Press, 1995), p211
Page 157: Bryans, R., *Trinidad and Tobago: Isles of the Immortelles* (Faber, 1967), p242 and *"Food and other maintenance and allowances under the apprenticeship system"* from the appendix to a report published by the Committee of the London Anti-Slavery Society on negro apprenticeship in the British Colonies (Anti-Slavery Society, 1838)
Page 176: Winer, L., *Dictionary of the English/Creole of Trinidad & Tobago: On Historical Principles* (McGill-Queen's University Press, 2009), p4
Page 178: Younger, P., *New Homelands: Hindu Communities in Mauritius, Guyana, Trinidad, South Africa, Fiji, and East Africa* (Oxford University Press, 2010), p96
Page 178: Thomas, C. Y., "Plantations, Peasants, and State: A Study of the Mode of Sugar Production in Guyana", *Afro-American Culture and Society*, v. 5. (Los Angeles: Mona, Jamaica: Center for Afro-American Studies, University of California; Institute of Social and Economic Research, University of the West Indies, 1984), p3
Page 178: Peoples of the Historic Slave Trade, *Stories: Sandy* accessed at https://enslaved.org/fullStory/16-23-126818/
Page 178: del Pilar Kaladeen, M., "Hidden Histories: Indenture to *Windrush*" (The British Library website, 11 April 2019)
Page 178: Bissessar, A. M., *Ethnic Conflict in Developing Societies: Trinidad and Tobago, Guyana, Fiji, and Suriname* (Palgrave Macmillan, 2017), p46
Page 179: Thomas, C. Y., *Sugar Economics in a Colonial Situation: a study of the Guyana sugar industry* (Studies in Exploitation. Ratoon Group. No.1, 1969), p1

ROTI

Page 199: Winer, L., "Indic Lexicon in the English/Creole Of Trinidad", *NWIG: New West Indian Guide / Nieuwe West-Indische Gids* (79, no. 1/2, 2005), p20
Page 200: *Atlantic's Urdu English Dictionary* (Atlantic Publishers and Distribution, 1995), p368
Page 200: Mishra, V., *The Literature of the Indian Diaspora* (Routledge, 2007), p91

PRESERVES & JUICES

Page 221: McKenna, T., *Food of the Gods: The Search for the Original Tree of Knowledge: a Radical History of Plants, Drugs and Human Evolution* (Rider, 1999), p17
Page 221: Ojimelukwe, P. C. and Ugwuona, F. U., "The traditional and medicinal use of African breadfruit (*Treculia africana Decne*): an underutilized ethnic food of the Ibo tribe of South East, Nigeria", *Journal of Ethnic Foods* (8, 21, 2021)
Page 222: Handler, J. S. and Jacoby, J., "Slave medicine and plant use in Barbados", *Journal of Barbados Museum and Historical Society* (Vol XLI, 1993), pp74–98
Page 222: Noll, R. G., "The Wines of West Africa: History, Technology and Tasting Notes", *Journal of Wine Economics* (3, no. 1, 2008), pp85–94
Page 222: Achaya, K. T., *A Historical Dictionary of Indian Food* (Oxford: Oxford University Press, 1998), p25
Page 222: O'Brien, J., *Raise the Bar – The Home Distiller's Guide* (Lulu.com, 2018), p57
Page 240: Lovelace, E., *The Dragon Can't Dance: A Novel* (Persea Books, 1998), pp13–14
Page 240: Warner-Lewis, M., *Guinea's Other Suns* (Second edition, University of West Indies Press, 2015), p34
Page 240: Howard, N., "Yoruba in the British Caribbean" in Falola, T. and Childs, M. D. (eds.), *The Yoruba Diaspora in the Atlantic World* (Indiana University Press, 2004)
Page 240: Nunley, J. W. et al., *Caribbean festival arts: each and every bit of difference* (University of Washington Press, 1988), p26
Page 241: Nunley, J. W. et al., *Caribbean festival arts: each and every bit of difference* (University of Washington Press, 1988), p26
Page 241: Ferkiss, V. C. and Ferkiss, B., "Race And Politics in Trinidad And Guyana", *World Affairs* (134, no. 1. 1971), p11
Page 241: Creighton, A., "The Importance of Ethnic festivals in Guyana", *Arts on Sunday*, 2003. Accessed at https://www.landofsixpeoples.com/news304/ns311094.htm
Page 241: Trotman, D. V., *Crime in Trinidad: Conflict and control in a Plantation Society, 1838-1900* (University of Tennessee Press, 1986), p86, p136, p224
Page 241: McNeal, K. E., *Trance and Modernity in the Southern Caribbean* (University Press of Florida, 2011), p64
Page 241: McNeal, K. E., *Trance and Modernity in the Southern Caribbean* (University Press of Florida, 2011), p65
Page 241: Anthony, M., "South's Canboulay Riots Hotter than North's", 4 March 1984. Accessed at http://www.triniview.com/articles/canboulay.html

Index

Acknowledgments

AUTHOR'S ACKNOWLEDGMENTS

First, initial thanks go to my Uncle Saladdin, Angelicque Eastman Owhoka and Byrl Anetha Harvey, and Bernard "Roti King" Miller, whose connections made this book possible.

In Guyana: Kirk, Cousin Ryan, Shelly and Uncle Morris, Cousin Sherman and in spirit the amazing work done by Life ARD, who you can find on YouTube.

In Trinidad and Tobago: Dominic, down in Moruga – Giselle, Noriga and the entire Granger family and village including Cliff, Franklin and frequent incredible cooking tips from Monty, Ms. Patsy, Ms. Rose, and Ms. Asha.

In Suriname: Driver Terry for insanely quick driving from Parbo to the ferry port.

In Jamaica: Sharmaine, Thomas and the entire Lovegrove family.

Family: Joshua, Laurelle, Misha, Aunty Nats, Aunty Bev, Aunty Phyllis, Uncle Eddie, Anthony, Uncle Keith, Sophia, Fabienne, Bianca, Aunty Dianne, Uncle Tony, James, Reece, Grace, Aunty Sandra, Aunty Bridget, Uncle Ian, Aunty Leslie, and Dad and Bob.

Again the group of people that keeps me sane most days and always support – Charles Dorrance-King, Mickey Down, Konrad Kay, Tom Lazenby, Jack Gove, Joby Weston, Otis Clarke, Harry Mitchell, Eji Onuchukwu, Josh Bernie, Jenny Taygeta, Olubiye Thomas, Nick Daley, and Matilda Bah.

Always thanks to Niki Chang, Stephanie Milner, and David Evans.

Thanks again to the great service from the Bodleian Library, Lady Margaret Hall Library and the British Library.

Book team: Cara Armstrong, Lucy Philpott, Vicky Orchard, and Barbara Zuniga.

PUBLISHER'S ACKNOWLEDGMENTS

DK would like to thank Stephanie Milner for acquiring *East Winds*; Izzy Poulson for design assistance; Marsha Gomes-Mckie for providing the sensitivity read; Katie Hardwicke for proofreading; Angie Hipkin for indexing; Alice Hughes for food styling assistance; Oliver Goodrich for photography assistance; and Adam Brackenbury for repro work.

CREDITS

The publisher and Riaz Phillips would like to thank the following for their kind permission to reproduce their text:

68 Michael McMillan: *The Front Room: Migrant Aesthetics in the Home,* © Michael McMillan, Black Dog Press (1st edition), Lund Humphries (2nd edition). **132 Edgar Henry:** Lyrics are of African / Guyanese Folk Song origin translated by the author Edgar Henry of "The Guyanese Slang Alphabet". **150 Kross Kolor Records:** Extract from the song Jimmy black pudding and souse written by Augustus Hinds aka Bill Rogers. **179 Permission granted by Railroad Town, SCAP/Zalytron, BMI:** Permission granted by Railroad Town, SCAP/Zalytron, BMI. **239 Fox Fuse:** "Like It Hot" written by Shertz James, Parry Jack and Patrice Roberts. Licensed courtesy of Fox Fuse, LLC.

The publisher and Riaz Phillips would also like to thank the following for their kind permission to reproduce their images:
(Key: a-above; b-below/bottom; c-centre; f-far; l-left; r-right; t-top)

13 The National Archives: The National Archives (UK), ref. CO323 / 733 (tr). **81 Alamy Stock Photo:** Chromorange / Bernd Juergens (clb). **241 Alamy Stock Photo:** Fazimoon Samad.
Cover images: *Front and Back:* **True Grit Texture Supply,** *Front:* **Caitlin Isola**

All other photography by Riaz Phillips except recipe images on pages 33, 36–37, 60–61, 64, 67, 72–73, 86–87, 95, 96–97, 98, 101, 110–111, 115, 116, 125, 126, 129, 139, 142–143, 145, 146–147, 150–151, 152, 155, 168–169, 184–185, 187, 188, 191, 196–197, 206, 208, 216, 219, 226, 228-9, 231, 236–237 by Caitlin Isola.

All other images © Dorling Kindersley

DK LONDON

Project Editor	Lucy Philpott
Senior Designer	Barbara Zuniga
Production Editor	David Almond
Senior Production Controller	Stephanie McConnell
DTP and Design Co-ordinator	Heather Blagden
Jacket Co-ordinator	Abi Gain
Editorial Manager	Ruth O'Rourke
Editorial Director	Cara Armstrong
Art Director	Maxine Pedliham
Publishing Director	Katie Cowan

DK DELHI

DTP Coordinator	Pushpak Tyagi
DTP Designer	Umesh Rawat
Pre-production Manager	Balwant Singh

Design concept and jacket design	Evi O. & Susan Le | Evi-O.Studio
Editor	Vicky Orchard
Photographer	Caitlin Isola
Prop Stylist	Nyasha Haukozi-Jones
Food Stylist	Alex James Gray

First published in Great Britain in 2023 by
Dorling Kindersley Limited
DK, One Embassy Gardens, 8 Viaduct Gardens,
London, SW11 7BW

The authorized representative in the EEA is
Dorling Kindersley Verlag GmbH.
Arnulfstr. 124, 80636 Munich, Germany

Text copyright © Riaz Phillips 2023
Images copyright © Caitlin Isola 2023
Copyright © 2023 Dorling Kindersley Limited
A Penguin Random House Company
10 9 8 7 6 5 4 3 2 1
001–328116–Oct/2023

A CIP catalogue record for this book
is available from the British Library.
ISBN: 978-0-2415-5243-8

Printed and bound in China

For the curious
www.dk.com

This book was made with Forest Stewardship Council™
certified paper – one small step in DK's
commitment to a sustainable future.
For more information go to www.dk.com/our-green-pledge

About the Author

Riaz Phillips is an award-winning writer and documentary maker. His previous book on Jamaican food, *West Winds*, won the Fortnum and Mason Cookery Book Award 2023 and the Jane Grigson Award 2022, plus was listed as one of the best cookbooks of the year by *The Guardian* and *Independent*.

Born and raised in London and now based in Berlin, Riaz self-published and released his first book *Belly Full: Caribbean Food in the UK* in 2017, for which he was marked as one of the Observer Food Monthly 50 "Things we Love" annual list, and awarded a Young British Foodie (YBF) Award.

When not moonlighting in kitchens or bars, his freelance writing can be found in the *Evening Standard*, *Vice*, Waitrose magazine, Eater and Resy, among other publications and blogs. His YouTube channel of short films and mini-docs, focused on food and travel, has garnered millions of views.

In 2020, he edited the Community Comfort cookbook, a collection of over 100 global recipes from cooks of immigrant backgrounds raising funds for the families of Covid-19 victims in their own community. Through his works Riaz has been featured on *MasterChef*, BBC News, ITV News, Channel 4 News, and Channel 5 News.

Follow his food journey @riazphillips on most platforms.

Dedicated to
Great Aunt Salima (Minnie Gafoor) Ishmael